Sport and Physical Education in Germany

Sport and physical education represent important components of German national life, from school and community participation, to elite, international level sport. This unique and comprehensive collection brings together material from leading German scholars to examine the role of sport and PE in Germany from a range of historical and contemporary perspectives.

Key topics covered include:

- Sport and PE in pre-war, post-war and re-unified Germany;
- Sport and PE in schools;
- Coach education;
- Elite sport and sport science;
- Women and sport;
- Sport and recreation facilities.

This book offers an illuminating insight into how sport and PE have helped to shape modern Germany. It is fascinating reading for anyone with an interest in the history and sociology of sport, and those working in German studies.

Roland Naul is Professor of Sport Science and Sport Pedagogy, Essen University. He is ICSSPE Regional Director for Western Europe and Vice-President of ISCPES. **Ken Hardman** is a Reader in Education at the University of Manchester. He is a former president of ISCPES and a Fellow of the UK Physical Education Association.

International Society for Comparative Physical
Education and Sport Series
Series Editor: Ken Hardman
University of Manchester

Other titles in the series include:

Sport and Physical Education in China
Edited by James Riordan and Robin Jones

Sport and Physical Education in Germany

Edited by Roland Naul
and Ken Hardman

International Society for Comparative Physical Education and Sport

London and New York

First published 2002
by Routledge
11 New Fetter Lane, London EC4P 4EE

Simultaneously published in the USA and Canada
by Routledge
29 West 35th Street, New York, NY 10001

Routledge is an imprint of the Taylor & Francis Group

Typeset in Sabon by Taylor & Francis Books Ltd
Printed and bound in Great Britain by MPG Books Ltd, Bodmin

British Library Cataloguing in Publication Data
A catalogue record for this book is available from the British
Library

Library of Congress Cataloging in Publication Data
Sport and physical education in Germany / edited by Roland Naul
and Ken Hardman. (International Society for Comparative Physical
Education and Sport)
Includes bibliographical references and index.
1. Sports–Germany–History. 2. Physical education and
training–Germany–History. I. Naul, Roland. II. Hardman, Ken, 1938-
III. ISCPES book series.

GV611 .S635 2002   2001048825
796'.0943–dc21

ISBN 0–419–25390–4 (hbk)
ISBN 0–419–24540–5 (pbk)

Contents

Illustrations

Tables

Figures

Contributors

Martin-Peter Büch took a doctoral degree in economics after graduating in economics, law and psychology. He has experience as a coach and in sports management. He has lectured in sport economics at the Sport University in Cologne and the University of Saarland. From 1978 to 1994 he served in the Federal Ministry of the Interior in the area of sport issues, and since 1995 has been Director of the Federal Institute of Sport Science (BISP).

Ken Hardman is a Reader in Physical Education at the University of Manchester. He is a member of several international committees, including the International Committee of Sport Science and Physical Education, the International Committee for Sport Pedagogy, and the Physical Education Curriculum Development Committee of the European Network for Sports Science Institutes of Higher Education, and is a former President of the International Society for Comparative Studies in Physical Education and Sport. He is also a member of a recently established Council of Europe Working Group on 'Access to physical education and sport'.

Ilse Hartmann-Tews is Professor and Chair of Gender Studies in the Institute of Sport Sociology at the German Sport University, Cologne. She studied in the area of social sciences at the Universities of Cologne and Essex. She obtained her Ph.D. in sociology in 1989, and in habilitation in the sociology of sport in 1995. Her main areas of teaching and research are: processes of social differentiation in sport in the international perspective, focusing on changing patterns of demand and supply in leisure sport in European countries; graduate careers in sports sciences and physical education; professionalisation and gender hierarchies in sport; and media and the construction of gender in sport.

Arnd Krüger is Professor of Sport Science at the George-August University in Göttingen, where he is also Head of the Society and Training section of the Sport Science Department. He has served as Dean of the Social Science Faculty of his university. After his studies in History, Philosophy,

English and Sport, he received a B.A. (UCLA, 1967) and a Ph.D. (Cologne, 1971) before he worked for the Elite Sport section of the German Sport Federation. He started his university career as a lecturer in Physical Education at the Berlin Teacher Training College, and was then Professor of Coaching Science at the University of Hamburg. He is Vice-president of the European Committee for the History of Sport, and Chairman of the Lower Saxony Institute for Sport History. He was a semi-finalist at the 1968 Olympics (1,500 metres) and is active in many types of endurance sport. He has authored or edited more than 30 books and 250 articles.

Roland Naul is Professor of Sport Science and Sport Pedagogy at Essen University, and is Director of the Willibald Gebhardt Research Institute. He is a long-standing member, and currently Vice-president, of the International Society for Comparative Physical Education and Sport, and is a former president of the International Committee for Sport Pedagogy. His major research and teaching interests are the history of European physical eduaction, comparative physical education, youth sport and Olympic education. He has written over 200 papers and has published 18 books.

Gertrud Pfister is currently a Professor at the Institute for Sport and Sport Science at the University of Copenhagen. She studied Latin, physical education, history and sociology in Munich and Regensburg. She has doctorates in history (University of Regensburg 1976) and sociology (Ruhr University, Bochum). From 1981 to 2001 she was Professor of Sport History at the Free University in Berlin. She holds a number of international offices, including President of the International Society for the History of Physical Education and Sport, Vice-president of the German Gymnastic Federation, and Head of the Scientific Committee of the International Association for Physical Education and Sport for Girls and Women. She has published several books and more than 200 journal articles. Her main area of research is in the domain of gender and sport. She loves all kinds of sports activities, but particularly skiing, tennis and long distance running.

Frieder Roskam is an architect and landscape architect as well as a physical education teacher. He is a lecturer at the German Sports University in Cologne, and for forty years was responsible for sports facilities guidelines, standards and promotion in the Federal Republic of Germany. He has been Honorary Secretary of the General International Association of Sports and Leisure Facilities, Cologne, since 1965, and Editor-in-Chief of *Sports Facilities and Swimming Pools*, a bi-monthly journal, since 1967. He is a member of the IOC Sport and Environment Commission.

Foreword

Ken Hardman and Roland Naul

The idea for this book was conceived on the occasion of meetings of the International Council of Sports Science and Physical Education (ICSSPE) and the International committee for Sport Pedagogy (ICSP) in Ottawa in 1995. The need for such a book is self evident: there is a shortage of material published in English; there are the significant historical influences on developments in physical education in German-speaking states and throughout Europe, in the nineteenth century and inter-war era of, first, the social democracy of the Weimar Republic, then National Socialism under Adolf Hitler, followed by the post-World War II period of sport and sport pedagogy; and there is the availability of English-speaking German scholars, each of whom has expertise in specific areas of sport and physical education in Germany.

All the contributing authors have first-hand experience and scholarly knowledge of specific aspects of the sport and physical education delivery system. Collectively, they provide a balanced picture of past and present initiatives and developments, as well as themes of topical interest. Hence the content of the book has a contextualising introduction, followed by chapters respectively focusing on historical developments; organisational structures; policies and programmes in physical and sport education in school settings; professional preparation of physical education teachers and sports coaches; sport delivery systems, including issues of institutional development of elite sport and 'sport for all' structures and policies; women and sport; and sports facilities. A short bridging chapter, which provides an outline of developments in the decade (1990–2000) following re-unification, is included between historical and present contexts in sport and physical education. All chapters contain essential references, for which full bibliographic details are provided. In addition, there is a 'Further reading' section at the end of the book, which cites additional literature sources for specific chapters.

Series editor's preface

Ken Hardman

A major initiative in the development of comparative and international studies in physical education and sport was the formation of the International Society for Comparative Physical Education and Sport (ISCPES) in 1978, since when it has been the leading body in the promotion of comparative, cross-cultural and cross-national physical education and sport studies. The Society is a research and educational organisation with the expressed purpose of supporting, encouraging and providing assistance to those seeking to initiate and strengthen research and teaching programmes in comparative and international physical education and sport throughout the world. ISCPES holds biennial international conferences, publishes conference proceedings, an international journal and monographs, sponsors (in the form of patronage) research projects and, in conjunction with E&F Spon and Routledge, has launched a book series.

The idea for the book series originated in a concern about the dearth of published analytical literature in the comparative transnational and cross-cultural domains of physical education and sport. With few exceptions, there was a predisposition towards description rather than analytic interpretation in early textbooks with a 'first order' comparative or international approach. Concentration was on the 'what' and there was neglect of the essential ingredients of 'truly' regarded comparative study – the 'why' and 'how'. The volumes in this book series are aligned with the expressed puposes of comparative and cross-cultural study, and serve to progress comparative and international studies beyond mere description.

The primary purpose is for the titles in the series individually and collectively to extend knowledge of national systems and issues' themes and topics. Thus the present volume, with its focus on the national system of *Sport and Physical Education in Germany* complements the first title in the series, *Sport and Physical Education in China* (Riordan and Jones, 1999: E&F Spon). Future titles will address themes such as women and sport, adapted physical activity, and sport and religion, amongst others. These and other titles will represent a significant contribution to the progress of comparative, cross-cultural and transnational studies. The intention with all titles in the series is to present explanations and/or inter-pretations so as to provide an analytic dimension rather than mere descriptive narration. The over-riding aim is not only to provide texts, which will cover constituent elements of cross-cultural and international aspects of physical education and sport, but also to facilitate deeper aware-ness and understanding in a variety of geographical, political, regional and thematic contexts and issues. Each text can be used on an individual/sepa-rate basis to extend knowledge and understanding. More importantly, the volumes can be taken together as an integrated basis for informed compar-isons, thereby serving the overall purpose of contributing to critical awareness and analysis amongst confirmed and potential comparativists and young scholars at graduate and postgraduate level. This text on the Federal Republic of Germany (including the former German Democratic Republic) is the second of two volumes taking an 'area' study approach by examining sport and physical education in a national political entity. It has a similar format to the first title in the series on sport and physical educa-tion in China. Such a format provides consistency within the book series, and facilitates awareness of similarities, variations and differences between the countries.

Acknowledgement

This book series was made possible by a generous donation to the ISCPES Trust Fund for publications and to establish a book series, from Sheikh Ahmad-al-Fahad al Sabah, President, Olympic Council of Asia, member of the International Olympic Committee, President of the National Olympic Committee of Kuwait and Vice-President of the Association of National Olympic Committees. Sheikh Ahmad's donation is dedicated to the name and memory of his father, Sheikh Fahad al-Ahmad al-Sabah, who was tragically killed at the outset of the Gulf War.

Sheikh Ahmad, like his father, the late Sheikh Fahad, is a strong advocate of fair play in sport, and believes in the special role of sport and physical education in contributing to global peace, harmonic co-existence and prosperity. In associating with these ideals, ISCPES is indebted to Sheikh Ahmad for his support of the Society, one tangible result of which is this book series.

Ken Hardman,
Editor-in-Chief, ISCPES book series

Abbreviations

APW	Akademie der Pädagogischen Wissenschaften (Academy of Pedagogical Sciences)
ASK	Armeesportklub (Army Sport Club)
BAV	Bereit für Arbeit und Verteidigung das Friedens (Prepared for Labour and Defence of the Peace)
BDM	Bund Deutscher Mädel (German Young Women's Federation)
BISp	Bundesinstitut für Sportwissenschaft (Federal Institute for Sport Science)
BLSV	Bayerischer Landessportverband (Bavarian Land Sports Association)
DHfK	Deutsche Hochschule für Körperkultur (German College of Physical Culture, Leipzig)
DRAfOS	Deutscher Reichsauschuss für Olympische Spiele (German Reich's Committee for Olympic Games)
DSHS	Deutsche Sporthochschule, Köln (German University of Sport, Cologne)
DOG	Deutsche Olympische Gesellschaft (German Olympic Society)
DS	Deutscher Sportausschuss (German Sports Committee)
DSB	Deutscher Sportbund (German Sports Federation)
DSSV	Deutscher Sportstudio Verband (German Sport Studio Association)
DTB	Deutscher Tennis-Bund (German Tennis Federation)
DT	Deutsche Turnerschaft (German Gymnastic Federation)
DTSB	Deutscher Turn- und Sportbund (German Gymnastic and Sports Federation)
DVS	Deutsche Vereinigung für Sportwissenschaft (German Association for Sport Science)
ENSSHE	European Network of Sport Science Institutes in Higher Education
EOS	Erweiterte Oberschule (extended upper polytechnic school)
EU	European Union

FDJ	Freie Deutsche Jugend (Free German Youth)
FDGB	Freier Deutscher Gewerkschaftsbund (Federation of Free German Trade Unions)
FES	Forschungs- und Entwicklungsstelle für Sportgeräte (Research and Development Centre for Sports Equipment)
FKS	Forschungsinstitut für Körperkultur und Sport (Research Institute for Physical Culture and Sport)
FRG	Federal Republic of Germany
GDR	German Democratic Republic
GST	Gesellschaft für Sport und Technik (Society for Sport and Technology)
IAKS	Internationaler Arbeitskreis für Sportstättenbau (International Working Group for Sports Facilities)
ICSP	International Committee for Sport Pedagogy
ICSSPE	International Council of Sports Science and Physical Education
IOC	International Olympic Committee
KJS	Kinder-und-Jugend-Sportschulen (children's and youth sport schools)
KMK	Ständige Konferenz der Kultusminister der Länder (Standing Conference of the Ministers of Education and Cultural Affairs)
KPD	Kommunistische Partei Deutschlands (German Communist Party)
LSB	Landessport-Bund (Land Sports Federation)
MfS	Ministerium für Staatssicherheit (Stasi) (Ministry of State Security)
NOK	Nationales Olympisches Komitee für Deutschland (National Olympic Committee)
NSDAP	Nationalsozialistische Deutsche Arbeiterpartei (National Socialist German Workers' Party)
POS	Polytechnische Oberschule (general polytechnic school)
PETE	Physical Education Teacher Education
SA	Sturmabteilung (assault division)
SED	Sozialistische Einheits Partei Deutschlands (Socialist Unity Party of Germany)
SMAD	The Soviet Military Administration
SMD	Sport Medizin Dienst (Sports Medicine Service)
SPD	Sozialdemokratische Partei Deutschlands (Social Democratic Party of Germany
SS	Schutzstaffel (defence squadron)
SSG	Schulsport Gemeinschaften (school sport societies)
SWS	Semesterwochenstunde (semester week hours)
TZ	Trainingszentrum (Training Centre)

| VDDT | Verband Deutscher Diplom-Trainer (Association of German Diploma-Coaches) |
| VEB | Volkseigener Betrieb (state companies) |

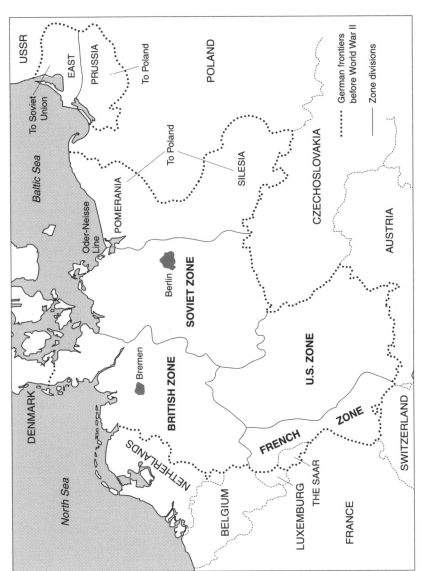

Map 1 Germany in 1945

Map 2 Federal Republic of Germany post-reunification

Chapter 1

Context for sport and physical education in Germany

Ken Hardman

Introduction

Since the late eighteenth century, German contributions to developments in sport and physical education have been significant and widespread. GutsMuths' natural form of gymnastic exercises, shaped from a range of pan-European ideas and practices, provided a conceptual framework, which became a springboard for subsequent initiatives both in sport and physical education initially throughout the European region and later beyond. The Jahn-inspired gymnastics movement was a singularly Germanic activity, which had socio-political significance at the time of its evolution in the quest for a unified German nation. Jahn's *Turner* gymnastics in its translated form gave the world 'Olympic gymnastics', which has endured the passage of time into the present millennium as an area of activity engagement from local to international levels. The thread of socio-political links with sport and physical education continued in the Hitler-led National Socialist period and in the German Democratic Republic (GDR). A pre-eminent role was assigned to physical and sporting activity, both in schools and the wider society, exemplified of course by the successful but notoriously infamous Berlin Olympic Games of 1936, and by the post World War II era of a divided Germany, in which, in the GDR in particular, sport was employed to achieve political goals in nation- and national consciousness-building as well as being a demonstration of ideological supremacy. Alongside its template-setting 'big brother', the Soviet Union, the GDR, with its relatively small population of around 17 million, set benchmarks in elite sport structures and delivery systems which served to bring about a shift in sporting power and became a catalyst for changes elsewhere in the world. Pre- and post World War I planning concepts, largely driven by Carl Diem, laid foundations for policies on community facilities for sport, recreation and physical education using basic principles around *per capita* space provision. The principles were later adapted when the German Olympic Society (DOG) fostered the 'Golden plan in the communities' (1961–75) in the Federal Republic of Germany (FRG) as well as in other countries. Another significant German contribution to the world of sport was the trail-blazing German Sports Federation's (*Deutscher SportBund* or DSB) 'Second way' (*Zweiter Weg*) campaign launched in 1959 at about the time that the GDR was flexing its sporting muscles. As an initiative to promote popular or mass sporting activity, it was intended to complement the proven forms of sporting activity in clubs and associations and serve the recreative and sporting needs of a broader social spectrum. Without doubt, it was an influential forerunner of one of the first national 'Sport for all' programmes established in 1967 in Norway under the name of 'Trim'. Variations of the Norwegian programme quickly spread south, with the then West Germany itself introducing a *Trim dich durch Sport* programme in 1970. Countries from all continental regions have gradually adopted the concept, albeit under a range of different titles.

With the exceptions of the National Socialist era (1933–45) and in the GDR in the years of separation of the two Germanies (1949–90), pervasive features of sport and physical education delivery systems in Germany have been the principles of federalism, subsidiarity and autonomy of sport as a social institution. Cultural autonomy (including education and sport) has been divested to territorial states or *Länder* with national (i.e. federal) government adopting a subsidiary role but supporting the traditionally established autonomy of voluntary sector sports organisations. The developments in the domain of sport in the nineteenth and early twentieth centuries, from clubs to *Land-* and federal-level single, multi-sport and umbrella agencies, were potent antecedents in this process. The potency is seen in the West German federal government's (1949–90) recognition of such historically embedded autonomy, which led it to take on a subsidiary role in a partnership with sport, i.e. give support 'from the flanks....The aim of all federal government efforts is to create a climate favourable to sport, enabling its optimal development' (Bundesminister des Innern, cited in Hardman 1982: 60) with 'the State furnishing an important functional service but not ruling sport, not regulating it nor subordinating it to state goals' (Kohl, cited in Hardman 1982: 60). This principle of government subsidiarity, but functioning as a supporting partner, has been maintained in post-1990 re-unified Germany. The broader significance of subsidiarity and partnership between sports bodies and government is further explored in ensuing chapters of this book which deal with various aspects in the context of sport and its delivery. An overview of the principles of federalism and subsidiarity as they apply to education is provided here, as a context for better understanding the physical education delivery systems in the pre-divided, divided and re-unified national settings.

The concept of federalism, which is at the very heart of the geo-political administrative framework of present-day Germany, is not new in its applicability. Federalism has a long constitutional tradition in Germany.

Historically, various models of state organisation developed within the framework of the federal order: the Holy Roman Empire of the German Nation (to 1806), the German Confederation (1815–66), the German Empire (1871–1918) and the Weimar Republic (1919–33). Such constitutional tradition was sustained in what was to be over forty years of a divided Germany, when in 1949 the founders of the constitutional order, established by the Basic Law (*Grundgesetz*), created a federalist order in the newly founded Federal Republic of Germany, not only in order to carry on a constitutional tradition but also to make a conscious break with the centralist National Socialist state of 1933–45. This federalism was countered in the German Democratic Republic by democratic centralism of a socialistic orientation, grounded in Marxism-Leninism. It is important to understand this background because of its consequences for developments in sport and physical education between 1945 and 1990.

The immediate aftermath of the Second World War and the National Socialist order in defeated Germany in 1945 was one of incalculable human misery, low morale, social disorder and confusion, which was exacerbated by material devastation, a void in government and reparations confiscation. The American, British, French and Soviet Union allies, as the European Advisory Commission, which was equally determined to destroy militarism, eradicate Nazism and politically decentralise the state, signed an agreement at Potsdam in 1945 to divide Germany into four zones, administered by Control Councils. The four-zone division, however, was short-lived: early Cold War politics effected a separation of the Soviet zone from the three western zones and the consequent emergence of two Germanies (Hardman 1981). Soviet aspirations to dominate the whole of Germany focused the political minds of the three western allies on striving to recruit the West Germans into the 'Atlantic camp' by granting financial assistance, mainly through the mechanism of the Marshall Plan. The 'western' inspired initiatives towards economic union and associated increasing economic conflict, together with the antagonistic political tensions between 'East' and 'West', effected the withdrawal of the Soviet zone from the proposed union. The separation of the Soviet zone from the three western zones heralded the political division of Germany into East and West. Whereas western Germany evolved and developed into a liberal, so-called western democratic administrative order, the eastern part of Germany became firmly rooted within the 'Soviet Union camp'. This separation was confirmed in 1949 when the promulgation of the *Grundgesetz*, or Basic Law, created the Federal Republic of Germany (FRG, or West Germany) as a 'social democracy of federated states', and was shortly followed by a Soviet-Union supported constitution which established the German Democratic Republic (GDR, or East Germany) as a 'socialist democracy' – the 'socialist state of the German nation'. What resulted was an administratively decentralised Federal Republic, made up of ten federated

Länder plus the specially related *Land* of West Berlin, and a centralised, consolidated socialist Democratic Republic, comprising fifteen administrative regions. The reality of two separate political entities was underscored by the construction of the Berlin Wall in 1961. It was a forty-year-long separation that lasted until the GDR's accession to the Federal Republic of Germany on 3 October 1990.

At the outset of its establishment, the Federal Republic of Germany (comprising the three 'western' zones) retained a major share of the former Germany's industrial base and natural resources. The immediate post-war years presented an acute problem for economic policy: infrastructural, industrial and housing damage; stagnation under allied military occupation, with further depletion due to demolition and reparations confiscation; workforce losses and internments; an influx of refugees (by the end of 1950, around 12 million German exiles and refugees from the former German eastern provinces and eastern Europe had moved into the territories of West and East Germany); shortages of essential supplies such as food, fuel and clothing; and low morale. A little more than a decade later the economy had experienced a substantial recovery; the 'economic miracle' (*Wirtschaftswunder*) laid the basis for one of the highest standards of living in Europe. This healthy national economic situation enabled government at all levels to invest, and sport was one beneficiary.

The German Democratic Republic (GDR), a geographically much smaller entity, was predominantly agricultural, with few natural resources. In the immediate aftermath of World War II, Soviet policy was ruthless because of its own wartime losses in men and materials; it sought compensation and revenge through confiscation, expropriation, dismantlement and demolition, and the Soviet zone became virtually a Russian industrial colony. Gradually, as the process of communising the political life of the state was extended and control seen to be in the hands of reliable party men, the Soviet Union handed over greater discretion to the GDR authorities, with exploitation giving way to partnership. The widely reported East German sports successes were matched by economic achievements. By 1966 the GDR had become the fifth largest producing country of Europe, and by 1970 was the eighth largest industrial power, with the highest standard of living of all Eastern Bloc nations. Politically and economically, the GDR became a consolidated socialist state, led by the Socialist Unity Party. It comprised 15 administrative regions with 217 districts subdivided into 9,021 communes. The supreme state body was the People's Chamber (*Volkskammer*), which had 500 elected deputies. The Council of State was responsible for implementing the decisions of the People's Chamber. The forty-year period of its existence saw two constitutions: the 1949 constitution legislated for the prevailing situation; the political realities of the 1960s necessitated a new formulation, which was adopted in 1968. The constitution provided a clear definition of the state, as well as its function and powers, and its relationship to the individual citizen.

Since 1990 re-unified Germany, under the label of the Federal Republic of Germany, has embarked upon a modern odyssey of reconciling differences embedded in different politico-ideological systems evolved and developed over a period of forty years. Re-unification was viewed as a victory of capitalist democracy over socialist authoritarianism, for the reality of re-unification was the absorption of a centrally controlled and administered state into a federally decentralised country, initially established as an anti-dote to the twelve-year period of Nazi rule under Adolf Hitler.

Present administrative organisation

Since 1990, the Federal Republic of Germany has comprised sixteen *Länder*: Baden-Württemberg, Bavaria, Berlin, Brandenburg, Bremen, Hamburg, Hesse, Mecklenburg-Vorpommern, Lower Saxony, North Rhine-Westphalia, Rhineland-Palatinate, the Saar, Saxonia, Sachsen-Anhalt, Schleswig-Holstein and Thüringia. As of 31 December 1998, administratively Germany has been divided regionally into these 16 *Länder* (including 3 city states), 32 administrative regions (*Regierungsbezirke*), 440 districts (*Kreise*) comprising 117 municipalities with the status of a district (*kreisfreie Städte*), 323 rural districts (*Landkreise*) and 14,197 municipalities (*Gemeinden*). The city states of Berlin, Bremen (2 municipalities) and Hamburg are also counted as local authorities. Some *Länder* also have inter-municipal corporations (*Gemeindeverbände*), where members agree to share resources with each retaining its individual rights.

In accordance with the Basic Law, governmental powers and functions are divided between the Federation and the *Länder*. At federal level, executive functions are discharged by the Federal Government and legislative functions by the German *Bundestag* and *Bundesrat*. At *Land* level, they are discharged by the *Länder* governments and parliaments respectively. The principle of federalism applies, i.e. both the Federation and its constituent *Länder* have the status of a state in Germany, a core element of which is cultural sovereignty (*Kulturhoheit*).

Education

Historically, educational provision has had two distinct roots: the Church (which has been involved since the early Middle Ages) and the state (the *Länder* or equivalent responsible political entity). Compulsory education was in evidence in the late seventeenth century in some areas, and was extended throughout the ensuing centuries. As the various political forces increased their determining influence on education, so the influence of the

Church generally and gradually declined. This was particularly the case in the GDR, where religion was replaced by dialectical materialism. Where religion has been able to retain an organisational presence is in the area of private education, and a significant number of the 3,000 private schools are under denominational control.

The Unification Treaty (31 August 1990) contained provisions designed to establish unity in the areas of culture, education and science, with a common and comparable basic structure in education and a common, though differentiated, higher education and research landscape in the re-unified Federal Republic of Germany. Cultural sovereignty provides the *Länder* with predominant responsibility for education, science and culture, with the proviso that policies, in line with the federalist principle, 'lend expression to the historical, geographical, cultural and socio-political aspects specific to their *Land* and thus to diversity and competition in the education system and the field of culture' (Eurydice 2001: 3). Each of the three main levels of government (federal, *Land* and local) has its own responsibilities for education. The constitutional powers at federal level in the area of education are limited to specifics such as legislation on general principles for education, regulation of grants, promotion of research, and regulation of working conditions, etc. for teachers.

The FRG system of education (1949–90)

In 1949 the Federal Republic's Constitution (Article 28) guaranteed the integrity and authority of each *Land* and devolved responsibility for educational and cultural affairs. The educational sovereignty granted inevitably led to differences in types of school and system. Educational federalism virtually produced an elevenfold centralism at *Land* level, though in general the structure of the system came to have a four-year primary school phase (*Grundschule*), followed by a three year 'orientation' transitional stage (*Orienteerungsstufe*) leading to the secondary school phase, variously comprising Grammar (*Gymnasium*) and comprehensive schools (*Gesamtschule*) and two types of general secondary school (*Realschule* and *Hauptschule*) with associated pathways into higher education institutions, technical colleges and vocational schools (full and part time). The specific pattern of types of school varied from *Land* to *Land*: some *Länder* perpetuated the more traditional grammar schools, whereas others promoted comprehensive schools. These tendencies reflected the cultural autonomy enjoyed by each *Land*, political demographics, and the influence of the former zonal legacies. Pervasively though, the *Länder* adopted an early guiding principle of equal opportunity (*Chancengleichheit*), and with a view to coordinating cooperation in the area of education and cultural matters, the *Länder* established the Standing Conference of the Ministers of Education and Cultural Affairs (the *Ständige Konferenz der*

Kultusminister der Länder or KMK) in 1949, which has served as a forum for permanent cooperation ever since.

The GDR system of education (1949–90)

The GDR had an educational system at once characterised by themes common to all communist education systems, and by features which may be termed German. The latter, however, were not readily discerned mainly due to the peculiar political situation which existed in the immediate post-war period, and which resulted in rapid upheaval to convert the then Soviet zone into a 'socialist democracy'. Hence politics and ideology were intertwined, and were significant determinants in the shaping of all aspects of life in East Germany.

The educational ideals of the Nazi period had to be completely eradicated; the pre-1933 education system, which had resulted in an entire nation being misled so disastrously, had to be suspect – thus it was arraigned. Scepticism for the system of education of the social democrats led to a sovietised form of redevelopment of the education system grounded in Leninist principles of communism. Already in 1944, the underground German Communist Party had drawn up a plan for the reform of education. The western allies refused to countenance the plan when presented at the end of hostilities, and so it could only become operative in the Soviet zone, particularly as its underlying ideology coincided with that of the Soviet occupants. In contrast to the federal structure of education and the cultural sovereignty (*Kulturhoheit*) enjoyed by the *Länder* in the (original) Federal Republic and characterised by ideological and social pluralism, the education system in the GDR was administered centrally and organised on a strict ideological basis in accordance with the doctrine of the Socialist Unity Party of Germany (SED). All fundamental issues relating to education, socialisation and science in the GDR were shaped not just by the monopoly of the Marxist-Leninist party ideology, but also by the fact that the GDR's education policy was connected to the central state control of the economy. The Soviet Union, with its experience in building up schools in a socialist society, moved to lay down the basis for centralist organisation and the ideological ties of the future education system in the GDR, when it established the German Central Administration for National Education (later transferred to the Ministry of National Education with the foundation of the GDR in 1949). The Soviet Military Authority's Order no. 40 of 25 August 1945, set the provisions legislated for in the 1946 Law on the Democratisation of German Schools. This law introduced state controlled, uniform and secular eight-year schools, provided free education, and granted equal access rights for all people throughout all stages of education. These principles were embodied in the 1949 Constitution (Articles 34 and 35) and in subsequent revisions in 1968 and 1974 (Articles 25[1] and 26[2]). Unlike its western Federal Republic counterpart, responsibility for education in the politically centralised Democratic Republic was strictly with the state, in which the Council of State implemented decisions of the SED-led People's Chamber; consequently, education was centrally controlled and administered. From 1959 to 1990, there was a gradual transition from the eight-year system followed by three years of vocational training to the ten-year system followed by two or three years of vocational training. The Law on the Socialist Development of the School System (1959), reinforced by the Law on Integrated Socialist Education (1965), established a fully integrated socialist education structure. The closely knit system comprised pre-school establishments (crèches and kindergartens), one-type co-educational ten-year general polytechnic high school, two-year extended high school and two/three year vocational school, tertiary and higher education institutions, which included vocational institutions, engineering and technical schools, colleges, universities and further education institutions for the general adult working population (Hardman 1980). Figure 1.1 shows the uniform and integrated system of education from crèche to adult- and higher education institutions.

Of the compulsory schooling years (age 6–16), generally the first three years (classes 1–3) were devoted to primary work, the next three (classes 4–6) to intermediate studies and the last four (classes 7–10) to secondary schooling; extended secondary schooling (including vocational school) lasted for two or three years (classes 11–12/13). It was a science-based education related to life in a technological age. As part of their general education, pupils were expected to spend some time in a factory or business. The basis of study was mathematics and natural sciences, with other subjects catering for aesthetic, artistic, physiological and emotional development. The German language and a study of at least one foreign language were included in the curriculum. Approximately 13 per cent of the school population went on to follow a two-year course in the extended high school (*Erweiterte Oberschule* – EOS). Criteria for admission to this phase of schooling included the ten-year leaving certificate (*Abitur*), demonstration of potential for further studies, and performance in 'Olympiad' schoolwork competitions.

The education system since re-unification in 1990

The Unification Treaty of 1990 (*Einigungsvertrag*) between the Federal Republic of Germany and the GDR required the five *Länder* in eastern Germany to reorganise education. Under the Establishment of *Länder* Act (*Ländereinführungsgesetz*) of July 1990, the five *Länder* in eastern Germany set up their own ministries of education, cultural affairs and science, joined the KMK in December 1990, and embarked on a mission of

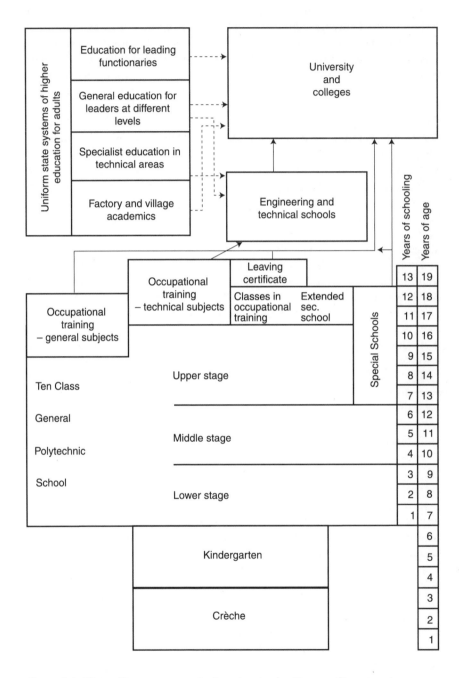

Figure 1.1 The uniform system of education in the German Democratic Republic

attaining a common and comparable basic structure in the education system of the Federal Republic. With the adoption of school legislation by the eastern German *Länder* parliaments, western Germany's differentiated system was introduced in all five *Länder* in eastern Germany at the beginning of the 1992–3 school year. For vocational training, the existing FRG regulations for the dual system of vocational education and training (*duales System*) were extended to the five new *Länder* in eastern Germany with effect from 1 August 1990. This laid the foundation for a reform of vocational training. Since the re-unification of the two German states, a central task of educational policy has been the reorganisation of the school and higher education system in the eastern *Länder*.

When the Basic Law placed educational sovereignty with the *Länder*, pluralism with variations in types of school, curricula, methods and examinations, etc., was inevitable. The 1949 KMK core task of fostering unity of purpose and coordination in cultural policy matters of supra-regional importance is still prevalent: the KMK continues to bring together the ministers and senators of the *Länder* responsible for education and training, higher education and research, and also cultural affairs in a broad sense, which includes sport. The KMK has no authority in itself, and its resolutions, which have to be unanimously agreed, become binding only if they preserve cultural federalism. Agreed resolutions are implemented in the individual *Länder* in the form of administrative action, ordinances or laws, with the *Land* parliaments playing a role in the legislative procedure.

The *Hamburger Abkommen*, a KMK agreement reached in 1964 (and amended in 1971), remains the cornerstone on which the joint fundamental structures of the school system in the Federal Republic of Germany are based. It incorporates, amongst other general provisions, the beginning and duration of full-time compulsory education; the designation of the various educational institutions and their organisation (types of school, etc.); the recognition of examinations and leaving certificates; and the designation of grade scales for school reports. On the basis of the *Hamburger Abkommen*, the KMK has agreed through supplementary resolutions other fundamental common features for the school system, as well as mutual recognition of leaving certificates for schools in all *Länder*. Of particular relevance to the 1990s is that further structural development in school education in general has been stimulated by German unity, and, in particular, by the framework agreement of 1993 (last modified in 1996) on types of school and courses in lower secondary education and their leaving certificates, as well as by the framework agreement on the standards in German, mathematics and foreign languages required for the *Mittlerer Schulabschluss*, which was adopted in 1995. The KMK also discussed the structure of the upper level of the *Gymnasium* (*Gymnasiale Oberstufe*) and of the *Abitur* following German unity, and in February 1997 a revised version of the agreement on the structure of the *Gymnasiale*

Oberstufe in upper secondary level (*Sekundarstufe II*) was adopted, which not only reinforces the importance of acquiring knowledge in major subjects such as German, mathematics and foreign languages in preparation for higher education, but also takes into account new educational findings in learning methods and class organisation.

The present system of education in the Federal Republic is essentially that of the pre-1990 situation extended to sixteenfold *Land*-level centralism, in which the structural organisation from kindergarten to tertiary and continuing education institutions varies between each of the *Länder*. Pre-school and primary phases are consistently similar throughout the country and it is mainly in the secondary schooling phases that variations occur, but even here an element of uniformity is discernible from their categorisation into two stages: secondary I and secondary II. Pre-school education (*Kindergarten*) caters for children aged 3–6. In all *Länder*, schooling is compulsory from age 6 and remains so in most *Länder* full-time until age 15 (in Berlin and Brandenburg, Bremen and North Rhine-Westphalia until 16) and part-time until 18. The system provides a general education in a common primary school (usually class grades 1–4; in Berlin and Brandenburg, grades 1–6) for all children. Transfer to one of the four types of lower secondary school (secondary I) depends on *Land* legislation. In principle there is an element of parent/pupil choice, but transfer may also be dependent on pupil ability, primary school recommendation, and capacity of preferred school. The organisation of the secondary school system (grades 5(7) to 12/13) is characterised by division into various educational pathways, with their respective leaving certificates and qualifications for which different school types are responsible. In the majority of *Länder* the following types of school exist: *Hauptschule, Realschule, Gesamtschule, Gymnasium* and in some *Länder*, *Förderstufe* and *Orientierungsstufe* amongst other variations. For pupils with special needs, there are various types of special school (*Sonderschule, Förderschule* or *Schule für Behinderte*) for different types of disability available within the organisational framework of general and vocational education.

Post-15/16 education is in the upper secondary stage (secondary II). The type of school entered depends on qualifications and entitlements obtained at the end of secondary I education. The range of schools available includes full-time vocational school or technical college, or the so-called 'dual system' combining vocational training with school attendance or schools offering an academic education. The majority of *Länder* offer the following types of school: *Gymnasium, Berufsschule, Berufsfachschule, Fachoberschule* and *Fachschule*; and in some *Länder, Berufliches Gymnasium /Fachgymnasium, Berufsoberschule, Berufskolleg* and *Fachakademie*. Pupils who do not attend a general education school at upper secondary level or enter training are required in some *Länder* to remain in full-time education and attend some sort of vocational school. The tertiary sector encompasses institutions of higher education and other establishments that offer study courses qualifying for entry into a profession to students who have completed the upper secondary level and obtained a higher education entrance qualification. Figure 1.2 illustrates the present system of education in the Federal Republic of Germany, the template for which evolved in pre-1990 West Germany.

Physical education ('sport') is a required curriculum subject during the compulsory years of schooling and features as one of four required general education subjects in the vocational schools. At upper secondary school level, sport can be taken as an *Abitur* subject. The evaluation of a pupil's performance is a pedagogical process; but it is also an administrative act based on legal and administrative regulations, whereby the teachers and the teaching staff as a whole are given some scope for discretion. Practical achievements serve as the basis of evaluation, particularly in such subjects as sport, music, and arts and crafts. Performance is assessed according to a six-mark system adopted by the KMK: 1 (very good); 2 (good); 3 (satisfactory); 4 (adequate); 5 (poor); and 6 (very poor). In the upper class stages of the *Gymnasium*, there is a credit point system, which ranges from 15 (very good) to 0 (unsatisfactory).

A pupil's progression to the next grade depends on the level of achievement at the end of the school year, as documented in the report received in the middle and at the end of the school year. An adequate mark or better is required in each of the subjects that have a bearing on promotion. Compensation for poor marks in a subject by good marks in another subject may apply. In some *Länder*, pupils who have not been promoted may, in certain school types and in certain grades, be promoted if they pass a subsequent examination at the beginning of the next school year. A pupil who has not been promoted is obliged to repeat the year. Generally speaking, it is possible to transfer between courses of education or school types, e.g. from *Realschule* to *Hauptschule* or even *Gymnasium*. Leaving certificates are awarded on successful completion of grade 9 (*Hauptschulabschluss*) or 10 (*Real-* or *Mittelsschulabschluss*). The entitlement to proceed to the upper level of the *Gymnasium* is obtained, as a rule, if certain standards of achievement are met at the end of the tenth grade at the *Gymnasium* or *Gesamtschule* (in two *Länder* at the end of the ninth grade at the *Gymnasium*). However, an entrance qualification required for transfer to the *Gymnasium* may be obtained by way of a *Mittlerer Schulabschluss* if a certain level of performance is achieved or, alternatively, via qualifications from a vocational school. Qualifications and entitlements obtained after grades 9 and 10 are mutually recognised by all the *Länder* provided they satisfy the KMK-stipulated requirements in accordance with the 1993 (amended 1996) 'Agreement on types of schools and courses of education at lower secondary level' (*Vereinbarung über die*

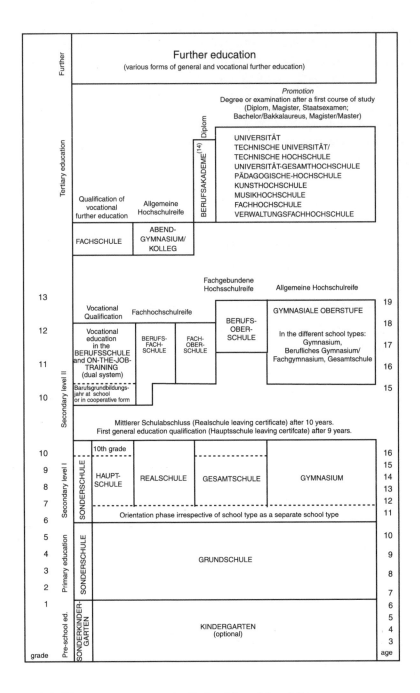

Figure 1.2 Education system in the Federal Republic of Germany

Source: adapted from Eurydice 2001

Schularten und Bildungsgänge im Sekundarbereich I) and the 1995 'Standards for the *Mittlerer Schulabschluss* in German, mathematics and a first foreign language' (*Standards für den Mittleren Schulabschluss in den Fächern Deutsch, Mathematik und erste Fremdsprache*).

This overview of the various geo-political settings of Germany and its education systems in the period of the two divided nation states (1949–90) and since re-unification in 1990, provides a contextual framework for past and present developments in sport and physical education. These developments will be presented in detail in the following chapters.

References

Eurydice (2001) *Germany*, Eurydice Information Unit.

Hardman, K. (1980) 'The development of physical education in the German Democratic Republic', *Physical Education Review*, 3 (2) autumn, 121–6.

——(1981) 'The development of physical education in West Germany', *Physical Education Review*, 4 (1) spring, 44–60.

——(1982) 'The development, structure and promotion of sport in the Federal Republic of Germany', *Physical Education Review*, 5 (1) spring, 45–61.

Strych, E. (1975) *Der Westdeutsche Sport in der Phase der Neugründung, 1945–1950*, Schorndorf: Hofmann.

Chapter 2

History of sport and physical education in Germany, 1800–1945

Roland Naul

GutsMuths and Jahn gymnastics

The first roots of German physical education were marked by the publication of J. C. F. GutsMuths' book *Gymnastics for Youth* in 1793. Translated versions of this book soon came to have widespread significance as a stimulus for the practice of physical education within school curricula in other European countries such as Denmark and Sweden. A distinct influence on GuthsMuths were his studies at the University of Halle, where A. H. Wolff was elected as the first German Professor of Pedagogy, a new type of science separated from religious studies. However, the influences on GutsMuths were not uniquely German. Other determinants included the work of several French physicians, but especially the educational philosophy embedded in naturalism and drawn from the gymnastic exercises of Ancient Greece and pedagogue Jean-Jacques Rousseau. The assimilation process and the formulation of a collection of gymnastic exercises with running, jumping, playing, swimming, etc., were assisted by the various contributions of GutsMuths' European students emanating from Austria, France, Denmark, Hungary and Portugal amongst other countries. Thus GutsMuths' 'system' of physical education was the culmination of an assimilation of pan-European ideas, requested vocational qualifications and implemented practices during his professional career in the Philanthropium at Schnepfenthal in the 1780s (see GutsMuths 1793).

After the experiences acquired in teaching at the Schnepfenthal Philanthropium, GutsMuths tried to persuade the authorities to incorporate his form of gymnastics into the Prussian school system after 1805. The attempt was subsequently supported by the likes of officers such as Hardenberg, von Humboldt, Süvern and Schulze in the Military Department and the Department of Education, who promoted 'gymnastics' as a subject within the new syllabus of the Prussian Education Reform Act from 1809 onwards. However, at about this time F. L. Jahn, a teacher in the city of Berlin, began (in 1811) to develop his more patriotic system of

German gymnastics (*Turnen*) with students on the open area of the Berlin suburb, the Hasenheide grounds (*Turnplatz*), which quickly superseded GutsMuths' gymnastics in popularity. Jahn borrowed many of his gymnastic exercises from GutsMuths' collection, but the underlying purpose and intention of the exercises and his supporters (e.g. Friesen, Beck and Follen) was linked with nationalistic notions of unifying the different German states and liberating them from French occupation by Napoleon (see Jahn and Eiselen 1816).

The Jahn 'gymnastic' model for school physical education received support from politicians between 1810 and 1820. Jahn himself was critically reluctant to have his system of 'folk' (or 'popular') gymnastics included within regular school education, because the ideal of social attitudes developed by gymnastic exercises did not fit into the frame of the rigorously controlled hierarchical Prussian education system. Conflict with Prussian State officials exacerbated by the assassination of one of their members by a student linked with the *Turner* movement brought closure of the gymnastics grounds and an associated ban (the so-called 'Ban on *Turnen*') on Jahn's gymnastics from 1820 to 1842. In practice the ban was gradually lifted in the late 1830s when the Prussian Ministry of Education was alerted to publicly reported health problems amongst school children. Gymnastic exercises have been regarded as an appropriate form of health promotion intervention since that time in German physical education history. The political uncertainties of the times persuaded the Ministry of War to give strong support to the Prussian Ministry of Education's Bill (1844) to promote physical education in schools, and saw the beginnings of Swedish influences on developments in physical education. Two military officers, Major Rothstein and Lieutenant Techow, were sent to study for a couple of months at the Royal Gymnastic Institute of Stockholm (1844–5). Rothstein became a strong supporter of the Swedish *Ling* system, which he recommended to the Prussian Ministries after his visit. In late 1847 the first gymnastic course for military personnel started in the newly founded Central Gymnastic Institute in Berlin. Rothstein was elected as Director and he himself taught the *Ling* form of gymnastics to his military students. Although the first course suffered because of the bourgeois revolution of 1848, in which Jahn supporters were involved, it signalled the beginning of training physical educators within the military system (Grossbröhmer 1994).

Lingian Swedish influence

A clear Swedish phase can be discerned between 1851 and 1863 when the Central Gymnastic Institute was under the direction of Rothstein. In 1851 the Prussian Central Gymnastics Institute also allowed entry for non-military students, and the Institute was divided into two departments, one for future officers in the military branch and one for future gymnastic teachers in schools in the civil service department. Rothstein headed the two departments. Kluge and Kawerau, both of whom were heavily involved in the Berlin Club of Gymnastics Teachers, which offered vigorous support to the new system of school gymnastics developed by Spiess, tutored the civilians. Spiess, German born, first studied Pestalozzi's elementary system of gymnastics in the 1830s and later taught his system, based on Pestalozzian methods, in the early 1840s in the Swiss city of Basel. At the time of the immediate end of the Jahn period and when the Ministry of War sent Rothstein to Stockholm, the Prussian Ministry of Education consulted with Spiess over the re-introduction of gymnastics in Prussian schools. At the Central Institute, somewhat contrary to Rothstein's views, Kluge and Kawerau became advocates of the Spiess system, which included traditional Jahn gymnastic exercises, particularly apparatus work on horizontal and parallel bars. In fact, the gymnastic training for the 'civilian' students given by Kluge and Kawerau was more similar to the Spiess system than to the officially approved Swedish system of Rothstein. When Rothstein banned horizontal and parallel bars from class instruction because these pieces of apparatus were excluded from the system of Swedish gymnastics, a clash of the respective ideologies of Swedish and German gymnastics arose – the so-called 'Quarrel of the parallel bars'. For Rothstein, horizontal and parallel bars were not conducive to health promotion in gymnastic exercises, but for the likes of Kluge and Kawerau, the foreign, unpatriotic Swedish system was inappropriate for the education of physically good and mentally strong German gymnastic teachers. The Berlin Club of Gymnastics Teachers challenged Rothstein by inaugurating a medical evaluation of the quality of the two gymnastic systems in health promotion. The clash became a political issue with discussion in the Prussian parliament. Finally, esteemed physicians and members of Parliament, like Virchow, criticised the Swedish system and recommended the German gymnastic apparatus as a necessary element in training German gymnastics teachers. In 1863 Rothstein vacated his position as Head of the Berlin Central Gymnastic Institute. Five years later, when the second Prussian physical education curriculum for folk schools was published, exercises on horizontal and parallel bars were included. Previously in the first Prussian syllabus of *Turnen* (1862), prescribed by the Prussian Act of 1860 to be delivered regularly for two hours per week in boys' schools, these had been ignored under Rothstein's rule. After the initial clash of German and Swedish gymnastics ideologies in Germany, the *Ling* system decreased in importance over a period of about ten years, to be generally replaced by the Swiss-German admixture developed earlier by Spiess. The Spiess system, which gained prominence in all German states between 1870 and 1914, comprised three parts: exercises to order like marching, free exercises of arms and legs, and apparatus exercises on horizontal and parallel bars. However, even as the system became standard in the training of gymnastics teachers in many German states, the waves of English games and sports were already approaching German schools (Grossbröhmer 1994).

The impact of English games and sports

English sports like rowing were already known in German cities such as Hamburg and Frankfurt as early as the 1830s and 1840s. Two groups were primarily responsible for introducing English sport into Germany: English-born traders, businessmen and their sons, who lived in commercial centres such as Hamburg, Bremen and Hanover; and German-born intellectuals, philologists and grammar school teachers, who had spent some time in England improving their English language skills and who became acquainted with English culture and lifestyle practices in the 1850s and 1860s. A German translation (1859) of Hughes' *Tom Brown's Schooldays* brought the essence and flavour of reformed English public school education, with its emphasis on organised sporting activity in which games (and particularly football) had an important role to play, to a wider audience. German grammar school teacher advocates of gymnastic exercises were deeply impressed by the cult of 'athleticism' and ideas on 'muscular Christianity' during their visits to English public schools. The perception was that the English type of physical activity (athletics, football and rowing), pleased the English boys much more than the ordered drills and free-standing exercise of arms and legs experienced by their German counterparts. By the 1870s, despite the efforts of some grammar school teachers to supplement the now widespread Spiess gymnastic system by re-introducing the former '*Turner*-games', the activities had little appeal for young German grammar school pupils, who were not too well disposed to participate in what they essentially regarded as mere running events. Such lack of interest in traditional Jahn *Turner*-games prompted Brunswick gymnastic teachers August Hermann and Karl Koch to introduce their pupils to football after Hermann had visited a number of English public schools and returned to Germany with a ball at the time a rarely seen item of games equipment in the country. In 1874 football was included in the physical education curriculum at the famous Brunswick public grammar school, the Martino-Catharineum. After 1878 all classes at the school had to participate in a weekly 'games afternoon', in which cricket also featured. The German gymnastics teachers' increasing antagonism towards the lack of regular games in physical education in grammar schools gained wider support from German colleagues for the initiatives taken by Hermann and Koch (Hamer 1989). In 1882 von Gossler, the Prussian Minister of Education in Berlin, sponsored a Bill to promote outdoor gymnastics lessons, rather than indoor ones in small gymnasia, with more vigorous support for rambling and *Turner*-games as physical education activities and football were included as a supplement to afternoon gymnastics lessons. The 1882 Act, the Games Act, officially recognised that games should be compulsorily taught outdoors at least every two weeks during gymnastics lessons on Wednesday and Saturday afternoons. Von Gossler decreed that the 'games afternoon' should be taught outdoors rather than in the gym, to improve health. From 1883 onwards, local head teachers were obliged to provide games lessons every fortnight. In many German grammar schools during the 1880s, *Turner* activities such as running events, stickball and English football featured regularly in physical education programmes. This, however, was not the case in folk schools, especially in Prussia, where lack of resources (space and equipment) inhibited even Spiess-method gymnastic exercises (Jonischeit 2000).

Rowing became popular from the late 1880s in Germany's grammar schools. Student self-governance was much in evidence in the school-based rowing clubs. Generally, many head teachers and other grammar school staff supported games and other sports, including rowing, because of their over-riding educational purpose as a form of 'preventive social medicine' to socialise students away from imitating the depredations of young university students, whose lifestyles were epitomised by tobacco smoking, excessive beer drinking and amoral social habits, then perceived to be characteristics of a 'strong German'. In spite of support from the Prussian Ministry of Education, in 1892 the 'games afternoon' became optional for all grammar schools. It was to be a non-governmental organisation which would become the real advocate for English games and sport for German school children (Eisenberg 1999).

The German Gymnastic Federation (*Deutsche Turnerschaft*) was founded in 1868. The first national sports association on German soil, the German Rowing Association, was founded in 1883, and was soon followed by the German Swimming Association (1886), and the first German Football and Rugby Association (1890), which after a decline in membership was re-established as the German Football Association in 1900. In 1902 the German Lawn Tennis Association was established. The last two decades of the nineteenth century were of great importance in the establishment of sport clubs, in the development of the first networks of regional and later national sports associations, and in bringing sports and games into the frame of school-based physical education. One national umbrella association became the leading institution in promoting English sports and games in Germany, inside and outside the school systems – The Central Association for the Promotion of Folk and Youth Games (*Zentralausschuß zur Förderung der Volks- und Jugendspiele*). The Association was founded in Berlin in 1891 and immediately started to promote English games and sports throughout Germany. Advocates, officers, and teachers like Hermann and Koch served on its executive board. The Association organised numerous short-term internships for gymnastics teachers in many urban locations over the next twenty years. Instruction books and booklets with the rules of games like tennis, cricket, football and many traditional German games (such as stickball) were distributed to schools and teachers free of charge. In this way Prussian federal and regional school authorities spent less money on fostering games education in grammar schools, leaving some local city school boards, and in particular the Central Association, as the only real promoters of the English games movement in Germany from the 1890s up to the outbreak of World War I (Jonischeit 2000).

Common ground was shared by the Central Association and the German Gymnastic Federation in opposing Pierre de Coubertin's and the Greek representatives' invitation for Germany to participate in the first modern Olympic Games in Athens in 1896. It was an individual, Willibald Gebhardt, supported by the court of the German Emperor, who arranged Germany's participation in the Games. In 1904 Gebhardt, together with some of his former Central Association adversaries, founded the first German standing Olympic committee, the German Reich's Council for the Olympic Games, which existed until 1917 when Carl Diem changed its name to the German Reich's Council of Physical Activity, under the premise that he and other members could not envisage any German participation in the Olympic movement after the end of World War I. As a national equivalent, the German Combat Games were celebrated in the 1920s and 1930s, and the Reich's Council continued to function as a national sports council, representing the different German sports associations until the beginning of the Nazi period in 1933 (see NOK 1999).

Meanwhile, the German Gymnastic Federation remained antagonistic towards 'English' sport and was joined by German gymnastics teachers, who were strongly opposed to any English kind of physical education. The British concept of sportsmanship, striving for excellence and record performance in any one physical activity, was altogether different from the attitudinal spirit embraced by German gymnastics. Football, for example, was criticised as a typical 'English disease'. Kicking a ball was like kicking a dog in the rear in the view of many *Turners*; it was not perceived as the kind of bodily exercise which readily fitted into the spirit of good posture which was a favoured feature of German gymnastic exercises. Indeed, between 1911 and 1914, there was some decrease in English games and sports in German schools. Football was never unanimously accepted by teachers because of the 'wild, rough uncontrolled activities', which sometimes led to injuries, for which teachers were privately made responsible by parents. Another reason why teachers remained reluctant to develop the game of football relates to the state authorities' refusal to pay any insurance fees for their teachers whilst teaching at school. Although many student-organised football clubs existed in grammar schools around 1900, the decline of football in schools continued up to 1914 (Naul *et al.* 2000).

German gymnastics teachers were not trained in games (and particularly not in English sports) at the Prussian Central Institute for Training Gymnastics Teachers in Berlin before 1908. The adoption of English games and other sports in German grammar schools was more or less a private initiative of anglophile teachers, supported by the non-governmental lobby, the Central Association for the Promotion of Folk and Youth Games, and some city school authorities, which either rented playing fields or financed the provision of playgrounds at newly founded local schools. The Prussian school authorities did not financially support this movement, but rather remained as a subsidiary partner for non-governmental activities. The relationship between state education authorities and the Central Association was good: teachers who wished to undertake further education course units provided by the Central Association for games teaching training could officially do so, but incurred expenses were not reimbursed. Without the independent efforts of the Association, none of the many boys and girls in German folk schools, to which about 95 per cent of all students belonged at the turn of century, would have had the opportunity to be involved in organised games afternoons during their school career. Prussian education authorities, because of their perceived propensity to prepare future German gentlemen and officers, supported English amateur sports.

Spiess German gymnastics and Swedish gymnastics

Before the end of the nineteenth century, it was already clear that English imports were supplementing the classical Spiess type of gymnastics in German grammar schools. Students enjoyed athletics, football, rowing and tennis as alternative physical activities to German gymnastics. Frequently the third gymnastics lesson per week, which became compulsory in Prussian schools in 1892, was used in many grammar schools as a 'games lesson', even though official curriculum policy dedicated this additional lesson to German gymnastics. German gymnastics on Spiess lines was under pressure. Representatives of the German Gymnastic Federation were aware of the implementation of games and sports in grammar schools, and as a patriotic alternative they tried to revive the 'sacred cow' of the former *Turner*-games with the inclusion of 'stickball' within the school physical education programme: GutsMuths' and Jahn's traditional activities were not to be replaced by the English game of football! However, the games and sport movement was not the only challenge to German gymnastics in schools. After 1900 there were increasing reports of new developments in Swedish gymnastics (*Törngren*) and the Danish (Knudsen) interpretation of Swedish gymnastics in the monthly journal, *Turnwesen*. The leading German physician, F. A. Schmidt, at that time a member of the executive board of the German Gymnastics Federation as well as of the Central Association for Promoting Folk and Youth Games, undertook a short study visit to Stockholm in 1899–1900. During this fact-finding tour, he observed Swedish gymnastics teaching at the Royal Central Gymnastics Institute in Stockholm, just as Rothstein had done some sixty years earlier. Schmidt also observed gymnastics teaching in Stockholm's folk schools. His short visit left him deeply impressed with the Swedish system from a physiological point of view. On his return to Bonn, he wrote a couple of articles about the new Swedish gymnastic system together with a book about his visit. The publications highlighted the physiological benefits of Swedish posture exercises and the use of Swedish gymnastic apparatus like the beam and the box. As a medical authority and an executive board member of the German Gymnastic Federation, Schmidt's recommendation of Swedish exercises as a supplement to German gymnastics was not regarded as unpatriotic. The door was now open for other gymnastics teachers to reform the old Spiess system, not only through sport and games but also by new forms of gymnastics (see Schmidt 1912).

Reform of German gymnastics commenced around 1904–5, when gymnasts met at three conferences, the so-called 'Hamburg art education days', at which Schmidt was an invited speaker. In 1909 the Prussian Ministry of Education passed a new Act on 'Gymnastics for schools without a gymnasium'. Then for the first time modern Swedish posture exercises were introduced in a state physical education curriculum in Germany. Whilst the traditional Spiess system of order-based, free- and apparatus exercises as the form of physical education in folk and grammar schools still dominated the structure of the curriculum prior to World War I, athletics and sports together with Swedish posture exercises already supplemented the 'German system'. Without these European influences before the War, the decline of the traditional Spiess system would have been less rapid in the early 1920s.

'Natural gymnastics' and the spirit of competition

At the end of the 'Great War' in 1918, political revolution ushered in the social democrats, who were responsible for the constitution of Germany's First Republic (the Weimar Republic). Reforms of the education system were considered and changes made. Physical education attracted interest from groups with different motives. Liberal groups of reformers and educationalists wanted to promote new 'natural' methods in school physical education for its new status as an integral part of general education and its role in developing the mentally and physically (i.e. harmoniously) developed individual. On the other hand, some more right-wing orientated *Turners*, sportsmen, and politicians supported school physical education as a counter to the prohibition of any military training for young Germans according to the Treaty of Versailles. From the outset of the Weimar Republic, therefore, school physical education was dually entwined with new educational purposes and curriculum initiatives, and with traditional, more law-and-order orientated, disciplinary and gymnastic exercises to offset the loss of military service (Naul *et al.* 2000).

In 1920 the 'games afternoon' became compulsory for all pupils every fortnight. Sports and games were implemented in folk schools. Examinations in gymnastics and athletics became obligatory in grammar schools at matriculation (*Abitur*) for entry into university-level study. Once again, however, football, seen as one of the new sports of the proletarians, did not gain the support of many grammar-school teachers. *Turner*-games like stickball and fistball dominated games education at school. A new *Turner*-game, field handball, was developed by leading gymnasts and became popular in clubs and at school in games afternoons. It was played 11 *v.* 11 on a football pitch and received the general support of physical education teachers. Field handball now became the true 'German game' for the *Turner*s. Exclusion of football from the new Prussian physical education curriculum for grammar- and middle-school boys was discussed in the mid-1920s. Meanwhile, many of the schoolboys played their beloved game in youth teams within one of the now numerous German football clubs.

English-style athletics almost replaced gymnastics during the summer term. The Spiess form of German gymnastics was officially omitted from the new physical education curriculum, but relics were still mixed with 'natural' types of gymnastics in lessons during winter. In primary schools, gymnastics lessons were largely revamped using exercises drawn from 'natural gymnastics', with a child-centred instruction strategy based on the 'Austrian school of gymnastics', developed by Margarete Streicher and Karl Gaulhofer from Vienna. Both scholars and their approach to teaching gymnastics were supported in Germany by such reforming *Turner*s as Erich Harte and Fritz Eckhardt. Through the officer, Ottendorf, at the Berlin Ministry of Education, several aspects of Streicher's and Gaulhofer's 'Austrian natural gymnastics' approach were included in the new physical education curriculum for girls in 1926. The reforming gymnast Erich Harte and the traditional *Turner* Edmund Neuendorff both became responsible for the new physical education curriculum for boys, published in 1925 (Gessmann 1987). Whereas Harte promoted the Austrian system of his friends Streicher and Gaulhofer, Neuendorff preferred the new 'Bukh approach' of the Danish system. However, Neuendorff put together elements of athletics, traditional German apparatus work, and the Danish type of more physiological-functional floor exercises into one new curriculum area, 'competitive gymnastics'. Competitive gymnastics according to Neuendorff was a mixture of German-English-Danish styled physical education elements, which were not regarded, especially by Gaulhofer, as systematic. What was clear, however, was that whilst the elements did not sit comfortably together as one system, the spirit of competition to achieve personal records, excellent postures and a shaped body was pervasive (see Gaulhofer and Streicher 1922; Neuendorff 1927).

Body shape, linked with Bukh's gymnastics, was viewed as a basic performance level for training athletics and apparatus gymnastics. Neuendorff and Harte replaced the classical tripartite structure of the Spiess system with a new structure: 'body training', which in the main encompassed various types of running and Bukh gymnastics; 'competitive gymnastics' with athletics and apparatus work; and games, including the German games of stickball, field handball and fistball. Swimming and rambling were also included, with both playing an important role as outdoor activities in school-based physical education in the 1920s. Nonetheless, there was also a strong resurgence of patriotism in the late 1920s and early 1930s, which resulted in military preparation within physical education before Adolf Hitler and the National Socialists (Nazis) came to power in 1933. Edmund Neuendorff, responsible at the turn of the 1920s for physical education teacher training in Berlin, became a fervent supporter of the patriotic resurgence, with marching securing an important place alongside rambling.

Aryan body training and political physical education

Adolf Hitler had already pointed out in his book *Mein Kampf* (1924) the purpose of Nazi-ruled physical education: a German boy should become as strong and stainless as Krupp manufactured steel, as durable as leather and as quick as a whippet. But before the education system was changed from what was considered to be an inferior training of the mind to the strong physical education of the body, all sports organisations were placed under the political control of the newly elected Reich Sports Leader, Hans von Tschammer und Osten. Federal sports associations (e.g. those for gymnastics, athletics and football) lost their independence and had to join the newly founded German National Socialist Reichsbund of Physical Activities. All sports organisations which were linked in any way with political parties other than Hitler's National Socialist German Workers' Party (NSDAP) or Church sports organisations were legally obliged to close down. The Hitler Youth organisation and paramilitary Nazi organisations like the SA ('Assault division') and SS ('Defence squadron') became the new leading organisations for training the young Aryan body ready to serve 'his leader Adolf Hitler' (see Bernett 1966; 1983).

School-based physical education became less important for the Nazi authorities when compared with their efforts to train young Germans in the Hitler Youth organisation and special Nazi-elite schools (the 'Adolf Hitler Schools'). Nevertheless, physical education became the most important school subject at that time and was strongly controlled by the new Department K (K being the abbreviation of the German term 'body education') of the Ministry of Public Education. In 1934 the third weekly lesson of physical education, discontinued by the Weimarian Ministry of Education a decade earlier due to financial problems, was re-introduced. The third lesson was financed by the Reich Military Ministry, and was dedicated to particular sports: in the lower physical education classes (grades 5–7) swimming; in the middle physical education classes (8–10) football; and for the upper physical education classes (11–12) boxing, which became compulsory for physical education graduation as a prerequisite for obtaining the school general certificate and gaining entry into university. In 1937 a new physical education curriculum was introduced for boys, and lesson allocation was extended to five hours per week. Pupils who failed in physical education were not permitted to continue their studies at grammar schools. Physical education was used to develop a 'hygienic Aryan race', to foster the 'mentality of a soldier' and to build strong 'leadership qualities'. Techniques, skills, good posture or individual performance were less important. The role to be aspired to was a strong fellow who disregarded risk of physical injury as a challenge for the individual body, who did not fear man-to-man combat as an integral part of the 'national body', and who would pursue whatever his leader, Adolf Hitler, wanted him to do. Engaging in the new German 'combat games' of football and field handball as a team member and fighting individually in the boxing ring at school, together with pre-military exercises in outdoor activities with marching, learning to spy, and to attack and defend in 'war games' in the countryside were the physical activities which dominated the curriculum. A role model for girls' physical education was also established in the Nazi schools, although it was late 1941 before the new syllabus for girls' physical education was published. The girls were educated in new German gymnastics, athletics and field hockey: the strength to bear children dedicated to the *Führer* was as important as the 'beauty of the race' (Bernett 1985).

Building the Aryan body with the spirit of the Nazi ideology was successful in German schools, even though there were a number of problems in delivering the physical education syllabus. Four to five hours of physical education were frequently provided, but it was only possible because classes were combined. Mass exercises ensued from shortages of teachers and the lack of available sports facilities. Physical education immediately declined in the years 1939–40 because many physical education teachers were recruited for military service in the war (Peiffer 1987). In many cities, physical education classes were closed after two or three years of war: gymnasia were used either to house people whose homes had been damaged or destroyed by bombing, or to store food or equipment salvaged after the allied bomb attacks. Many school buildings were also closed, and school children were separated from their parents and sent with their teachers to youth hostels and lodges in Alpine regions to protect them from the frequent bombings at home. Without doubt, physical education in the National Socialist period was implemented in accordance with the Aryan ideology, just as the Berlin Olympic Games of 1936 were utilised to demonstrate the superiority of Germany's 'national body'. However, the ideology of the Aryan body culture inside and outside the school system remained an enduring threat for post-war re-education and democratisation processes in the Federal Republic of Germany, especially in the 1950s when reactionary forces inhibited the renewal of physical education in schools.

Conclusion

German gymnastics systems developed by GutsMuths and Jahn were assimilated in the nineteenth century in other European countries such as Denmark and Sweden (GutsMuths), in the Austro-Hungarian Empire, and in the Netherlands and Belgium (Jahn) by immigrants after the bourgeois revolution of 1848, just as in the case of the United States of America. In the second half of the nineteenth century, however, the concepts of Lingian gymnastics from Sweden and the British games and sports movement supplemented the development of school physical education in Germany. Nevertheless, the rather mechanical German system of Spiess gymnastic excercises overtook all previous forms of gymnastics and new European influences up to World War I. The renewal of gymnastics via the different approaches of natural gymnastics (Austria, Denmark, Sweden) in the 1920s was accompanied by strong support for athletics and games, which finally formed the classic structure of German physical education, with gymnastics, athletics and games supplemented by swimming and other outdoor activities like rambling.

It is clear that state authorities gave special support for physical education in schools in the different pre-war periods (i.e. after 1900 and after 1933). Pre-military preparation with gymnastics and sports, and later with games and sports, shaped young male German bodies physically and mentally in readiness for each challenge – to serve either the Emperor Wilhelm or the *Führer* Adolf Hitler. There were of course several reform concepts and strategies implemented to teach physical education, but the more sophisticated educational aspirations were subjugated by political agendas and by prominent gymnastics and sports leaders who opened the doors of national gymnastics and sports associations to receive the influence of political instrumentalisation and guidance.

References

Bernett, H. (1966) *Nationalsozialistische Sportpolitik*, Schorndorf: Hofmann.

——(1983) *Der Weg des Sports in die nationalsozialistische Diktatur*, Schorndorf: Hofmann.

——(1985) *Der Sport an der nationalsozialistischen Schule*, St Augustin: Academia.

Eisenberg, C. (1999) *'English Sports' und Deutsche Bürger*, Paderborn: Schöningh.

Gaulhofer, K. and Streicher, M. (1922) *Grundzüge des österreichischen Schulturnens*, Vienna: Deutscher Verlag für Jugend und Volk.

Gessmann, R. (ed.) (1987) *Schulische Leibesübungen zur Zeit der Weimarer Republik*, Cologne: Strauss.

Grossbröhmer, R. (1994) *Die Geschichte der preussischen Turnlehrer*, Aachen: Meyer & Meyer.

GutsMuths, J. C. F. (1793) *Gymnastik für die Jugend*, Schnepfenthal: Druckerei der Anstalt.

Hamer, E. U. (1989) *Die Anfänge der Spielbewegung in Deutschland*, London: Arena.

Jahn, F. L. and Eiselen, E. (1816) *Die Deutsche Turnkunst zur Errichtung der Turnplätze*, Berlin: Selbstverlag.

Jonischeit, L. (2000) *Spielerziehung in der Schule. Zur Geschichte der Bewegungsspiele*, Aachen: Meyer & Meyer.

Naul, R., Jonischeit, L. and Wick, U. (2000) *Turnen, Spiel und Sport in Schule und Verein. Jugendsport zwischen 1870 und 1932*, Aachen: Meyer & Meyer.

Neuendorff, E. (1927) *Methodik des Schulturnens*, Leipzig: Quelle & Meyer.

NOK (1999) *Deutschland in der Olympischen Bewegung. Eine Zwischenbilanz*, Melsungen: Bernecker.

Peiffer, L. (1987) *Turnunterricht im Dritten Reich. Erziehung für den Krieg?*, Cologne: Pahl-Rugenstein.

Schmidt, F. A. (1912) *Die schwedische Schulgymnastik*, Berlin: Weidmannsche Buchhandlung.

Chapter 3

Sport and physical education in the two Germanies, 1945–90

Ken Hardman and Roland Naul

Introduction

The realities of developments in educational, economic and social systems
in the two Germanies from 1949 on were embedded in politico-ideological
differences: in the administratively highly decentralised western Federal
Republic of Germany these mirrored the democratic and market economy
ideals of so-called capitalist western democracies; and in the centrally
controlled eastern German Democratic Republic, they reflected an idea of
democratic centralism based on socialist (some would argue communist),
Marxist-Leninist inspired principles. International recognition of the
sovereignty of the Federal Republic of Germany was not long in coming, a
major influence on which were the Cold War political interests of the West
and the early-1950s economic union and political intitatives in western
Europe. In the GDR, Soviet exploitation directly associated with compensation for wartime losses in men and materials only gradually gave way to
the partnership and economic recovery for which the Democratic Republic
came to be regarded in the mid-1960s as a shining example of communist
economic planning. Contributory to its international political recognition
were the considerable international sporting successes of the GDR, manifest in the progressive acknowledgement of its national sports associations
by international organisations, for example the recognition of an independent national Olympic committee in 1965 and the participation of its
athletes as the GDR team in the Olympic Games from 1968 on. With the
establishment of the *Deutscher Sport Ausschuss* (German Sports Committee
or DS) in the Soviet zone of occupied Germany in 1948 (it was later replaced in the GDR by the German Gymnastics and Sports Federation, the
Deutscher Turn- und Sportbund or DTSB, in 1957) and the German
Sports Federation (*Deutscher Sportbund* or DSB) in the FRG in 1950 in
Frankfurt-am-Main as the umbrella association for all sports associations
and their member clubs, the post-World War II division of Germany was
officially extended into the realm of sport. The result was the existence of
two completely different sport structures and systems in the two German
states, which persisted until re-unification in 1990. Therefore, the develop-

ment of sport and physical education in Germany should properly be dealt with in two separate sections (Federal Republic of Germany and German Democratic Republic). First though, there follows a review of developments from the end of the National Socialist era to the constitutional arrival of two new nation states.

Early post-war developments

The development of organised sport, 1945–50

The total collapse of the Third Reich and the subsequent chaos, coupled with a rejection of everything Nazi, were dominant factors in developments in sport and physical education. Under the leadership of Adolf Hitler, physical activity had enjoyed pre-eminent status in assisting the *Führer*'s aims of a fit and superior Aryan race, and so it was entirely consistent with post-war anti-fascist attitudes that sporting activity was officially disregarded. The four-zonal command affected sport as much as any other social institution. The revival of sport was difficult under the prevailing circumstances of the dissolution of Third Reich institutions, the disqualification from public and semi-public office of former active Nazi Party members, and the requirement of a special licence from the military command to practise organised sporting activity. Officially, no member of a former Nationalist Socialist organisation was allowed to participate in a sports meeting. However, despite malnutrition, poor living conditions and the allied imposition of anti-fraternisation regulations, sport was soon taking place among the inhabitants and troops, and some relaxation in restrictions were evident as early as September 1945. Allied Control Power policies and interpretation of Directives were not uniformly consistent. Early on it became clear to German sports personnel that they could expect little from the French and Russians, whereas the Americans and British showed a greater degree of tolerance. The first *Länder*-level sports organisations emerged in the American zone in 1946; in the French zone they were not allowed until 1948 (Sorg 1955). Generally, however, despite the zonal variations, initial uncertainties were partly allayed through Allied Ordinances 8–13, which were implemented by Directive no. 17 on 15 September 1945. The Directive foreshadowed rapid developments in organised sports structures, and within five years both the Democratic and Federal Republics had 'umbrella' organisations promoting and fostering the cause of sport. In essence, Directive no. 17 permitted the establishment of clubs without prior consent of the military rulers; mistrust, however, was mirrored in the Directive:

> The military commanding officers are reminded that the history of sports clubs under the Nazi regime shows that they formed a powerful

tool in the spread of Nazi doctrine and militarism. It is clear that the present relaxation in the restriction of their activity contains a danger that they will again be misused in this way.

(Sorg, cited in Hardman 1982: 45)

Control Directive no. 23 (17 December 1945) progressed the cause of sport. It aimed to erase the pre-capitulation organisation of sport, to impose a ban on the practice of paramilitary sport and to restructure sport in a decentralised, democratic and non-military form. Sports organisations were permitted up to local district level but only with local Allied Control Authority permission. Interpretation varied from zone to zone with regional sports officers: some were liberally minded, others restrictive. Ordinance no. 104 on 'Control of sport' of 18 June 1946 granted permission to hold inter-district competitions subject to military commanders' agreement. Within two years Ordinance 104 had been annulled and Control Directive 23 had become largely ineffective, but by the end of 1948 the British military rule was publicly disposed to approve a sports association at zonal level. It was a progression which fell short of German aspirations for an umbrella organisation of at least the three western zones. Before such an organisation could be established, major difficulties had to be overcome: reconciliation of different opinions; removal of occupying forces' prejudices; and initiation of democratic processes. One major problem was finding sufficient numbers of experienced administrators to manage clubs and association affairs, because Directive 24 excluded all active Nazi Party members from public and semi-public office and this included sports organisations. The Directive was soon superseded by Directive 38, which established five categories of levels of guilt (1. principal offenders; 2. incriminees [activists, militarists, profiteers]; 3. less incriminated; 4. 'camp followers'; 5. those persons cleared) and in accordance with Ordinance 79, which was reinforced by Ordinance 122 on removal from office of former Nazis, only category 5 persons were allowed to be active in the executive of a sports club or organisation. However, despite the strong exclusion measures, the reality was that some ex-party members were in evidence (Strych 1975).

The early post-war years witnessed some conflict between *Land* sports federations and the governing bodies of sport, but especially between the gymnasts and footballers. The sources of conflict were embodied in the developments and clashes in the late nineteenth and early twentieth centuries when sports activities were challenging the introspective *Turner* associations, and in finance. The *Land* federations required clubs to pay dues to finance regional activities and for distribution to the sports associations. The Football Association in particular, as the largest member organisation and with a substantial income, objected to any form of financial control. Whereas the great majority of sports bodies sought a new organisational structure which would bring unity, the gymnasts pressed ahead with forging first their own bi-zonal (American and British) committee in autumn 1947, and eventually as part of a process of rationalisation bringing together all gymnasts, the German Gymnastic Association (DT) was established in 1950. Meanwhile the footballers had officially re-established the German Football Federation (DFB) as the first post-war German Sports Association on 10 July 1949 after a process which had seen a football championship planned as early as the 1946–7 season (the occupying powers objected to the scheme), the formation of a bi-zonal (British and French) committee in December 1947, an extension into the German Working Committee for Football (DFA) on 10 April 1948, followed by a constitution and the renewed structure of the former German Football Federation.

The zonal organisation of sport

In their zone, the Americans allowed sport to recommence quickly. The Bavarian Worker Sports group attempted very early on to revive sport, and representatives of other politically neutral bodies aligned themselves with the promotion of reconstruction. As early as July 1945, club administrators founded the Bavarian *Land* Sports Association (BLSV), which was granted its licence in June 1946. In order to achieve a democratic structure, the clubs became direct members. The Association's Council, with a majority of club delegates, elected and controlled the management committee and decided on statutes and finances. The sports representatives, who were organised in branches, were sports-wise and financially independent. With the exceptions of North Rhine-Westphalia and South Baden, which went other ways, this formula, derived from a desire for uniformity and unity, was adopted by all other *Land* sports associations.

In the British zone, the early post-war months were epitomised by confusion and different opinions. Hugo Grömmer propagated the idea of people's sport associations. In the Westphalia region a *Volkssport* association was founded in December 1945. Swimmers, footballers and gymnasts were allowed to form 'interest societies', but the British authorities were not always lenient and occasionally vetoed requests to form a federation. Gradually, however, new forms of organisation developed. Of these the Zone Sports Council and *Land* Sports Federation were of particular importance. After Directive 23 came into force, the British permitted the creation of a non-executive body to discuss matters of general concern and compliance with the requirements of the military rule. The Zone Sports Commissioner convened the first assembly in February 1946. The meeting called for the creation of a unified sports organisation, the establishment of a sports college in the zone, and supra-regional organisations. This small assembly was the forerunner of the Zone Sports Council, which was constituted at Detmold in May 1946. Four sub-committees were set up: school sport, youth sport, adult sport – men and women. The founding of the Council was contrary to the views of those single-sport associations, particularly football, who wanted to retain their autonomy. At its assembly in Marl in November 1946, the Zone Sports Council produced an organisational model, which represented a compromise between the single associations and the unified umbrella organisation. The Marl scheme envisaged clubs becoming direct members of the unified body, which would be financed through a poll tax on the incomes of the sports associations. With the discussions at zonal level proving fruitless, events switched to *Land* level: in Lower Saxony, Hamburg and Schleswig-Holstein unified associations were founded; clubs, in line with the Marl model, had direct membership. By the middle of June 1947, all *Land* sports federations in the British zone had been established. With the exception of North Rhine-Westphalia they were modelled on the Marl plan.

In the French zone there was a quite different picture. The French sports officers were fully aware of the nationalistic orgins of the German *Turner*. Their somewhat negative attitude seriously hampered the development of the supra-regional organisation of sport. Sports activity was strictly limited, and hence opportunities to influence others at inter-zonal conferences remained way behind those of the other two western zones. It was not until 1948 that the French occupying forces thought the time ripe to permit sports organisations at *Land* level. The *Land* sports associations which came into being followed the south German model of organisation.

In the immediate post-war period Soviet policy ruthlessly sought compensation and revenge for its own war-time losses in men and materials, and the Soviet zone became virtually a Russian industrial colony. The entrenchment of the East Germans in the 'Soviet camp' inhibited progress in developments in sport, but gradually, as the process of communising the political life of the state was extended and control was seen to be in the hands of reliable party men, the Soviet Union handed over greater discretion to the East German authorities. A partnership evolved, in which the later GDR came to be regarded as a shining example of communist economic planning.

In its anti-Nazi stance, the Soviet Military Administration (SMAD) gave considerable support to the German Communist Party (KPD). Its Order no. 2 of 10 June 1945 permitted the (re-)establishment of non-Nazi political parties and trade unions, and the KPD took on a vanguard role in the Berlin-based Central Sports Committee and Main Sports Office, formed under the Berlin *Magistrat*. Sport in Berlin at that time was organised on the basis of communal groups, administered by the local sports offices of the municipal districts. By way of contrast, in Leipzig, attempts by former Workers' Sports Movement officials to establish a united 'popular' sports movement were temporarily prevented by the US occupation forces.

However, with the change in occupying power on 15 July 1945, Soviet-backed communal sports groups were developed in Leipzig. In practice, the communal sports groups were the only organisational forms tolerated by the authorities. The Allied Control Council Directive no. 17 of 15 September 1945 merely formalised the role of the new communal sports groups in the Soviet zone, and Directive 23 of 17 December 1945 primarily reinforced the *status quo* with its restrictions on activities to local level and proscription of para-military sports such as boxing, judo and shooting. The dearth of non-Nazi affiliated sports personnel resulted in responsibility being placed on those whose political reliability was more highly valued than their experience. In Mecklenburg, for example, responsibility for sport was granted to the anti-fascist youth groups in December 1945 and later to the Free German Youth (FDJ) organisation after its foundation in March 1946. Although officially an independent organisation, the FDJ became closely associated with the Socialist Unity Party, founded in April 1946 by a merger between the KPD (German Communist Party) and the SPD (German Socialist Party). At its first assembly, the FDJ laid down 'Basic Rights' for young people, one of which was the right to sport, a right later to be enshrined in a series of 'Youth Laws'. The importance of the FDJ in the domain of sport was underlined when the SED's Cultural Committee placed responsibility for sport in FDJ hands. In May 1948, the FDJ Central Council drew up new guidelines for sport, amongst which was removal of the Control Council Directive 23 limiting competition to regional level, thus permitting Soviet zone championships for the first time in 1948 (Eichel 1983). The SED continued to politicise sport when it increased the influence of the Free German Trades Union (FDGB) through greater involvement in sport. In August 1948, the FDJ and FDGB joined forces in a 'Call for the creation of a democratic sports movement', the culmination of which was the creation of the German Sports Committee (*Deutscher Sportausschuss* or DS) in October 1948 by the FDJ Central Committee and FDGB Executive. The rhetoric of political activism associated with the developments in sport in the Soviet zone effectively condemned to failure any attempts to create a unified sports movement of East and West. The reality of division was confirmed with the declaration of intention, at the Allied Sports Conference in Bad Schwalbach on 16–17 July 1949, to create an umbrella organisation for sport in the three western zones, the detail of which is presented in the next section below. The *de facto* division of Germany with the founding of the Federal Republic and the GDR in 1949 coincided with a greater emphasis on the role of sport as a vehicle for expression of ideology. The ideological underpinning of the sovietisation process and its relationship with sport had been previously evidenced at the 1948 constituent assembly of the German Sports Committee. Erich Honecker, then Chairman of the FDJ, linked sport with politico-social affairs, when he called for a politically orientated sport movement to assist in the process of nation- and national conscious-ness building. It was a process envisaged to embrace the creation of a new culture through holistic development, a democratic renewal of the nation in the interests of peace and international understanding, improvement of the nation's health and efficiency (specifically amongst young people) and promotion of broad participation in mass sport as well as club-based competition (Hardman 1980). Honecker was clearly establishing a direct relationship between politics and physical culture in the pursuit of socialist aims. This relationship was later underlined by Manfred Ewald's (1973) comment that 'One principle has been ... valid ... from the very beginning: the active share in educating the athletes to become conscious builders of the workers' and farmers' state, our socialist G.D.R., has been, and continues to be, one of the basic aims' (Ewald 1973: 9–10). Subsequently, key politicians and leading administrators and pedagogues continuously reinforced the constitutional principles and particular significance of sport and physical education. On the occasion of a meeting of the State Council in September 1968, for example, Walter Ulbricht, Chairman of the Council, identified physical culture as a part of the national culture and as a main feature of humanistic culture policy; he also intimated that all-round education of mind and body was central in forming a new type of man, i.e. a 'socialist personality' (Hardman 1980).

The emergence of the German Sports Federation (DSB)

In November 1946 the first sports conference was held in Frankfurt with the object of initiating a unitary sports association for the whole of Germany. Non-obligatory (and therefore ineffective) resolutions on restructuring and educational re-orientation of sport encompassed the promotion of the Olympic ideal through a National Olympic Committee, the re-establishment of international relations for which a unitary associa-tion was necessary, regular physical education with qualified teachers, re-institution of a broadly based sports badge scheme, emphasis on lifetime activities, and sport for women (Strych 1975). Following the next inter-zonal conference in July 1947, when the assembled body was made up of *Land* sport associations' representatives, the first supra-regional sports organisation, the German Sports Union, was set up, albeit for a short period of time. In February 1948, the South German *Land* Sports Association's representatives formulated proposals for the formation of *Land* sports federations and by implication an umbrella organisation. At the next conference held in Munich in April 1948, to which the South German *Land* Sports Associations' Union had invited two representatives from each *Land* sports association and one representative from each governing body of sport in order to reconcile any differences, the assembly set up an acting committee to work out a model for an umbrella organisation. The route to the eventual establishment of such an organisation was rather tortuous: for instance, because of the cessation of communication with Soviet Zone sports personnel and the restrictions imposed in Berlin and in the French zone, it fell to the American and British zones to carry on the work, and they were only joined by the French initially with three delegates at a sports conference in Bad Schwalbach in July 1949, and later at a plenary session in August 1949, when the French zone representives took a full and equal part. In the meantime, the occupying forces continued to oppose progress towards the creation of an umbrella organisation, and it took meetings in Cologne in May 1948, at Bad Homburg in October 1948 and Bad Schwalbach in July 1949 to reach agreement on a range of contentious issues. Fuel was added to the fire on 24 September 1949. In Schwalbach, the sports officers had advised the German functionaries to wait until an umbrella association had been established before forming an Olympic Committee. But the Germans were impatient and, with the cooperation of the newly formed Federal Government, the National Olympic Committee of West Germany (NOK) was founded. In spite of this potentially confrontational development, an inaugural assembly of the umbrella organisation was called for 19 March 1950, but further delay occurred because of conflicts of interest in relation to a draft constitution. Ultimately, after revision of the draft constitution and concessions to large organisations over the voting franchise, the inaugural meeting was held in Hanover on 10 December 1950, when the constitution and thereby the foundation of the German Sports Federation (*Deutscher Sportbund* or DSB) as it was finally called, came into being. This was the body

> to secure unity in German sport and to achieve ... set goals ... namely the promotion of the aims of sport and the interests of its member organisations in relation to state and communities and publicly oversee the control and conduct of supra-associational matters and tasks.
>
> (Strych, cited in Hardman 1982: 49)

The situation of physical education

The 'womb of sport', physical education, did not enjoy a similar rapid rise to prominence, rather the contrary, especially in the western part of Germany, where contemporary educationalists lacked the courage to bring to physical education the dignity which had been so denigrated and misused by the National Socialists. Hence physical education did not appear on the immediate agenda of the reconstruction of education. Moreover, shortages in the supply of teachers, equipment and buildings added to the chaos. In Berlin alone, 50 per cent of schools had been destroyed and only 26 out of 332 gymnasia had survived the ravages of war (Hardman 1981). Restoration to a position of relative respectability was slow, and even when the KMK was established it was rather ineffective in making progress, especially as the cultural and political individualism of the *Länder* conflicted with uniformity and standardisation. Essentially, it was left to the DSB and other voluntary or private sector bodies to reveal the plight of the subject in schools and promote its situation and cause through advocacy and action. The post-1950 developments are addressed below and in Chapters 4 and 5.

Concluding comments

A consequence of the two different directions in which the two new nation states moved after the 1945 Potsdam agreement is that the evolution and development of physical education and sport in the period of separation up to 1990 have to be considered in two parts and have to address two separate entities: the Federal Republic of Germany and the German Democratic Republic. It is possible to discern some similarities, but the principal and significant differences between the two Germanies are such that it is impossible to make direct chronological comparisons in their respective progressive developments. The decentralised/centralised polarisation of the two countries embedded in post-war politics and ideology profoundly influenced all developments, some of which were pervasive and persistent, while others occurred in relation to specific events or within different periods of time. Hence, in dealing with the two states as separate entities, some persistent issues in the GDR, such as extra-curricular programmes and the politicisation of sport, are addressed outside the general (but not identical) chronological structure followed.

Physical education and sport in the Federal Republic of Germany

Material crisis and individual character-building (1949–65)

The consitutional stranglehold on the KMK of unanimous agreement of all *Länder* ministries of education and the arts ensured that reforms in education in general, and physical education in particular, were slow to materialise. At the outset of the newly constituted Federal Republic, the position of physical education in schools was largely determined by adverse reactive anti-Nazi opinion, a shortage of teachers and gross deficiencies in provision of facilities. The first curricula published, for example, in the federal *Land* of North Rhine-Westphalia in 1949 (see Naul and Grossbröhmer 1996) expressly rejected the 'inhuman' National Socialist concepts of physical education. Re-education policy and efforts to deal with the legacy of National Socialism caused education authorities to revert to the ideas which had resulted in school physical education reform during the period of the Weimar Republic, and whose educational concept had been converted by the Nazis into their own political ideology. The true aim of the Weimarian years of reform had in fact been the harmonious intellectual and physical development of the individual in the interests of an all-round education, and it was this heritage which inspired the first curricula for physical education in schools in the new federal states (Naul *et al.* 2000).

Many of the initiatives in developments in physical education stemmed from organisations outside the education sector. Thus the German Olympic Society (DOG, a voluntary 'interest group', not to be confused with the National Olympic Committee) and the German Sport Federation (DSB) were instrumental in drawing public attention to the deplorable situation of physical education in schools, citing KMK indifference to its plight, and ascribing descriptors to it such as a 'misery', 'a step-child', a 'catastrophe'. At federal level, in the early 1950s, the DSB was already becoming the key proponent of physical education. In an initial stock-taking of the progress of physical education in West German schools (1955), the DSB ascertained that only 0.9 hours a week of instruction were actually being provided. Many federal states had still not incorporated physical education into their new schedules as a compulsory subject with a specified number of teaching hours. The DSB endeavoured to establish contacts with the 'central partners' and to persuade the KMK, as the body responsible for general education policy, and the local authorities responsible for the construction of sports facilities (the German Congress of Municipal and Local Authorities) to work together to promote physical education. The adverse exposure of physical education's situation caused the KMK, with the support and approval of the DSB and leading munic-ipal authorities, to issue *Recommendations on the Promotion of Physical Education in Schools* in 1956, which emphasised the role of physical education within education as a whole, particularly its contribution to the preservation of health. The *Recommendations* called for appropriate recognition of physical education on the timetable, a reappraisal of teacher training, provision of facilities and closer school/club cooperation (Arbeitskreise der Kultusminister der Länder *et al.* 1956). Specifically, the recommendations included a call for a daily period for physical education and games during the first two years of primary school; three hours a week from the third year onwards, plus a further games afternoon providing two hours of sport a week. Looking to the future, the recommendations called for daily physical education and sport to be introduced for all school years. These recommendations were justified until the mid-1960s on the basis of an educational ideal, in which physical education had an essential role: 'Physical education forms part of the overall education of the young; if physical education is non-existent or inadequate, education and development as a whole are placed in jeopardy' (Wolf 1974: 6). The implementation of these recommendations varied with each *Land*: Hesse and North Rhine-Westphalia, for example, introduced curricula which allocated three hours a week to physical education before 1960 (see Mester 1962; Kurz 1977). But overall nationwide, there was little other response in practice, though several *Länder* were sympathetic in theory.

The general reluctance to act caused the DSB once again to publicly deplore the lack of progress and to challenge the KMK to be more proactive in fostering the cause of physical education. In 1961, Willi Daume, then President of the DSB, accused the KMK of 'intellectual secularisation' in their 1956 joint recommendations, because far too little had been done in the meantime by the *Länder* ministries for education and the arts to promote physical education in the course of their numerous educational projects. A statistical study conducted by the DSB in 1965 showed that a decade on from the *Recommendations*, on average only about 25 per cent of the jointly agreed time allocation targets had been met (Wolf 1974). Nonetheless, despite this discouraging record, physical education had gained some ground in the Federal Republic's schools during the period between 1950 and 1965, even though there was still a serious lack of qualified instructors and the provision of aid for the construction of sports facilities was still in its infancy. The Federal Youth Games, composed of indoor sports in winter (if a gymnasium was available) and athletics in summer, using school playgrounds and playing fields, had been held regularly since 1951. These Games were compulsory for all boys and girls from the fifth year onwards. The term 'games', however, is somewhat of a misnomer, because the content comprised track and field activities such as running, jumping and throwing in the summer, and gymnastic exercises (floor and apparatus work) in the winter terms. During the period from the mid-1950s to the mid-1960s, the requirements of the Federal Youth Games in physical education became the *de facto* curriculum of school sport. At the same time, the syllabus was extended to include, especially on games afternoons (usually Wednesdays), outdoor sports for girls (especially team games such as Völkerball and stickball) and for boys (especially football and handball). At the very least, every pupil was supposed to pass a fifteen-minute swimming test, introduced as a safeguard against the risk of drowning on bathing trips to rivers and lakes in the summer. At different times of the year, hiking expeditions and school excursions supplemented the physical education programme, which was sexually segregated and followed a seasonal cycle in the same way as the Federal Youth Games. The over-riding aim of this physical education curriculum was the development of individual personality. Qualities such as enthusiasm and determination, developed through regular activity and competition, were deemed to assist character formation in general. Many physical education theorists in the early 1960s were convinced that these individual qualities, fostered particularly by physical education, would extend to, and shape, the whole personality of each pupil and so make an important, formative contribution to a general code of behaviour (this was the 'transfer hypothesis'). Thus the theories applied to physical education at this time were very much in line with the social context of post-war Germany, where accelerated reconstruction and the 'economic miracle' of the 1960s found expression in career qualities such as determination, enthusiasm and competitiveness. Viewed in this light, this era of physical education in the Federal Republic may, in retrospect, have been more successful in shaping minds and characters in the context of a competitive society than its many critics (amongst whom were Daume, Balz and Mester), assumed in the 1960s, when they considered the minimal extent to which its aims were met. In this regard, it is hardly surprising that in standard reference works, this first developmental phase of physical education in West German schools was labelled 'the school sports crisis' (Paschen 1969). Historians like Krüger (1979) characterised this early stage of crisis in physical education development in the Federal Republic of Germany as reminiscent of the Weimar period, both because of the educational concepts and traditional purposes, and the lack of financial support.

Education in leisure sports activities for all and the training of the gifted for elite sport (1966–80)

Economic prosperity and political change in the early 1960s left their mark on the development of sport and physical education in schools. The building of the Berlin Wall in 1961 intensified the East/West conflict, which became the driving force behind the rise of elite sport in West Germany. In 1963 the *Bundesliga* marked the arrival of the era of professionalism in football. Other branches of sport rapidly followed this example of concentration on elite sport and the division between amateur and professional at federal level. After the internal trials to select a combined German Olympic team in 1964, East German athletes formed a majority for the first time. The international recognition of the East German sports associations, with their own NOC, meant that two German states were allowed to participate on equal terms in world championships and the Olympic Games (1968). Economic growth and tax revenues made it possible for West Germany to bid to stage the 1972 summer Olympics, and in 1966 the IOC decided in favour of Munich. Prosperity and economic growth had also made it possible by the early 1960s to reduce the working week from 48 to 42 hours. It was not long before school children, too, had Saturdays off. These free Saturdays were available for leisure and recreation.

In the domain of physical education, the DSB's early 1960s challenge to the KMK resulted in the *General Guidelines for Physical Education in Federal German Schools* (1966). The *Länder* were urged to support standardisation, to examine their existing guidelines with a view to adapting, or even reformulating, them in accordance with the principles expressed. The *Guidelines* embraced the tasks of physical education, regarded 'as an essential element of education' (KMK 1966: 2), principles of teaching method and syllabus content, students' voluntary activities, teachers' responsibilities and duties, assessment of students and exemption from physical education lessons. Eventually, the *General Guidelines* principles were adopted by three *Länder* (Baden-Württemberg, Bavaria and Rhineland-Palatinate), whilst in three others (Hesse, Lower Saxony and North Rhine-Westphalia) measures had already been implemented prior to the announcement of the general plan. Elsewhere and outside of the education sector, two new, forward-looking approaches to both school and club sport were specifically promoted by the sports associations and, in particular, the DSB: more sport for all in the increased available leisure time, and additional training and financial incentives for particularly gifted athletes. These two new developments, which would have a decisive influence on school sport from the late 1960s, were launched by the DSB in 1966 with its *Charter for German Sport*. Interestingly, the *Charter*, which pointed to the indispensability of physical education in the education of people and suggested that 'Guidelines, curricula and proposals for school reform must take this fact into account' (Deutscher Sportbund 1966: 1), was published a year before the KMK's *General Guidelines* document. The *Charter* called for daily exercise in the first two school years, three lessons per week from the third year on, with two hours of afternoon games, and regular physical education in the vocational and technical schools; it sought closer school/club cooperation, active parental involvement and priority provision of facilities. The similarity of aims, purpose and content of the KMK's publication exemplifies the significance of the DSB as a persuasive and influential body. The DSB's charter also prompted Grupe (1968) to draw up a strategy for a new form of physical education, which in abandoning the view that its main purpose was the development of the individual through physical exercise, favoured a belief that it would serve to prepare for, and encourage, individual involvement in sport outside school or after school hours, with more communication, social contact and social cohesion in the new leisure society. With the Munich Olympic Games in 1972 in mind, the *Charter* also sought to promote achievement in elite sport, and it was no surprise that a few months after its publication, the year 1967 witnessed a change in DSB policy from promotion of the general cause of physical education in schools to a concentration on fostering competitive sport and excellence in sport. Notably, this was the year before the Olympic Games were scheduled to take place in Mexico City, and there was growing West German concern over the successes of East German athletes. The DSB formulated the 'Resolution on the promotion of competitive sport' on the promotion of sporting talent in schools. The 'Resolution' encompassed a series of measures to set up experimental sports schools, introduce streaming based on sporting ability, promote interest groups in schools and clubs more effectively, increase attention to the organisation of competitive sport in clubs, intensify systematic training, centralise resources to maximise effect, and train greater numbers of coaches (Hardman 1981). Federal support was sought mainly on account of the related financial implications. With one eye on the Democratic Republic, the Federal Government could hardly refuse.

A year later, in 1968, after discussions with the KMK, the DSB officially adopted the programme entitled 'Talent identification and promotion with the aid of schools'. Thus in the space of two years (1966–8) the new shape for physical education had been determined: preparation for leisure sport and promotion of competitive sport. Various agencies at Federal, *Land* and sports association level gave voice to action and talent promotion programmes. For educationalists, they were a pragmatic means to enhance the status of physical education. However, difficulties in achieving unanimous agreement between the different bodies concerned led to a five-year delay before discussions came to fruition in an 'Action programme' of 1972. Meanwhile, several *Länder* had already produced their own plans, thus illustrating both the independence of the individual *Länder* and the cumbersome nature of negotiations imposed by the federal structure on supra-regional bodies. Gradually, however, the *Länder* incorporated the spirit and intentions of the suggestions into their respective guidelines, and the innovations introduced brought a degree of uniformity across the country.

In the course of the process of change towards a sport-orientated physical education, proposals were also made in West German sporting circles for the introduction of special schools, *Sportsgymnasien* or sports grammar schools, to develop talent. They were to be modelled on the East German KJS system (children's and young people's sports schools). Such schools were actually set up in some West German *Länder*, but by the mid-1970s it had become apparent that they were failing to achieve as much as had been hoped for in the advancement of young top-class athletes. Instead, as part of the reform of sixth-form education, as mentioned earlier, sport was successfully introduced as a special major or a minor subject, carrying appropriate credits for the *Abitur*, with five or six lessons a week, including instruction in the theory of sports.

The new dual objectives of preparation for leisure and promotion of competitive sport for physical education in schools exerted an influence on the continuing development of the school sporting curriculum in all West German *Länder*, an influence which endured into the 1980s. In the course of various school reform programmes (the introduction of the secondary level, the reorganisation of post-16 education) new schedules and curricula offered greater differentiation of sporting activities to suit pupils' needs and abilities and, as proposed by the DSB, curriculum content was also extended to include new leisure-oriented types of sport such as tennis, table tennis, badminton, etc. The developments also ushered in a terminological change. As early as 1968, North Rhine-Westphalia had become the first *Land* to replace the term 'physical education' with 'subject sport', and was followed from 1970 onwards by all *Länder* adopting the name 'sports education' for the subject.

During the Cold War era, both before and after the Munich Olympics of 1972, West German society came to accept the public funding of elite sport at federal and *Land* level (e.g. the creation of the Federal Institute for Sports Science, and the construction of training centres). The DSB and *Land* sports federations (LSBs) and various specialist committees controlled and coordinated the initiatives. During this same period, too, the DSB, together with the KMK and the leading local associations, drew up an 'Action programme for school sport' that was introduced in 1972 to update the old 1956 programme for the promotion of physical education. This 'Action programme' expressly referred to a new form of school sport, designed to prepare children and young people in schools for participation in sport in society and later social life. It also critically referred to earlier time allocation targets for physical education in schools, which had not been achieved in several *Länder* after sixteen years of development. It called for more emphasis on learning for sports education, and also improvement of motor learning in primary schools, with sports lessons becoming more differentiated in accordance with pupils' personal interests and their level of peformance in secondary schools. Additionally, the plan sought the inclusion of new types of sport in the curriculum to foster life-long engagement in physical activity and increased cooperation between school-based physical education and sports club programmes for talented students. As a miniumum, three lessons of physical education in primary schools (ages 6–10) were requested in the 1972 'Action programme', as well as organised extra-curricular sport when physical education did not feature on the school day's timetable. For secondary I schools (ages 10–16), three lessons per week were demanded; in secondary II schools (16–18), the demand was for two hours per week for grammar schools and at least one lesson in vocational schools. Improvements in the construction of sports facilities and the provision of equipment also advanced the cause of sport in schools, as did the increasingly widespread appointment of qualified sports instructors by the *Länder* in the 1970s. Interestingly at this time, curriculum allocation to sports education was much closer to the theoretical target of three hours a week than it had ever been. The performance principle was taken seriously for the development of new physical education curricula in the early 1970s. Primary school children in North Rhine-Westphalia, for example, were introduced to basketball, football, team handball and volleyball via the concept of 'mini-games', just as their physical performance and technical skills in swimming were tested in the four Olympic disciplines of breast stroke, front and back crawl and dolphin stroke in grades 3 and 4.

Without doubt, sport in schools benefited from state aid to the education system and elite sport. The educational aims for school sport were revised, both in view of the success in terms of material and human resources in overcoming the earlier physical education crisis in schools, and in bearing in mind the statement of educational objectives for the new form of school sport. Many sports educationalists now believed it possible to dispense with having to justify sport as an essential part of a general education. Moreover, the attitudes of many students, who preferred the 'pleasure principle' to the 'performance principle', showed that the character-forming effect of physical education was clearly not as significant as had been assumed in previous years. In the second half of the 1970s, Kurz (1977), who reflected the views of other sports educationalists, took the lead in reformulating the educational function of sports education in more realistic terms. The aim was no longer the formation of an individual's moral character through physical exercise, but the more modest ambition of creating sporting *Handlungsfähigkeit* to prepare pupils for lifelong engagement in sport. The concept of *Handlungsfähigkeit* (literally 'capability of action') as a single word embraces a variety of concepts that were being voiced in professional circles during the second half of the 1970s as criticism of the one-sided sports orientation of physical education. The term *Handlungsfähigkeit* in sport represents three general objectives:

(i) the intention behind sports education cannot be exclusively based on the 'performance principle' but must also take account of other objectives;

(ii) the content of sports education must not be defined solely by the disciplines of competitive sport (e.g. the sprint in athletics) but must also take account of in the same context the fundamental forms of movement (running, jumping, throwing); and

(iii) *Handlungsfähigkeit* must not merely promote motor skills but must encompass the advancement of social skills and the intellectual approach to sport (see Kurz 1986).

In essence, 'Handlungsfähigkeit' implies a variety of purposes in physical education, and different perspectives on practising sports-based physical activities.

Typically in the late 1970s, each *Land* had developed its own physical education guidelines, though in practice the general framework of guiding principles and suggested syllabi were rarely applied. Initially the terminology employed differed amongst the *Länder*, but gradually came to be standardised as 'sport' or 'sport education'. Essentially throughout the

Länder, the fundamental aims were the preservation of health and the development of a high level of physical efficiency; other similar aims and objectives could be generally discerned. There was a common ideal of harmonious and optimum development of the individual. Specifically health, endurance, strength, performance, character, willpower – respectable, social values-related objectives – were in evidence (ironically, philosophical justification was seldom acknowledged) and excellence and participation came to be pervasive aims, with emphasis on competition, interest, aptitude and performance groups. In summary, the guiding principles of the individual *Länder* regarded physical education as a constituent part of school education, allowing the child in the school context scope for play and movement, through which spiritual and intellectual powers are acquired. It had a formulative task in the education of the all-round personality. The guidelines widely indicated three or four curriculum time lessons per week, but frequently figures suggested these were not being achieved in some *Länder* and some school levels – the situation was worst in vocational schools, where more than 90 per cent of schools offered either a minimal physical education programme or no programme at all.

Whilst physical education curriculum content was subject to specific *Land* variations, generally in the primary phase classes, there was a 'movement' orientation with emphasis on creativity and discovery learning, as well as exploration of small apparatus, but it was supplemented by special learning and training in sports activities. Basic skills (e.g. throwing and catching) were complemented by 'natural' activities such as running, jumping, climbing, etc., as well as by respective guidelines for sport activities. Swimming featured in all *Länder* guidelines and throughout the school years. The curriculum in secondary schools comprised athletics, games, gymnastics (with apparatus work for predominantly for boys and rhythmic and dance activities for girls), swimming and outdoor pursuits. With the accelerating trend towards choice in activity, the range of curriculum opportunities increased, especially in the 1980s, but spread of activities depended on staff availability, facilities, environmental conditions and traditions of the school and area. The range of games was expanded in schools by the promotion of basketball and volleyball, and by the introduction of racquet sports such as badminton and tennis and table tennis as new 'lifelong' sports activities. The proliferation in options offered stemmed from educational desirability of choice according to needs and abilities, and also from the attempts made by different organisations to encourage and promote sporting talent.

Physical education enjoyed compulsory subject status with annual student assessment (of effort and performance, general fitness, behaviour and attitudes, participation in extra-curricular activity, knowledge of rules, training programmes and safety precautions, etc.). After reforms in the late 1960s and early 1970s had led to the establishment of the gymnasial 'upper secondary level', it became possible to choose 'sport' as an elective specialist subject. This was consistent with the prevailing philosophy of the time, which was to enable students to select a school course corresponding to their aptitudes and talents. An outcome of KMK efforts to standardise requirements in the gymnasial upper secondary level was the 'Agreement on the application of uniform standards in the *Abitur* examination', which led to general stipulation for objectives and structure in instruction in physical education. At *Abitur* (school leaving certificate) level, 'sport' could be taken as a fourth subject, comprising four 'practical' and two 'theory' (biological, physiological and sociological aspects) lessons in the week.

Generally, throughout the West German *Länder* new 'leisure sports' were introduced into schools, and the range of 'competitive sports' designed to screen and promote talent also broadened in the early 1970s. For interested school pupils and for those with relevant aptitudes, there were opportunities to extend experiences through voluntary participation in extra-curricular recreational and competitive sporting activities available in school sports societies and clubs. The various 'action' and 'promotion' programmes after 1968 stimulated various initiatives and schemes, some of which required cooperation with outside-school agencies. Many of the initiatives were linked with the search for, and promotion of, talented young people. No doubt they were, in part at least, prompted by the Federal Committee for the Promotion of Sports' document (1971) 'General framework for the search and promotion of talent', which called for a systematic approach to provide a standard model for the promotion of talent. Schools were believed to have a lead role in the search for such talent. In addition to the programme related to talented pupils, there were diverse 'grassroot' activities such as *Trim* (health-fitness/active lifestyle related) and the German Sports Badge scheme (age-group related with bronze, silver and gold levels) as well as intra- and inter-mural, inter-school competitions, school sport festivals, local through to national championships including the Federal Youth Games and Youth Trains for the Olympics (*Jugend trainiert für Olympia*) competitions. The *Olympia* programme, introduced in 1968–9 with the 1972 Olympic Games in mind, not only gave competitive sport in schools an enormous stimulus, but it also helped to produce closer ties between schools and sports clubs. Every year, trials were held (and are still being held) in more than twenty different sports and in all age groups from 10 to 18, to identify the best school athletes, first at municipal level and then in each district, region and state, the *Land* champions going on to take part in the federal schools finals in Berlin.

Towards the end of the 1970s, a general disillusionment with school sport began to set in. As financial resources became tighter, less highly qualified instructors were recruited, the construction of facilities was cut back, and the great expectations of the promotion of competitive sport in schools had to give way to more realistic considerations. The structural features of the West German schools system meant that it simply could not afford to promote talent in the same way as the KJS system in the GDR. Additionally, increasing numbers of sports pedagogues were coming to regard the sports focus of physical education, even in normal school sport, as an educational restriction on children's upbringing. It was hardly surprising, then, that many sports pedagogues preferred a direction which offered alternatives to competitive sport in sport education.

Handlungsfähigkeit *in sports- and alternative sports education as physical experience, and open education (1980–90)*

In many physical education-related published materials, the 1980s is characterised as a phase of 'differentiation' (Grössing 1983). 'Differentiation' had come to encompass not only pupils' physical performance and personal interests, but also a variety of purposes in physical education and different concepts of physical education teaching approaches. The concept of *Handlungsfähigkeit* for grassroots leisure-time sports activities was assimilated by many physical education specialists (see Kurz 1986; 1987) and provided a basis for new physical education curricula in some of the West German *Länder*, and particularly in North Rhine-Westphalia (Kultusministerium NRW 1980–1). At the time, however, criticism arose that this approach was grounded too much in the spirit and structure of sport and restricted by its emphasis on motor skill learning, technique instruction and (competitive) games strategies. It was argued that the approach was not within the pedagogical frame, and that rather than serving the educational purpose of *Handlungsfähigkeit*, the real content of the objectives in the new physical education curricula were again limited to sport outside school (see Aschebrock 1986; Hübner 1986). As a consequence of the criticism of *Handlungsfähigkeit*, and in line with the strong support for social learning in physical education in the newly established comprehensive schools of the 1970s, Jürgen Funke (1980; 1983) developed a completely new approach to physical education teaching. The terms 'sport' and 'instruction' were dispensed with; both were linked with teacher-centred instruction to foster learning and promulgate exercise. Instead of teacher-directed instruction of physical skills in selected sport activities, pupils should experience and explore 'the body' and, assisted by their class peers, re-discover their lost 'sense of the body'. Total awareness of the whole body was the overall aim, and this had to be discovered through indirect teaching and the individual's experiences. Psycho-motor activities and motor tasks solved by a team were a real alternative to teacher-directed sports education. At this time also, the international 'new games movement' fitted neatly into this approach to physical education in Germany and was implemented in schools. Whilst this form of physical education orientation did not feature generally in *Länder* curricula (there were some exceptions in a few comprehensive schools), in the day-to-day situation of school physical education, parts of Funke's approach were implemented, particularly in the late 1980s, when Funke himself provided examples of how regular teaching of sports like gymnastics, track and field could be changed and supplemented by his methods (see Treutlein *et al.* 1986; Funke 1997).

Two other important 1980s trends in 'differentiation in physical education' are worthy of attention here: one is closer to the concept of Kurz's *Handlungsfähigkeit* in sport, the other is closer to Funke's alternative of 'experiencing the physical body'. Hildebrandt and Laging (1981) criticised the teacher-centred approach in school sport activities. Both wanted to have students as 'partners' of physical education teachers in discussing and deciding both on the purpose and content of physical education lessons. They were not critical of the sport approach *per se*, but rather the process of teacher-centred direction in decision-making and action-taking. They argued that agreement between the more open-minded teacher and students should be negotiated on ideas and intentions in the gymnasium. This student-centred concept of teaching physical education should be 'open ended' by unplanned teacher interaction processes. The intention was to have multi-purpose approaches in teaching sports activities, not limited by a single direction and kept flexible by heeding children's social interests and needs. This concept was taken up by others who introduced modifications, either in the direction of any unstructured possible physical activity, or linked with the skills and techniques of certain kinds of popular school sports. In this regard, the so-called 'open concept' shares some aspects (variety of purposes of sports practice) of the *Handlungsfähigkeit* approach.

More critical about the general structure of skills and techniques in sports activities, and more antagonistic to the modern sports system as a negative outcome of technological developments in society, was the so-called 'Frankfurt Group approach' (Frankfurter Arbeitsgruppe 1982; Landau 1996). The thesis is that basic movement competences with a variety of movement patterns like balancing and jumping, etc., have been over-socialised in terms of certain skills and techniques. Gymnastic apparatus, for example, should be re-structured and used for basic movement experiences. Because of societal developments, many children no longer have general motor abilities because they have been taught specific techniques at school without any experience of the variety of movement patterns, and without having the basic psycho-motor competences to move the body as a whole. New concepts of teaching have been developed for a range of movement activities, using ropes and other gymnastic apparatus, balancing on parallel bars, or moving with large plastic feet and balancing with sticks across a swimming pool (see Trebels 1983; Joeres and Weichert 1984). With the deconstruction of motor skills in some sports activities, in particular in gymnastics, this approach is close to Funke's concept of 'experience the body'. Both concepts have become the forerunners for a new physical education label in the 1990s, 'movement education' (see Marburger Sportpädagogen 1998), a label which has been criticised as an inappropriate term to replace the educational purpose of physical education (Krüger and Grupe 1998).

Despite these almost antagonistic developments in physical education, extra-curricular activities associated with the promotion of competitive school sports in the context of the old Federal School Games and the Youth Trains for the Olympics campaign still continued, as did the 1970s approach of teaching sport at school for students' participation in leisure sport activities within the sport club. However, there was increasing criticism of the insufficient educational purpose of *Handlungsfähigkeit*, and in particular of extra-curricular activity as the antithesis of 'body experiences'.

The 1980s was also a period when more attention was devoted to strengthening ties between schools and sport clubs, with a focus more on the 'sport for all' than the competitive sport perspective of the 1970s, as well as on extending the variety of extra-curricular physical activities offered within schools (e.g. table tennis in the school yard during breaks, etc.). Both of these aspects, along with other 1980s developments in teaching sport at school, were included in the *Second Action Plan for School Sport*, which was initiated again by the DSB and its partners (KMK and Council of Municipalities) in 1985 (DSB 1985) against a background of value-changes in society and a reshaping of educational philosophy. This 1985 *Second Action Plan* outlined principles and measures for the further development of physical education and sport. The underpinning principles were the enrichment of life in school, importance of sport in modern society, and concern at young children's decreased physical activity related to societal developments: 'das Spielkind wird das Sitzkind' ('the active, sporting child is becoming the sedentary child'). Special attention, different from previous progammes, was paid to the promotion of manifold extra-curricular physical activities as an essential part of daily school life and as bridge to sporting life outside school and beyond school years. It addressed curricular and extra-curricular sport at all levels, teacher training, facilities, school/club relationships, special needs groups, etc. The realisation of the principles was seen as a corporate responsibility, involving governments (federal and *Land*), educational, religious and other social institutions, sport clubs and associations, parents, trade unions and significant others. To some extent, the *Second Action Plan* incorporated the approach of *Handlungsfähigkeit* and communicated this essentially

North Rhine-Westphalian physical education curriculum approach to a wider federal audience. It was proposed to increase the amount of hours in primary physical education movement activities, as in other subjects such as music and fine art. For secondary I schools there was a continued demand for a minimum of three lessons weekly, as well as for the promotion of sport as an optional fourth subject for *Abitur*-graduation.

The elements of 'body experiences' and their association with deconstruction of the school sport disciplines were also implemented, not so much through official *Land* physical education regulations but more by schoolteachers (and school-based physical education in-service training) who wanted to improve social learning in physical education, in particular in primary schools. The 'new games movement' entered the physical education curriculum and new types of school-based games festivals with fun-orientated physical activities also emerged in this context (Brodtmann and Landau 1984). But there was controversy about the direction of this 'alternative' concept of a new physical education (see Krüger 1988).

In the second half of the 1980s, in academic circles and at conferences, a new/old orientation for physical education was discussed: the renaissance of character building through physical activities as a pre-requisite of general education, with a view to re-introducing moral attitudes and values in teaching physical education (see Meinberg 1986; 1987; Naul 1985; 1987; Beckers 1987; 1996). For some years, the impact of education in physical education had been lost because the approach of *Handlungsfähigkeit im Sport* supplanted the character building purpose of physical education by the introduction of different perspectives in the practice of sports activities. But this 'back to educational basics' trend in physical education was only acknowledged and accepted after German re-unification in the 1990s. School-based physical education in the 1980s also suffered from severe budget cuts, with increasing unemployment rates for qualified physical education teachers (Heinemann *et al.* 1990). Since the mid-1980s, delivery of physical education has been by teachers untrained in the subject, particularly in primary schools, and there has been a marked reversal of the general increases in physical education curriculum time allocation.

In summary, generally in the 1980s no paradigm of physical education teaching was without contention and criticism. It was a decade of 'anything goes' in teaching methods, a phenomenon which can be seen in the broader societal context of postmodernism and its associated changes in norms and values towards more individualism and hedonism in sports activities (Fernandez-Balboa 1997). They were developments which also brought changes and innovative practices in the sport system outside schools. Not only did concepts of physical education become more diversified, but so also did sport and the sport system. The early 1980s saw a new wave of American sports reach German soil: aerobics and jogging without any social sport club affiliation emerged, and American baseball and football spread. New clubs, leagues and associations were founded. Following private sector provision of facilities and the international successes of Boris Becker and Steffi Graf, tennis club playing membership numbers increased rapidly in the late 1980s, as did membership of the National Tennis Federation (DTB). Outside the domain of traditional German sport clubs based in community sports facilities and overseen by municipal authorities, commercial leisure sport facilities opened their doors to anyone and at any time, a development which fed the new individual fitness fashion, and which led to the establishment of the German Sport Studio Association (DSSV), the umbrella for fitness clubs and commercial leisure sports centres. Fitness courses and aerobics sessions, and racquet games such as squash, tennis and badminton produced a new type of individualised and Americanised sporting lifestyle movement in Germany, which was based in the new private sector of sports programmes and facilities (Dietrich and Heinemann 1989). This new sports movement also became linked with present-day public and commercial health and nutrition promotion campaigns, where singles meet singles in their 'second homes', the leisure sport centres (Dietrich *et al.* 1990).

Meanwhile, elsewhere in the sports-related domain, after an evaluation of the outcome of the 1984 Olympics in Los Angeles, the system of elite sport came under scrutiny. There was a need to concentrate and integrate the many 1970s-constructed federal and regional sports facilities and to bring in a more professional management structure. The DSB's committee responsible for the promotion of elite sports re-organised the system after 1985 with the establishment of 'Olympic Centres', each offering biomedical support including training facilities and personnel, scientific guidance, control and social support, needed by athletes for their sporting and vocational careers (Naul 1990). Athletes came to be based for their specific sport at one of the regional Olympic Centres, located in the same city as or close by the sport club to which the athlete belongs.

Physical education and sport in the German Democratic Republic

Introduction

Politics and ideology were significant determinants in the shaping of all aspects of life in the German Democratic Republic (GDR). The GDR had educational and sport delivery systems at once characterised by themes common to all communist education systems, and by features which may be termed German. The latter, however, were not readily discerned, mainly due to the peculiar political situation which existed in the immediate post-war period, and which resulted in rapid upheaval to convert the then Soviet zone into a 'socialist democracy'.

The Constitution, socialist ideals and status of sport and physical education (1949–62)

Article 18 of the GDR Constitution accorded physical culture and sport an important place within the socialist system of development; paragraph 3 recognised that as elements of socialist culture, they contributed to the all-round physical and intellectual development of the people; and Article 25 (3) referred to the role of state and society in encouraging participation in physical culture and sport for the complete expression of the socialist personality. Special mention was made of the right of health preservation, and measures were stipulated to implement this: Article 35 (2) guaranteed this right by planned improvement of working and living conditions, public health, a comprehensive social policy, the promotion of physical culture, school, and public activities and tourism.

Physical education (in the guise of 'physical culture') and sport were constitutionally important elements of socialist culture in serving the harmonious and balanced development of mind and body, and as such had an essential role in cultivating the 'socialist personality'. Thus both state and society had a responsibility to encourage participation in physical activity, and health maintenance was regarded as a constitutional right. In this way the socialist state viewed physical education as an integral part of the means to achieve it. Consequently, physical education enjoyed enhanced status in the hierarchy of the GDR's affairs, testimony to which were the references within the Constitution and associated state legislation: Article 18 (3) recognised the contribution of physical education to the 'all-round physical and intellectual development' of the people; Article 25 (3) acknowledged its role in 'the development ... of socialist personality traits'; Article 35 (2) guaranteed the right to health preservation and stipulated measures to apply the principle such as 'the promotion of physical culture, school and popular sporting activities' (Hardman 1987: 20). Sport was overtly linked with politics in the pursuit of socialist aims; it was to play a leading role in nation building and the development of a national consciousness. This link was explicitly seen in the aim of 'educating the athletes to become conscious builders of the workers' and farmers' [GDR] state' (Ewald 1973: 9–10). Clearly, physical education and sport were inextricably entwined with ideology and politics in the pursuit of socialist aims. The importance of physical education was reflected in its position as a compulsory curriculum subject and its status as a principal subject. The importance of sport was seen in the perceived roles of athletes as 'diplomats in tracksuits'.

The state control of the education delivery system ensured that the curriculum, with its core focus of a 'socialist education', and integrated into which was physical education and sport, was centrally laid down and administered by a state organ for schools (*Ministerium für Volksbildung*). The first physical education curriculum plan was drawn up in 1946 (allegedly by Carl Diem) but was replaced in 1951. Early models of physical education (from 1952 literally entitled 'body education' – a Russian term) curricula incorporated training for the Prepared for Labour and Defence of the Peace (*BAV für Frieden*) Sports Badge Award. The preamble of the 1950 Youth Law had ascribed a duty to all state organisations to further the 'democratic sports movement'. Paragraph 36 ordered a sports performance badge. As an indication of the total sovietisation of all areas of life, BAV was a clear imitation of the 1931-initiated Soviet military sports badge, Prepared for Labour and Defence (GTO). It was applied to four age groups, and in the main comprised athletics events; in addition the scheme included questions such as 'Why do we love the Soviet Union?'. It is significant that the GDR state authorities quickly recognised the value of health through sport for productivity, but it also indicates the value attached to physical activity in the cultivation of the 'socialist personality'.

The exclusion of the GDR from the 1952 Olympic Games and the Soviet successes at Helsinki were a shot in the arm for greater efforts in the area of physical education. The zonal administration years, 1946–9, had seen a concentration, in the secondary phase of schooling, on fitness and the development of an all-round personality. In 1946 the Law on the Democratisation of German Schools (*Gesetz zur Demokratisierung der Deutschen Schule*) had called for a tightening up of the physical education curriculum: swimming became obligatory; classes 1–3 had one physical activity lesson per week and classes 4–12 two lessons per week. At the beginning of each year all pupils were medically examined so that the sports teacher had ready information regarding the health and development of each boy and girl. Already at the beginning of the 1950s, the governing SED was promoting a new doctrine of patriotism along the lines of patriotic awareness and pride in the traditions of the German people. As a consequence, the activities in the Prepared for Labour and Defence scheme were extended to include obstacle courses and orienteering. In the 'Official decrees for the extension of the curriculum in physical education' (*Amtliche Verfügungen über die Erweiterung des Lehrplanes Fach Körpererziehung*), the Ministry of Education demanded that the young people train in physical education lessons for the Sports Badge, and that the new activities be included in the curriculum of the common schools.

The curriculum for the academic year 1951–2 included physical education as a principal subject, which specified BAV requirements to be met. The latest addition to an already crowded syllabus (it included athletics, games, gymnastics and swimming) was openly criticised by the teaching profession because the common economic, material and personnel deficiencies in schools were preventing the tests being fulfilled. These criticisms did not go unheeded by the State Committee for Physical Culture and Sport, and in April 1953 a decree 'On the physical education of pupils in general schools' emphasised physical education as a principal subject. In July 1953, the Sports Badge training activities were removed from the syllabus (though preparation for it continued to underpin the physical education curriculum into the 1980s). This military-style sports training was then initially taken on by the Society for Sport and Technology (*Gesellschaft für Sport und Technik* or GST, founded in 1952) and later after further directives from the Central Committee, by school sports societies (*Schulsport Gemeinschaften* or SSG) and the German Gymnastic and Sport Federation (*Deutscher Turn- und Sportbund* or DTSB).

An abortive popular uprising in 1953 led to physical education once again being allocated the task of promoting 'democratic patriotism'. In all areas of education, children were directed to hate the enemy, love their homeland and be ready to defend it. In this context, pre-military and para-military training was re-instituted in the school physical education programme and incorporated into the revised curriculum of 1954, which preceded increases in physical training curriculum time allocation by 1957 to three lessons in classes 6–10 and two lessons for other classes. As an area of curriculum activity, para-military training received greater emphasis as a result of the February 1956 ministerial 'Resolution on the further development of physical education and sport in the German Democratic Republic'. The content of the BAV scheme was extended to include the additional, but elective, activities of cross-country and obstacle running and small-bore rifle shooting, the requirements of which could only be met by extra timetable space. Hence for classes 6–12 an obligatory 'play and sports afternoon' was introduced. However, its existence was short-lived after parental opposition, pupil apathy and teacher antagonism caused a ministerial rethink, which resulted in alternative possibilities being offered, such as active participation in school or factory sport societies or German Gymnastic and Sports Federation clubs. Significantly, and in anticipation of the impending changing order of events, 'body education' was replaced by the old German patriotic term *Turnen* in 1957. This represented an order inclined to revive the historical German spirit. The political impact of Jahn's gymnastics was interpreted by GDR physical education and sport historians as the first step in socialism in the development of societal body culture in Germany up to the then stage of development of the first socialist German Republic. *Turnen* was taken to mean socialist patriotism involving physical strength and mental awareness, in preparation for immediate readiness to defend the development of socialism.

The events of 1958–9 proved deeply significant in future developments in the GDR. Reparation repayments to the Soviet Union came to an end at the same time as an upturn in the economy, but a serious drought in the summer of 1959 culminated in a recessive set-back and the collectivisation of agriculture. Loyalty to the state rapidly waned, and half a million people fled to the West: the social and economic drain was halted by the erection of the infamous Berlin Wall. The changes, which occurred at this time, were so effective that in them lay the roots of the system which prevailed until the Wall was breached in 1989. A change in the conception of school physical education (sport) coincided with the wishes of the SED to catch up with, and even surpass West Germany in *per capita* consumption and production. Concomitantly, the transformation in the concept of physical education signified that Soviet influence was on the wane in the attempt to establish a more concrete national identity for the GDR. In sport there was the opportunity to demonstrate the superiority of socialism in joint German Olympic teams. Thus a closer relationship between school physical education and extra-mural sport was demanded, and performance in sport and competition were increasingly emphasised in new syllabi: the 'three T's' (Training, Technique and Tactics) were the basic themes in the plans. The new syllabus now included versatility in athletic movement (strength, endurance, speed and agility); increased intensity of activity in lessons to maximise the use of time; earlier specialisation; and each session was punctuated by glowing reports of the successes of East German teams and individual sports stars (Hinsching and Hummel 1997).

Conceptual changes, the 'new man' and cultivation of 'socialist personality' and nation consciousness (1963–80)

At the State Council's eleventh session in 1968, Chairman Walter Ulbricht (1968) articulated the basic socialistic aim of forming 'the new man', a 'socialist personality' of all-round education of mind and body. It was an aim to be achieved by building a 'developed system of socialism'. In theory, socialist education was intended to create the necessary conditions for coming to terms with changed situations at work and in changing situations in life. In essence, it was to make a decisive contribution to the harmonious development of all aspects of the personality. Therefore, such education embraced an introduction to natural and social sciences (native and foreign languages, mathematics, culture and art, the relationship between school and production and physical culture and sport). Five years earlier at the SED's Sixth Congress in 1963, Ulbricht had already articulated the importance of physical culture and sport in the all-round development of people, indicating that all-round physical training should be in the forefront of the schools' new curriculum, and that a change in the content and form of physical education would be necessary to link it more directly with sport outside of school. He also called upon all vested-interest bodies to coordinate their efforts to prioritise the goal of regular participation in sport. In November 1963, a congress was held in Karl-Marx-Stadt to discuss the theme of 'Fundamental changes in the content and form of sports training in the socialist school', and the foundations for syllabus modification already laid in 1958–9 were reinforced and firmly established. The specified syllabus aimed to give an all-round basic physical education, and was divided into the following areas: basic exercises, athletics, apparatus work, gymnastic floor work, games (girls either had handball or basketball; boys chose two from basketball, handball and football – often the choice of activity depended on local traditions), skiing (if conditions were conducive to this activity), and swimming, which was obligatory but not always possible; if a school had no access to a pool then the pupils were required to attend a swimming camp). In the period 1964–71, revised curricula were introduced for classes 1–10, with allocations of three lessons of physical education per week in grades 4–6 and two lessons in grades 1–3/7–12; there was also a daily period of fifteen minutes of gymnastics, as well as the opportunity of extra-curricular activity of up to two hours per day in a school or other sports clubs. These curricula remained in place until 1989. The syllabus for classes 11–12 (extended secondary school years) was introduced in 1980, and at the time of proposed revisions for class stages 1–10 in the late 1980s, there were no immediate plans to replace or modify it. The 1974 Youth Law gave a further fillip to physical education by guaranteeing fundamental rights: 'Physical culture and sport are a part of life for young people in a socialist society....The socialist state guarantees physical education and sport for young people in all walks of life' (Article 34). The Law (Article 35) also increased state responsibility to provide the means for sport in every sphere: 'Teachers shall encourage initiative and readiness on the part of pupils and students to engage in sports....Specific places to stimulate sports activities shall be included in the annual and enterprise plans as well as the enterprise collective agreements' (Hardman 1987: 20).

In the physical education curriculum in this period (and indeed up to 1989), for each class stage there was a syllabus handbook containing principles, areas of main emphasis, overview of content, allocation of time to activity areas, details of, and observations on, material to be taught, and recommendations on division of the year into activity cycles; for example, the syllabus for classes 1–4 was divided into thirteen 'cycles' with suggestions under the headings of 'Training and educational focal points' and 'Physical exercises/play activities'. Underpinning the content of the physical education curriculum were the two aims of *Können* (ability) and *Wissen* (knowledge in the sense of knowing how). More specifically, other aims and objectives embraced development of fitness in general and stamina, endurance, speed, agility, and mobility in particular; attainment of high performance standards; cultivation of qualities such as determination and will-power; fostering habits of regular lifetime participation in sporting activity; and the inculcation of socialist character traits, attitudes and convictions (Hardman 1989; 1992). The latter included socialist patriotism and proletarian nationalism, with young males in classes 11–12 being prepared physically, politically and morally for national service, 'for the defence of the socialist fatherland (was) the patriotic duty and honour of each young person' (Ministerium für Volksbildung 1980: 7).

Two lessons per week (sixty per year) were allocated to curricular physical education in all class stages except stage 4–6, which had three (ninety per year). The National Plan was much in evidence. Physical education teachers were assisted in planning and implementing schemes of work and individual lessons by class-stage manuals – 'instruction aids' (*Unterrichtshilfen*) which supplemented the syllabus handbooks (*Lehrplan Sport*). The manuals prescribed the functions and organisation of instructional aids, with detailed support material for each year's syllabus schedule in track and field, basic physical exercises, games/play activities (for younger age groups) and gymnastics (apparatus and rhythmic). The resource material increased in specificity with each class-stage. Games had the highest time allocation. After a broad introductory base at primary school, there was concentration in classes 4 and 5 on basketball, football, handball and volleyball, after which one game was selected, usually in accordance with local tradition. Wherever conditions or facilities allowed, swimming (a compulsory activity) and/or winter sports were incorporated into special syllabus guidelines. Children were normally inducted in swimming in class 2, when they began the first (of two) 'complex' in a two-year scheme. Prior to commencement, ability was tested and discussions on the swimming programme and the children's needs were held between swimming teachers and parents. Summer courses and camps provided alternative opportunities for swimming at nominal cost in locations where access to a swimming facility was not possible. In classes 9–12, pupils were required to take a course in 'instructions' and topics such as the organisation and tasks of the socialist sports movement, the traditions of German physical culture, and the life and achievements of outstanding German athletes were covered. Personal contacts with sports idols were encouraged because of their potential influence on the development of sporting interests and desirable character traits in children.

Co-educational groups were the norm in classes 1–4, after which segregation was recommended, and after class 7 demanded, unless local conditions of economies of scale, such as those found in small rural schools, prevailed. Teaching style was explicit and direct in applying practice to aims; it was formal, with strict standards of control and discipline. A mandatory sports greeting – *Sport Frei!* – punctuated the start and end of lessons, which were typically conducted in three phases: introduction of walking/running and free-standing exercises/aerobics to music and/or circuit training; technique and skill development or a game or equivalent for compensatory reasons; and a critical review and announcement of activity events.

Assessment was carried out twice a year, though it was essentially on-going. Practical performance ability and general conduct were taken into account. Criteria for assessment with scales of points were laid down by the education ministry in 'Recommendations for evaluation and grading in school sport'. The BAV scheme was often used either as a yardstick or to improve a grade. Grading was on a scale from 1 ('very good') to 5 ('inade-quate'); the latter, a fail grade (a rare occurrence) theoretically resulted in the repetition of the entire year's curriculum. At the end of classes 10 and 12, pupils were graded in physical education on the 1–5 scale. As physical education was a principal subject, a grade of satisfactory or above was required to qualify for the leaving certificate. Grades depended on a general mark given by the teacher for general behaviour and tests in athletics, gymnastics, swimming and games.

'Subject circles' (Fachzirkel), comprising physical educators, advisors and administrators, met mandatorily on a monthly basis to discuss (some-times with practical demonstrations and personal involvement) professionally related issues. Outcomes were incorporated into a head teacher's formal report to the appropriate education authorities, thus activating potential dialogue and interaction between state functionaries and practitioners.

New directions on the road to communism: redefinitions and education for leisure sport (1982–90)

In 1982 work began on preparing a new physical education curriculum with analyses of the syllabi then in force. A systematic scientific approach carried out under the direction of the Ministry of Education and involving the collaboration of the Academy of Pedagogical Sciences, sports scientists in university and teacher training institutes, physical education advisors and practising physical education (sports) teachers, resulted in the produc-tion of new syllabi for classes 1–10 and implementation in September 1989. An important basis for working out the new syllabi was also formed from international comparative investigations. These were not just restric-ted to comprehensive curriculum evaluations; they also employed knowledge and experiences gained through the exchange of study-tour knowledge, and experiences acquired through the exchange of study-tour delegations and through international conferences. Although the analyses indicated that no general change in the syllabi was necessary, the overall consensus of scientific opinion of the main aspects of the proposed new curriculum was that societal demands on health, physical performance capacity, psychological stability and motor adaptability, as well as the moral development and attitudes of young people, were changing. Generally, there was the view that social development required a more deep-seated incorporation of sporting activity into a healthy, cultured way of life.

The researchers' and practitioners' proposals for the new syllabi were combined in hypothetical concepts for lower, intermediate and upper classes. After experimental trials in schools, modifications were made. The revised forms of the curriculum proposals were published in the specialist journal *Körpererziehung* in 1987, and presented for public debate. This provided teachers with the opportunity to acquaint themselves with the entire set of new curricular requirements. The whole of 1987 was used for curriculum discussion in specialist groups concerned with school sport, in specialist commissions in the districts, and in conference debates and sports science institutions. Over 150 written, and a great number of oral, comments and suggestions were submitted for evaluation. The proposed curriculum for the lower, intermediate and upper stages was divided into four aspects:

(i)   lesson aims and tasks;
(ii) guidance on teaching methods;
(iii) distribution of lessons over the year; and
(iv) lesson content according to subject area.

At the beginning of what was destined to be the last full GDR school year, 1989–90, new aids on teaching methods and revised recommendations for the assessment and marking of pupils' performances were simultaneously introduced with the new curricular syllabi. Work had already commenced on a new edition of the textbook for higher education *Teaching Methods for Sport*, an important study text for the initial and in-service training of school sports teachers. Furthermore, proposals were drawn up for measures to improve the material requirements for curricular and extra-curricular sport (Hinsching and Hummel 1997).

In pursuit of the all-round development of personality, the new 'ten-year school' physical education curriculum's main aims included physical and psychological well-being and regular lifetime participation in leisure time sporting activity, to compensate for sedentary occupations and to overcome new work-related demands. Specifically, it aimed at the systematic age-related development of physical performance capacity and sporting ability, the development of positive attitudes, moral attributes (e.g. fair play, self-control, order and discipline) and psycho-social qualities (e.g. determination, perseverance, independence and collective behaviour), patriotic and internationalist education, and aesthetic appreciation.

Curriculum content was divided according to specific age and gender-related developmental characteristics of pupils by class stage. The lower stage (classes 1–3) was to be regarded as the basic (elementary) stage of physical/sports training. There was training in basic forms of movement as well as selected sports skills, which were modified for educational effect. The goal was to achieve general movement training and a balanced development of conditional and coordinative abilities. The areas were to include amongst others: 'small' games (18h); athletics exercises (running and jumping, 16h); apparatus gymnastics (including floor exercises such as forward and backward rolls and simple sequences, 12h); rhythmic gymnastics (including simple exercises with hand apparati such as gymnastic ball and ribbon, 9h); swimming (30h in classes 2–3) and winter sports (introduction to skiing or ice-skating, up to 12h). The intermediate stage (classes 4–6) prioritised learning of sports skills, with a focus on games (acquisition of basic techniques, skills and tactics in one game, 24h); athletics (22h); apparatus gymnastics (including balance beam and asymmetric bars for girls, horizontal bar and parallel bars for boys, floor for girls and boys, 22h); gymnastics (including single and combinations with each of two pieces of apparatus: ball, rope or clubs for girls; rope and medicine ball for boys); swimming (30h); winter sports (skiing or ice-skating, up to 18h); and options (6h). The upper school stage (classes 7–10) was to be orientated to the enhancement of physical performance capacity and development of sports ability through games (16h); athletics (10h); apparatus gymnastics (10h); rhythmic gymnastics (girls only, 10h); strength and combat sports (boys only, 12h); winter sports (up to 12h for classes 7–8; up to 10h for classes 9–10); and options (4h).

The proposed curriculum also allowed for differences based on local circumstances. For example, in only approximately 25 per cent of districts was there a guarantee of snow for winter sports. Similarly, the amenities available for swimming and combat sports were variable. Hence, for such reasons and in view of specific sporting traditions in schools and districts, the new syllabi allowed variations in subject material choice and organisation of lessons. In games from class 4 onwards, there was choice of handball or basketball or football (boys only), and in the interests of local traditions where corresponding facilities were available, one of the following could be introduced: volleyball, fistball, rugby or hockey. From class 7 onwards, on the basis of its particular suitability for leisure-time sports activity, volleyball was favoured as the second game to be introduced. If this sport had already been learned in the intermediate school stage, handball or basketball or football (boys only) could be considered. For both apparatus and rhythmic gymnastics, sequence variations were to be allowed. In strength and combat sports, there was a choice between judo, wrestling or boxing. Variations in the area of swimming related to availability and/or access to facilities and courses. In winter sports, tobogganing could replace skiing or ice-skating.

One interesting innovation, which significantly differentiated the 1989 curriculum model from its predecessors, was the opportunity for students for the first time in GDR curriculum development in the intermediate and upper school stages (classes 4–10) to have activity choice within the otherwise compulsory activity framework of games, athletics, gymnastics, combat sports, swimming and winter sports. The intention was to introduce pupils to popular and widespread forms of leisure-time sports activity, as well as to enhance opportunities for fostering school and local traditions. The general framework programme contained the following possibilities. At the intermediate school stage: introduction to badminton, table tennis or softball; hiking, winter sports exercises; and preparation for mass-level sports competition in schools or areas. At the upper school stage: badminton, lawn tennis or table tennis; games which were not taught as first or second sports; continuation of swimming; and winter sports, hiking, orienteering, and cross-country running.

In anticipation of the new curricular syllabi, a number of preparatory measures were implemented. These included early publication of plans and texts for familiarisation, events organised by the Central Institute for Further Education (in-service training) to disseminate additional guidelines to school directors, consultations in specialist subject groups, conferences and related in-service courses to help sports teachers gain confidence in the innovations. Additionally, syllabus interpretations and advice on teaching methods were published in advance. In most schools and districts, decisions on the application of variations of subject material choice were made a year before the introduction of the new curricula.

An overall curriculum plan, conceived from a set of transcending aims, united the syllabi of all subjects and class stages. The production of each curriculum, including that of the extended secondary school and the vocational training institutions, was the result of long-term and interdisciplinary cooperation. For example, nearly 3,000 experts from various disciplines were engaged in the production of the Ten Year General School Curriculum, which was progressively introduced between 1964 and 1971. A new uniform overall curriculum based on the needs and experiences of practice in schools, and on the latest scientific findings and societal trends, was scheduled for introduction by 1990.

A central point of reference for all subject syllabi was the transmission and acquisition of a sound socialist general education, directed at the fundamental and harmoniously balanced development of the 'socialist personality'. This education embraced an introduction into natural and social sciences: native and foreign languages, mathematics, culture and art, the relationship between school and production, and also physical culture and sport. It reflected the essential demands of all spheres of life. The proportions of the areas of education of the new curriculum to be introduced in 1990 coincided with these basic positions. They encompassed the following obligatory components: social science 10.9 per cent; German language 12.8 per cent; literature 10.1 per cent; foreign languages 11.0 per cent; natural science 12.2 per cent; mathematics 17.7 per cent; polytechnic education 11.0 per cent; art and music 6.8 per cent; and sport (physical education) 7.5 per cent.

Deriving from the overall concept of socialist general education, in the production of the new syllabus proposals for physical education, the role of the subject in the all-round personality development of pupils was re-defined. At the same time, its place in the educational areas was to be dealt with in regard to the proportions of time as above. In the lower stage (classes 1–3), the subject 'sport' (physical education), was to embrace two lessons, in the intermediate stage (classes 4–6) three lessons, and in the upper stage (classes 7–10) two lessons per week, and would be taught by subject specialists with higher education qualifications, or in the lower classes by 'primary' schoolteachers with extended training in 'sport'. For the compilation of the new physical education syllabi, extra-curricular sporting activity in unity with sports lessons was to have an essential role in pupils' all-round personality development.

Talent identification was an integral feature of the physical education curriculum, especially in early school years. Each child was tested in class 3, and results were recorded and screened by DTSB officials in Berlin. Selected children would attend a 'training centre' several times in the week for up to three years (though this was activity-dependent – in gymnastics, only one year). Monitoring procedures would then determine whether the child was suitable for entry into a Children and Youth Sport School (KJS). Despite the progressive developments in physical education manifest in the curriculum planning initiative immediately prior to its demise in 1990, it is clear that in the GDR, and particularly since the country embarked on a path of showing its superior system to the world, that sport, competition and performance, and not physical education, was the central concern. Sports successes in the GDR were not necessarily directly associated with the school physical education programme concerning the mass of children. Rather it was the extra-curricular activities, the *Spartakiad* festivals of sports competition, which not only played an important role in the moti-vation of children, but also in the detection and selection of young talent; and the Sports Schools, which were the reasons behind East Germany's sporting prowess.

The KJS schools, which had been initially set up in 1952–3 at the time of the Soviet Union's international successes, had a major function to bridge the gap between mass participation in sport and the process of producing champions. The Ministry of Education and the State Committee directly supervised the schools for physical culture and sport. Pupils from the age of eight up were selected on the basis of their scholastic records, social activities and the results of an entrance examination. The schools followed the same curriculum as the 10- and 12-year polytechnic schools, except that there was extra time devoted to 'physical education': five hours in classes 5–8, six hours in classes 9–10; and seven hours in classes 11–12.

For classes 11 and 12 the physical education curriculum was divided into two parts: first, 144 'hours' to all skill areas and course of instructions; and second, 66 'hours' to a specialist activity. The average work-out per week was 10–12 hours. In addition to the regular physical education classes, pupils had to participate once a week in a sports afternoon class to obtain the Sports Badge. They were also advised and encouraged to join one of the sports clubs to improve in their speciality.

For school children, performance was a main feature of the physical education programme alongside the cultivation of the all-round 'socialist personality'. The responsibility for this cultivation was a corporate one, and partially accounts for the support given by outside-school bodies. In sport the two-way interaction between school physical education lessons and extra-curricular activities provided incentives and guidance, first from the school where these were enhanced by the acquisition of skills, and second from the sports club. This interaction made up for the shortage of time on the timetable to achieve the required levels of performance.

Extra-curricular sport

Extra-curricular activity was part of the total programme. Increasingly, the school programme came to assist in the preparation of children for sport and other leisure activities after school hours and beyond it, but two or three lessons per week in school were considered inadequate for laying down the foundations. After 1956, School Sport Societies (SSGs), which were often linked with Factory Sport Clubs or German Gymnastic and Sport Federation Clubs, played an important role. In 1989, some 93 per cent of schools had such societies, with an average attendance of 72 per cent of school-age children. The highest attendance (over 83 per cent) occurred in the class stages 1–4 (Hardman 1990), when young children of working parents remained in after-school nursery centres (*Horte*) to enable participation in a range of activities designed to secure 'positive attitudes, interests ... knowledge and ability' (Honecker 1982: 22) and to 'develop each child optimally, to cultivate, to foster the aptitudes and abilities of each child in order to establish his/her individuality' (Honecker 1985: 10). Older children also had opportunities to engage in a range of school, district, regional and national competitions and festivals of sport, including *Spartakiad*, Pioneer and Free German Youth promotions. These features pervaded the system and were exemplified in annual vocational school competitions to find the 'Most athletic girl' and the 'Strongest male apprentice of the year' (Hardman 1992).

In the GDR, there were opportunities for age-related sporting and health-promoting leisure activity under educational guidance after school, for example in school nurseries (the *Horte*), to which more than 80 per cent of lower school pupils belonged. Opportunities also existed in school sports societies, which were found in 96 per cent of all schools, and in which, together with DTSB sports societies, over 80 per cent of pupils participated in organised sport. The new draft curriculum emphasised more strongly than hitherto the necessity of using these facilities effectively in addition to curricular sport for the all-round development of personality. The aim here was to encourage pupils from the first class onwards to lead a healthy life and to regularly participate in sport during leisure time (Lehrplan Sport 1987: 54). After-school sport was promoted as a contribution to the development of socialist behaviour patterns, in which not only regular participation in sporting activity but also improvements in performance levels were key aspects. In 1951 schools were directed to form a School and Pioneer club and to liaise with factory sports clubs. In 1956 the 'Resolution on the further development of physical culture and sport' established the SSG as the principal form of extra-curricular sport. By 1958 the State Committee saw its way to intervene because there was little sign of any deep-rooted improvements, but participation remained low and the sports societies were unable to flourish until school sport dropped its ideological weighting and militant patriotism from the syllabus content. 'Instructions for the development of extra-curricular sport in the secondary schools of the German Democratic Republic' and 'Working guidelines for the school sports societies of general schools in the German Democratic Republic' were received by the clubs in October 1961. Both Directives transferred to the school and its director full responsibility for the development and organisation of the clubs in place of the Free German Youth Pioneers. The 'Instructions' laid down the responsibilities of the school Director, gave information on the work and function of the SSGs, and determined the role of the Pioneer organisation. School heads and directors had the major responsibility for the scheduled and pedagogical work of the societies. Usually a sports (physical education) teacher directed the development but was answerable to the Director. The teacher was obliged to form a Sports Council, to which usually belong coaches, representatives of the DTSB, of parents' associations and Pioneers.

The SSGs were arranged into 'divisions' for general sport and in 'sections' for more advanced and specialist training. Generally speaking classes 1–4 participated in activities which were preparatory to the work of the 'secondary' level. In the sports sections athletes chose one, sometimes two, of the following activities: athletics, basketball, gymnastics, football, handball, table tennis, volleyball, fistball, swimming, skiing, chess and rowing. From these sections the youngsters moved on to Factory Sports Clubs or DTSB clubs. There were SSGs in 82 per cent of the extended schools and 85 per cent of the ten-year schools. In 1970 there were approximately 43 per cent and 34 per cent in classes 5–8 and 9–12 respectively, who were members of extra-curricular sports groups. By 1977 these figures had increased, and it was reported that about 60 per cent of young people between 6 and 16 years of age were members of such groups (i.e. about 1.5 million children). In charge of the afternoon club sessions were something in the order of 15,000 physical education teachers and 10,000 ancillary trainers/coaches. The development of after-school sports in both its forms effectively tied in with the aim of developing fit, healthy and balanced personalities among young people. At the same time, it provided important foundations for the further development of the DTSB, which over the years saw a growth in membership from 220,000 in 1948 in the then central sports body, the German Sports Association, to 2.6 million in 1975.

From the earliest days of the GDR there were efforts to institutionalise physical education and sports at all levels, so that everyone in the state was exposed to the influence of the various bodies of state. The 1970 Youth Sport Act obliged all state administrative agencies to assist in development of the democratic sports movement and to promote the education of a physically and morally sound younger generation. From 1948 to 1957 the cross-regional sport organisation, the German Sport Association, had central control. The DTSB succeeded this body. Its brief, outlined at its inaugural conference, was to recruit the whole nation, and young people in particular, to the practice of physical culture and sport, to promote the universal education of healthy and optimistic personalities, and so contribute to the successful development of the socialist society. Thus the DTSB was to play an important role in both the development of extra-curricular sport and the socialist construction of youth in particular. Essentially the DTSB was responsible for the practical application of state law, decrees, etc., in regional, district and local sports groups. It both coordinated and cooperated with its member organisations in the development of schemes to involve people in sporting activity on a mass scale, with the incentive of low membership fees which entitled members to free use of communal and factory-owned facilities.

Until October 1948 (the date of the founding of the *Deutscher Sportausschuss*), the FDJ organisation was jointly responsible with the Federation of Free German Trade Unions for the control of communal sports groups. As its title implies, the FDJ was a body which chiefly concerned itself with the promotion of activities for young people. It was also politically inspired through its undertaking to use its influence on young people to improve preparation in their studies of Marxist-Leninist principles, to keep alive the revolutionary traditions of the working class and the international communist movement. As early as 1946 the FDJ had actively engaged itself in youth activities: in October it had worked out a programme of sports events for youth associations, and issued guidelines to coaches and trainers in basketball, football, handball, swimming, skiing and skating, for both males and females. It also set about the reconstruction of sports facilities helping to coordinate the work of voluntary workers; its efforts in making good deficiencies in youth hostel provision enabled it to promote vacation and convalescent camps in use in late 1946. Its initiatives led to local and regional competitions in athletics, football and swimming, and in 1948 these culminated in youth championships in football at the zonal level. Throughout the 1950s, the FDJ gave impetus to projects involving facility, equipment, clothing and sports-schools provision, as well as the training of sports teachers and the institution of regular school sport. A feature of its work was the introduction of international youth competition with socialist countries, and after 1957 it cooperated with the DTSB in ventures to popularise physical activity, until gradually its activities became concentrated on mass sport and political-ideological work amongst youth participating in sport. By the 1970s its major responsibilities came to lie in working with the DTSB and Department of Education in children's and youths sporting activities; cooperating in mass measures in the common sports programmes of the FDGB, FDJ and DTSB; the regular guidance of the sport commissions of the Free German Youth grassroots organisations and Pioneers' Association in cooperation with the Education Department and DTSB; and in cooperation in the district and territorial *Spartakiad* movements.

Other agencies outside school also made a contribution to the development of children's and youth sport. In almost all districts there existed 'houses' of the 'Ernst Thälmann Pioneer Organisation', which, together with the state education authorities and the DTSB, supported the training of sports organisers, instructors, judges and referees, the organisation of mass sports competitions, and the after-school sports activities. Many secondary school level pupils, i.e. those up to the age of fourteen, attended one of the 750 central Young Pioneers' camps, or one of the 6,500 'enterprise' holiday camps, further specialists' camps, recreation and work camps.

In short, sports for children and young people were organised outside of the schools by the DTSB clubs, state-owned enterprises, cooperative farms, government offices, vocational schools and colleges, school sports clubs, the Pioneer organisation, the FDJ and the GST.

As seen above, indoctrination and uniformity via the standardised curriculum were supplemented by various institutions. National and local festivals of mass physical exercises reinforced this total commitment and endeavour – they were important collectivising devices! The increasing importance of competitive sport in the international arena had a double significance for the GDR. On the one hand it had to strive hard for diplomatic recognition, and on the other there was a desire to gain universal acknowledgement of the benefits of a social democracy. Effectiveness in elite sport demanded a structured system with a long-term plan for the development of sporting performance. This implied high demands on sport at all levels, but in particular in children's and young people's sports.

The Pioneer *Spartakiad*s, begun in the 1950s, were not the answer to these demands, though they did serve a useful function in providing relevant experience and knowledge regarding content and organisation. It was necessary to centralise sport in all areas in order to plan systematically for both the short and long term. The DTSB was allocated the task of persuading children and young people to engage in regular, organised sporting activity in the various sports associations. Associated tasks set encompassed talent identification and development, as well as raising the quality of the structure and organisation of practice, training and competition to increase participation in elite sport as well as mass sport. The new type of *Spartakiad*, begun in 1965 and organised jointly by the DTSB, the education authorities, the FDJ and the Young Pioneers, sought to increase numbers of participants in regular sporting activity and the systematic development of young talent.

Preparatory training for the *Spartakiad* competitions mostly occurred in schools, school sports societies and groups in the clubs of the DTSB. Every two years *Spartakiad*s took place in the schools – these were the very bases of the pyramid of participation. In each case, a year before the national championships, school competitions and competitions in local school sports societies or the DTSB clubs were held. The best ball-game teams were determined by 'knockout' competitions. The local contests were followed by area *Spartakiad*s, which produced qualifiers for the regional championships. These qualifiers spent three weeks in a training camp preparing for this next stage. Some four weeks after the area contests the regional championships were held. A year later the winners participated in the National *Spartakiad* Championships, in which the youngsters competed in one of four age groups: 12–14, 15–16, 17–18 and 19–21. Gradually, the programme came to concentrate on Olympic sports: whereas in 1966 there were twenty-three sports, in 1972 there were eighteen! That the *Spartakiad*s were successful on both counts (mass participation and top-class performance) was reflected in the statistics. Participation increased from 1.7 million in 1965 to over 4 million in 1974, and over 90 per cent of GDR medal winners in the Seoul Olympics of 1988 were *Spartiakiad* participants.

Annually, competitions for the Certificate of the State Council Chairman involved large numbers of secondary school children. This competition became obligatory in 1961. It comprised three events: 60m run, long jump and rounders ball throw (classes 5–6) and 75m run, long jump and shot put (classes 7–12). Points were allocated for performance, and certificates were awarded to all individual pupils with a score of 140+, to the best three schools, the best three districts, and the best three regions. Again, one can recognise the twofold purpose of such competition in engaging large numbers in sports activities and searching out talent.

The Swimming Association and the magazine *Zeit im Bild* jointly organised the Swimming Competition of Secondary Schools of the GDR. Points, on a percentage basis, were awarded to pupils who gained swimming badges. The best school, i.e. the one with the highest number of badges obtained, received a cup and 1,000 marks; the runner-up received 500 marks and the third 300 marks. There were three stages in this badge scheme: stage I – 25m one stroke, 25m a second stroke, dive in deep water; stage II – 100m one stroke, 50m a second stroke, a racing dive; and stage III – 100m one stroke with time limit, 100m a second stroke with time limit, a racing dive.

Reference was made earlier to the BAV award. The 1976 Ninth Assembly of the SED considered ways of developmental preparation for the demands of economic production and national defence. It discussed means of winning over more people, especially infants and school children, to regular participation in physical activity, and called for an extension of the measures to involve such people. Already there had been over six million participants in the Sports Badge scheme! The DTSB was given the task of restructuring and strengthening the Sports Badge programme. The new format embraced five areas: endurance or walking, pull-ups or press-ups, three hops or broad jump, shooting, and throwing. Successful completion qualified for a bronze award. For silver and gold awards, additional activities (long-distance swimming, sprinting, long or high jump, shot put or a distance throw, and a selected sports activity) had to be completed. There were three groups for children and youths and six groups for adults. It was extremely difficult for anyone to escape the network of this scheme because of the number of bodies involved in its administration: the DTSB, FDJ, FDGB, Pioneers, and universities and other higher education organisations.

There were a number of other schemes which aimed to involve young people in outside-school physical activities:

- The International Friendship four-event athletic competition, which was open to school teams in socialist countries. It was originally started in Poland in 1956. Six boys and six girls, (aged usually 12–13), participated in a 60m run, long jump, high jump and rounders ball throw contest. Annually the Pioneers organised preliminary rounds in schools. Schools notified the organisers of the number of points scored. The best schools then met in area competition to decide the winners, and next the best GDR school was determined by further competition. The national winner went on to compete against counterparts from Bulgaria, Czechoslovakia, Hungary, Poland and the Soviet Union.
- Whom Do You Overcome? was a five-event youth competition leading to national finals.

- The Cross Country Youth Race began at school level and progressed through district, area, regional to national levels.
- Cup competitions, run on a knockout basis, were held in several sports: gymnastics, swimming, handball, basketball, shooting, football, and so on.
- Miscellaneous activities which sought to engage the mass of population, including school children, were frequently organised, such as: *Lauf dich gesund* ('Run for Your Health'); *Eile mit Meile* ('Run a Mile Campaign'); the 'Jubilee Mile' (on the twenty-fifth anniversary of the Athletic Association); and the 'Festival Mile' (on the occasion of the Tenth World Youth Festival).

All of these competitions and mass activities support the notion of effectively spreading the net of participation of youth and the promotion of young sporting talent. They were an integral part of the GDR socialist cult.

The politicisation and role of sport

Measured by Olympic medallists' results, world and European athletics and swimming championships, the GDR, in simple arithmetical terms, was among the top three most successful countries in the world. If success is correlated with population it was ahead of its main rivals, the Soviet Union and the United States of America. Whilst the evidence has made it clear that many elite GDR athletes were exposed to performance-enhancing drugs, the international successes achieved by this country of less than seventeen million inhabitants, which faced almost total devastation at the end of World War II, and during a period when athletics standards improved at an unprecedented rate world-wide, cannot solely be ascribed to the skilful use of performance-enhancing agents. Sport was totally integrated into the social and political fabric of the country, in which meticulous state planning, strategic use of limited resources, and a sophisticated structural network of talent seeking, identification and development were important features.

Any analysis of the GDR sports system has to be seen in a wider context, first as one element of an all-encompassing social system, second as a means of establishing the nation as the equal of its fellow German state, the Federal Republic. A third factor was the need to achieve influence within the Warsaw Pact, comprising countries which had suffered grievously at the hands of Nazi Germany; and finally to achieve both political and sporting status on the world scene, that is within the United Nations and the Olympic movement. It is a measure of these objectives that final acceptance of the GDR by the IOC came in 1972, for the Munich Games, to be followed closely by the GDR's gaining membership of the United Nations. Both were the result of twenty-five years of intensive political and sporting diplomatic activity.

Sport in both post-1945 Germanies benefited from a tradition extending back to the eighteenth and nineteenth centuries, beginning with GutsMuths and Jahn. From the outset, sport and physical education had been associated with the regeneration of the nation and, overtly, with political organisations. In the nineteenth century, these included Jahn's *Frei Corps*, which fought against Napoleon, and in the twentieth century organisations from both left and right on the political spectrum. In the 1920s, German workers' sports organisations were the strongest in Europe; however, they were superseded in the 1930s by fascism. Sport was a major weapon in the Nazi armoury, attracting young people into the Party and then conditioning them to work on its behalf. At the 1936 Berlin Olympics, Nazi Germany gained the highest overall total of medals, 89, including 33 gold. Prior to such political instrumentalisation of sport, Germany had already in 1928 a sports medicine system in place under the guidance of Rector August Bier, an orthopaedic surgeon, and a chief administrator, Carl Diem, Secretary of the German Olympic Committee. Both appointments established a precedent for developments in the GDR.

In the development of sport in the new 'socialist democracy', its leader, Walter Ulbricht, was a key player. Ulbricht had been a member of the workers' sports movement in the 1920s, and he retained a fanatical interest in sport. Moreover, despite scepticism from his political associates, he saw sport as one of the main means of establishing the GDR as a recognised nation state, and also of giving it a place in world politics. Because of sport's former association with fascism, all clubs and national associations were disbanded and re-formed according to 'socialist' principles. The reorganisation of sport in general was given over to the youth movement, the FDJ, under the leadership of Erich Honecker, later to succeed Ulbricht as head of government. It was not long before sport came within the province of the trade unions and industry (this corresponded with a previously established model in the Soviet Union). They were charged with providing new facilities and working with the FDJ to promote participation at grass-roots level. But an effective central body for sport was missing; the SED at its Second Congress in July 1952 set about to remedy the situation and created the State Committee for Physical Culture and Sport (*Staatliches Komitee für Körperkultur und Sport*) to oversee sports affairs. It was directly controlled by decisions from the Party's Central Committee and made law through the Council of Members (*Ministerrat*). In 1957 a further reorganisation took place, which fundamentally changed the face of sport and particularly elite sport. On the initiative of the government's advisory body, the State Secretariat for Sport and Physical Culture, a new, all-powerful (it was given total authority for the planning and finance of sport) executive body was formed, the DTSB. This body had close ties with government and the ruling Socialist Unity Party, and thus ensured that future sports developments would be supportive of socialism/communism in the GDR. The DTSB had cross-representation in the FDJ, and at every tier of regional and local government. All national governing bodies of sport were reorganised and brought under its umbrella, and were subservient to it. The DTSB also absorbed existing organisations which had been set up to encourage elite sport, the network of sports boarding schools (the KJS) in 1952, the sports medicine service, and the German College of Physical Culture (the DHfK, in 1952). This included the staffing of KJSs with coaches within the elite sports system, the employment of sports medicine specialists, and perhaps more radically, the training of all professional coaches and sports doctors at the DHfK.

The Central Commission supervised elite sport for competitive sport, which worked through the DTSB. As was usual in socialist countries, with each Olympic cycle the Commission set targets for medals in each sport, the level of attainment of which determined future support. Children at KJSs trained up to twenty hours per week at the sport and also had to meet high academic standards. Prior to major competitions, school routine was broken up by attendance at 3–4-week intensive training camps. Adult athletes were classified into three groups. The master class and class I included all personnel in sports clubs organised by the DTSB. It was obligatory for employees to release such athletes for sixteen hours per week for training. In total, athletes were expected to log between 1,300 and 1,600 training hours per year. Class II athletes had to be released eight hours per week and class III athletes four hours. The school and school sports system fed both KJSs and sports clubs or a neighbourhood sports club (BSG) and special training centres (TZ) established by towns and cities for youngsters. Before acceptance into the system, all potential athletes were subjected to detailed prognostic physical tests. Selection was dependent on innate ability and potential, rather than existing levels of performance. Detailed physical assessments were maintained throughout an athlete's competitive career. The political orthodoxy of parents and athletes also had to be beyond reproach. Each sports club/KJS had its own staff of coaching and sports medicine specialists, but all had a common background, and therefore a consistent approach to training methods and technique. Promotion for coaches depended on how many successful athletes they produced and passed on to a higher class.

Whilst the two Germanies competed as one team, the GDR attempted to produce as many athletes as possible for that team, in order to hold key positions in team management. After 1972, when the country was officially recognised as a sovereign state in its own right, the GDR consciously fostered sports in which 'chance' was a limited variable, and especially those individual sports such as swimming, which gave more medals per competitor than team sports. Thus sports such as basketball and water polo were abandoned. In the same vein, research effort went into sports which gave a positive return, for example, the aerodynamics of bobsleighs and the luge. For the Olympic Games, it is not surprising that the GDR authorities targeted medals in three areas of sport – gymnastics, swimming, and track and field – because together they accounted for 70 per cent of the medals to be won.

Conclusion

Developments in physical education in the GDR paralleled those of the Soviet Union. The GDR enjoyed its rise to economic recovery and sporting prowess over a compressed time-scale: it had the benefits of Soviet experience; it was advanced industrially and had a literate population. That the system was modelled on the Soviet Union, though with some German features, is beyond doubt, for the form of socialism was based on Marxist-Leninism. Soviet and East German educators adopted the union of academic, technical and physical training which Marx had seen as the only possible method for producing the all-round and harmoniously developed individual. This can be seen in the provision of the polytechnical secondary school.

The *raison d'être* for the state's drive to involve all in sport was embedded in Marxist ideology: it was through the use of sport that social consciousness or 'collectivity' could be developed. The application of Marxist-Leninist principles through the system of mass physical education and sport, particularly high-performance sport, elevated the prestige of the nation. The triumphs over capitalist countries were seen both as a contribution to, and triumph of, the socialist cause. After 1949, Ulbricht saw the massive national involvement in sport not simply as a means of securing recognition outside the Eastern Bloc, but also as an expedient way of diverting young people from undesirable political activity – schools were no exception!

Physical development for the East Germans was an integral part of the process of shaping and developing an all-round personality. It was in this process that school physical education had such an important part to play, for the youth of the nation was viewed as the future of the nation. Physical education, alongside extra-curricular activities, mass participation measures and competition, served the cause of the Party, for they assisted in cultivating the socialist personality according to Marxist philosophy, and in demonstrating the superiority of the 'new man' in a socialist democracy over the capitalist bourgeois.

The two Germanies: concluding comments

From the position in 1949, which stemmed from the discrediting of the National Socialist era of 1933–45, and was accentuated by shortages of teachers and facilities, together with the reluctance of educationalists to give support, the restoration of physical education to a position of relative respectability in the FRG was slow: coordinating supra-regional bodies such as the KMK were rather ineffectual in initiating progress; and the cultural and political individualism of the *Länder* inhibited a cohesive and collective approach to resolving difficulties and problems. It was non-educational sector bodies such as the DSB and DOG which lobbied for progressive measures, and which exerted considerable influence on the developments which took place. The Nazis had aimed to deprive physical education of all individualism and make it nationalistically popular. In the post-war era, physical education has gradually come to serve to educate the whole person through physical activity within a democratic and humanistic framework. The sublime status of physical education in 1945 was transformed, and the subject, through the trials and tribulations of the 1950s and 1960s, was accorded a degree of educational credibility in its adoption as an examinable subject within the School Leaving Certificate framework.

Developments in physical education in the German Democratic Republic were markedly influenced by the application of Soviet-Union inspired Marxist-Leninist principles, albeit alongside some traditional German features. The physical development of young East Germans was an integral part of the process of shaping an all-round, developed personality. School physical education had a distinctive role to play in this process, for the youth of the nation was also the future of the nation. Physical education, along with extra-curricular activities, mass participation measures and competition, were used as an instrument to serve the interests of the Party for they assisted in cultivating the 'socialist personality' according to Marxist philosophy, and in demonstrating the superiority of the 'new man' in a socialist democracy over the capitalist bourgeois.

Developments in physical education in the Federal Republic of Germany were strongly influenced by the various DSB activities throughout the years and by KMK guidelines, which in fact supported the promotion of physical education at school rather ambivalently. The main purpose of physical education, the character-building of the independent individual, was a part of general education, but it changed after 1970 into the promotion of 'sport for all' and for lifelong physical activity as a central part of active leisure time. The change from traditional physical education to competitive sports preparation at all levels of the school system, including new extra-curricular activities like the Youth Trains for the Olympics campaign, with the attempt to set up special sports schools, has to be seen in the context of the development of the two German elite sport systems of the late 1960s and early 1970s. Whereas the spirit of competition in school sport was subjugated by alternative teaching approaches in the 1980s, it continued in the GDR through further developments of the broad system of extra-curricular activities. Nevertheless, the 'sport for all' movement did usher in a new physical education policy in the GDR of the 1980s.

If we look to official and unofficial interactions of the two German sport and physical education systems, there appears to have been in different periods some exchange of physical education concepts and developments between the two sides of the 'Iron curtain': the switch from patriotic *Turnen* to 'sports education' in the GDR after 1963 was more or less a result of the battle between the two systems which elevated competitive sport. The West German sport and education authorities changed their traditional physical education in the late 1960s to the sports concept, with new curricula in the early 1970s. At that time GDR teaching materials for physical education, with the respective textbooks, were even recommended in West German physical education curricula! The 'sport for all' movement in physical education in the West Germany of the late 1970s also appeared in the GDR around the mid-1980s, when the traditional competitive focus of sports education was supplemented by leisure/sport-related aims within the physical education curricula introduced in 1989. Nevertheless, both systems of sport and of physical education were diverse in general structure and purpose, and also of course in terms of general education and its philosophical-political background in supporting school physical education. Different systems were also developed for extra-curricular physical activities inside and outside schools, which enjoyed quite different levels of importance and state support in the two countries.

References

Arbeitskreise der Kultusminister der Länder *et al.* (1956) *Empfehlungen zur Förderung der Leibeserziehung in den Schulen*, Bonn: KMK, 1–4.

Aschebrock, H. (ed.) (1986) *Fachdidaktische Analysen zur Qualität des Sportcurriculums in Nordrhein-Westfalen*, Münster: Lit.

Beckers, E. (1987) 'Durch Rückkehr zur Zukunft? Anmerkungen zur Entwicklung der Sportpädagogik', *Sportwissenschaft*, 17, 241–57.

——(1996) 'Hermeneutics and Sport Pedagogy', in Schempp, P. G. (ed.) *Scientific Development of Sport Pedagogy*, Münster/New York: Waxmann, 203–22.

Brodtmann, D. and Landau, G. (1984) (eds) *Wettkämpfe, Sportfeste, Spielfeste*, Reinbek: Rowohlt.

Deutscher Sportbund (1956) 'Empfehlungen zur Förderung der Leibeserziehung in den Schulen', in Wolf, N. (ed.) (1974) *Dokumente zum Schulsport*, Schorndorf: Hofmann, 46–58.

——(1966) *Charta des deutschen Sports*, Frankfurt: Limpert.

——(1972) 'Aktionsprogramm für den Schulsport', in Wolf, N. (ed.) (1974) *Dokumente zum Schulsport*, Schorndorf: Hofmann, 182–90.

——(1985) *2. Aktionsprogramm für den Schulsport*, Frankfurt am Main: DSB.

Dietrich, K. and Heinemann, K. (1989) *Der nicht-sportliche Sport*, Schorndorf: Hofmann.

Dietrich, K., Heinemann, K. and Schubert, M. (1990) *Kommerzielle Sportanbieter*, Schorndorf: Hofmann.

Eichel, W. (1983) *Illustrierte Geschichte der Körperkultur: Band II – die Körperkultur in Deutschland von 1917 bis 1945; die Gestaltung der sozialistischen Körperkultur in der Deutschen Demokratischen Republik bis 1981*, Berlin: Sportverlag.

Ewald, M. (1973) 'Striding consistently and resourcefully on the tested path', *Sport in the GDR*, 3, 9–10.

Fernandez-Balboa, J-M. (1997) *Critical Postmodernism in Human Movement, Physical Education and Sport*, Albany: State University of New York Press.

Frankfurter Arbeitsgruppe (1982) *Offener Sportunterricht: Analysieren und Planen*, Reinbek: Rowohlt.

Funke, J. (1980) 'Körpererfahrung', *Sportpädagogik*, 4, 13–20.

——(ed.) (1983) *Sportunterricht als Körpererfahrung*, Reinbek: Rowohlt.

——(1997) *Vermitteln zwischen Kind und Sache: Erläuterungen zur Sportpädagogik*, Seelze-Velber: Kallmeyer.

Grössing, S. (1983) *Einführung in die Sport-Didaktik*, 3rd edn, Bad Homburg: Limpert.

Grupe, O. (1968) 'Kommentar zur Charta des deutschen Sports – Die Leibeserziehung in den Schulen', in Wolf, N. (ed.) (1974) *Dokumente zum Schulsport*, Schorndorf: Hofmann, 159–63.

Hardman, K. (1980) 'The development of physical education in the German Democratic Republic', *Physical Education Review*, 3 (2) autumn, 121–36.

——(1981) 'The development of physical education in West Germany', *Physical Education Review*, 4 (1) spring, 44–60.

——(1982) 'The development, structure and promotion of sport in the Federal Republic of Germany', *Physical Education Review*, 5 (1) spring, 45–61.

——(1987) 'Politics, ideology and physical education in the German Democratic Republic', *British Journal of Physical Education*, 18 (1) spring, 20–2.

——(1989) 'Physical education in the German Democratic Republic', *Physical Education and Sport under Communism. Monograph*, Manchester: University of Manchester, 18–30.

——(1990) ' "Sport in Hort": community provision and socialist personality', *British Journal of Physical Education*, 21 (2) 281–3.

——(1992) 'Physical education in the former German Democratic Republic', *Journal of the International Council for Health, Physical Education and Recreation*, XXVIII (2) winter, 5–10.

Heinemann, K., Schubert, M. and Dietrich, K. (1990) *Akademikerarbeitslosigkeit und neue Formen des Erwerbsverhaltens: dargestellt am Beispiel arbeitsloser Sportlehrer; eine empirische Untersuchung*, Weinheim: Deutscher Studien-Verlag.

Hildebrandt, R. and Laging, R. (1981) *Offene Konzepte im Sportunterricht*, Bad Homburg: Limpert.

Hinsching, J. and Hummel, A. (eds) (1997) *Schulsport und Schulsportforschung in Ostdeutschland 1945–90*, Aachen: Meyer & Meyer.

Honecker, M. (1982) 'Auch wir Pädagogen stellen uns der Herausforderung dieses Jahrzehnts. Für jeden Schüler den besten Start ins Leben sichern', *Protokoll des Zentralen Direktorenkonferenz des Ministeriums für Volksbildung vom 10–12 Mai 1982*, Berlin: Volkseigener Verlag.

——(1985) 'Die Schulpolitik der S.E.D. und die wachsenden Anforderungen an den Lehrer und die Lehrerbildung. Materialen der Konferenz des Ministeriums für Volksbildung in Erfurt 15–16 November 1985', *Deutsche Lehrerzeitung*, 28.

Hübner, H. (ed.) (1986) *Schulpraxisnahe Analysen zur Umsetzung des Sportcurriculums in Nordrhein-Westfalen*, Münster: Lit.

Joeres, U. and Weichert, W. (1984) *Schwimmen – Bewegen und Spielen im Wasser*, Reinbek: Rowohlt.

KMK (1966) *Rahmenrichtlinien für die Leibeserziehung an den Schulen der B.R.D*, Bonn: KMK.

Krüger, A. (1979) 'Turnen und Turnunterricht zur Zeit der Weimarer Republik – Die Grundlagen der heutigen Schulsportmisere?', in Krüger, A. and Niedlich, D. (eds) *Ursachen der Schulsportmisere in Deutschland*, London: Arena, 13–31.

Krüger, M. (1988) 'Was ist alternativ am alternativen Sporttreiben?', *Sportwissenschaft*, 18, 137–59.

Krüger, M. and Grupe, O. (1998) 'Sport- oder Bewegungspädagogik? Zehn Thesen zu einer Standortbestimmung', *Sportunterricht*, 47, 180–7.

Kultusminister des Landes Nordrhein-Westfalen (1980–1) *Richtlinien und Lehrpläne für den Sport in den Schulen im Lande Nordrhein-Westfalen*, vols I–V, Frechen: Ritterbach.

Kurz, D. (1977) *Elemente des Schulsports: Grundlagen einer pragmatischen Fachdidaktik*, Schorndorf: Hofmann.

——(1986) 'Handlungsfähigkeit im Sport – Leitidee einer pragmatischen Fachdidaktik', in Spitzer, G. (ed.) *Sport zwischen Eigenständigkeit und Fremdbestimmung: pädagogische und historische Beiträge aus der Sportwissenschaft; Festschrift für Hajo Bernett*, Bonn: Wegener, 28–43.

——(1987) ' "Vom Vollzug" der Leibesübungen zur Handlungsfähigkeit im Sport', in Peper, D. and Christmann, E., *Standortbestimmung der Sportpädagogik. Symposium zum Andenken an den Sportpädagogen J. N. Schmitz*, Schorndorf: Hofmann, 52–67.

Landau, G. (1996) 'Critical theory in German sport pedagogy', in Schempp, P. (ed.) *Scientific Development of Sport Pedagogy*, Münster/New York: Waxmann, 223–36.

Lehrplan Sport (1987) 'Entwürfe der Lehrpläne Sport der Klassen 1 bis 3, 4 bis 6 und 7 bis 10', *Körpererziehung*, 37 (2/3) 53–120.

Marburger Sportpädagogen (1998) ' "Grundthemen des Bewegens". Eine bewegungspädagogische Erweiterung der Sportlehrerausbildung', *Sportunterricht*, 47, 318–24.

Meinberg, E. (1986) 'Die Körperkonjunktur und ihre anthropologischen Wurzeln', *Sportwissenschaft*, 16, 129–47.

——(1987) 'Warum Theorien sportlichen Handelns Anthropologie benötigen!', *Sportwissenschaft*, 17, 20–36.

Mester, L. (1962) *Grundfragen der Leibeserziehung*, Braunschweig: Westermann.

Ministerium für Volksbildung (1980) *Lehrplan Sport: Abiturstufe und Berufsbildung*, Berlin: Volk und Wissen Volkseigener Verlag.

Naul, R. (1985) 'Sport in der Schule', in Twellmann, W. (ed.) *Handbuch Schule und Unterricht*, vol. 7.2, Düsseldorf: Schwann, 751–76.

——(1987) 'Sporterziehung als Bestandteil einer neuen Allgemeinbildung', in Heid, H. and Herrlitz, H. G. (eds) Allgemeinbildung (10. DGfE-Kongreß) 21, *Beiheft der Zeitschrift für Pädagogik*, Weinheim, 161–71.

——(1990) 'Olympic headquarters: a new challenge to sport pedagogy in the Federal Republic of Germany', in Fu, F. H., Ng, M. L. and Speak, M. (eds) *Comparative Physical Education and Sport*, vol 6, Hong Kong: Condor, 199–204.

Naul, R. and Grossbröhmer, R. (1996) *40 Jahre Schulsport in NordrheinWestfalen. Lehrplantheorie und Unterrichtspraxis*, Düsseldorf: Concepta.

Naul, R., Jonischeit, L. and Wick, U. (2000) *Turnen, Spiel und Sport in Schule und Verein. Jugendsport zwischen 1870 und 1932*, Aachen: Meyer & Meyer.

Paschen, K. (1969) *Die Schulsportmisere*, Braunschweig: Westermann.

Sorg, H. (1955) *Von der Stunde Null bis zum Deutschen Bund*, Frankfurt am Main: DSB.

Strych, E. (1975) *Der Westdeutsche Sport in der Phase der Neugründung, 1945–1950*, Schorndorf: Hofmann.

Trebels, A. H. (1983) *Spielen und Bewegen an Geräten*, Reinbek: Rowohlt.

Treutlein, G., Funke, J. and Sperle, N. (eds) (1986) *Körpererfahrung in traditionellen Sportarten*, Wuppertal: Putty.

Wolf, N. (ed.) (1974) *Dokumente zum Schulsport*, Schorndorf: Hofmann.

Chapter 4

Sport and physical education in re-unified Germany, 1990–2000

Roland Naul and Ken Hardman

In October 1990, almost a year after the symbolic breaching of the Berlin Wall in November 1989, German re-unification was sealed with agreements on the basis of the Unification Treaty (31 August 1990). The Treaty included one article related to sport. It was solely concerned with three elite sports agencies in the former GDR: the doping laboratory at Kreischa, the research unit for developing sports equipment (FES) in East Berlin, and the research institute for coaching and training (FKS) at Leipzig. All three agencies have been restructured and have become an integral part of the Federal Institute for Sport Science, headed by the Ministry of Interior. The DHfK, where after 1972 the former GDR coaches were trained, was dismantled along with the entire GDR sports system in the early 1990s. Former GDR sports associations joined West German sports associations after re-unification, one example of which was the GDR Football Association (DFV), which became the north-east regional branch of the West German Football Association (DFB) and included the five football associations of the five new *Länder* (Mecklenburg-Vorpommern, Brandenburg, Saxony-Anhalt, Thuringia and Saxony). All other former GDR sports associations were similarly merged with their West German counterparts on the lines of the football model. Many sports clubs, linked previously either with the army (ASK), the Ministry of State Security, the so-called *Stasi* (Dynamo) or with state companies (VEB) were closed down. The former state enterprises were privatised and their sports facilities were made available for employees.

The highly structured system of competitive sport linked with the education system was also dismantled (see Naul 1992a). Training centres for gifted athletes were closed. Some former KJSs were restructured and converted to private boarding schools (e.g. the former KJS in the city of Rostock); others in Potsdam, Berlin, Halle, etc. were adopted and supported by the new *Länder* ministries of education as sport schools linked with sport clubs to provide additional support for talented young people in specific sports. Physical education in the former polytechnic comprehensive schools and the extended upper secondary classes (grades

11–12) changed dramatically. All the new waves in physical education emanating from West Germany in the 1980s were brought to the attention of (and in some instances imposed upon) the remaining former GDR physical education representatives and teachers (many members of the SED had lost their jobs on political grounds). West German pedagogues gave lectures at teacher training colleges and university sport science institutes. Reconstruction involved critical evaluation procedures of physical education and sport science departments, in spite of the fact that some West German benchmark standards were somewhat dubious and in some areas in need of reform. Even the DSB took on an advocacy role and actioned a plan to support sport science units at universities in East Germany (DSB 1994). However, criteria and norms in the plan for academics included lower standards than had already been set and achieved in the former GDR, and somewhat ironically in this situation actually resulted in academic staff reductions.

The traditional conceptual and contextual criteria of West German models became the yardsticks for reform of the sport system of the East beyond the university-level institutions (see Naul 1993; 1994). They embraced a DSB campaign to set up a 'Golden plan for the East' to provide sport facilities to meet the needs of sports clubs (DSB 1995). The campaign was based on the successful 'Golden plan' for provision of community facilities in the 1960s and 1970s in West Germany (see Roskam, Chapter 11 in this volume).

On the occasion of the first bi-annual congress of the German Association of Sport Science (DVS) at the East German University of Potsdam 1993, the West German sport sociologist and new President of the unified German Track and Field Association commented in his keynote address that the old East German sport structures should be completely dismantled, and that little if anything could be used from a new structural point of view (Digel 1995). Digel's rationale was that West German society was 'postmodern' whereas East German society lagged behind and would need to copy and adopt West German norms. He argued that a pause in postmodern development of the sports system in the West, caused by reunification policy, might lead to a moratorium and a rethink on current developments of postmodern lifestyle concepts in sport, and that reunification could also re-shape the social role of the traditional sport clubs in the West; in turn, these should become the model for the new sport clubs in the East (Digel 1995). Thus the official sport politics of the West were directed to promote adaptation and imitation of western standards. Concomitantly, any aspect of the East German sport and physical education system, which after evaluation might be reconstructed (e.g. the physical education research unit of the former Academy of Pedagogical Science), was overlooked. The only exceptions remained the three former GDR elite sport institutions, which were protected by the Unification

Treaty, and a few elite sport schools, which, as previously indicated, were adopted by the respective ministries of education in the new *Länder* (Brettschneider and Klimek 1998).

The founding of new sport clubs and state sport associations progressed in the five new *Länder* during the 1990s. However, the development of sport clubs in the East was linked more with the traditional standards of competitive sport programmes rather than with 'modernisation' in the spirit of the 'sport for all' movement (see Baur *et al.* 1995; Baur and Burrmann 2000). This development runs counter to Digel's arguments, and has attracted criticism of sports associations in the eastern *Länder* because their sport programmes have been limited more to the traditional standards of sport in the former GDR. The development of sport in the East has not produced a moratorium on postmodernism; in fact economic growth and imitation of modern lifestyles to compensate for former restrictions on leisure sport activity, frequent travelling and holidays abroad have served to reinforce the developments. After ten years of German re-unification, representatives of the new federal sports associations appear to be content with what has been achieved; even the National Olympic Committee (NOK) views progress positively, regardless of the decrease in total Olympic medals won in Atlanta (1996) and Sydney (2000) compared with Barcelona (1992) (NOK 2000). The benefits of the former GDR's elite sport system, still visible in Barcelona in 1992, no longer exist in the unified Germany. On the other hand, there has been considerable progress in the 'sport for all' movement, as increased membership in sport clubs' activities in the East testify in several sports. However, many differences with the western *Länder* remain. In particular, young people are less involved in sports activities, in some instances even less than pre-1990, for which there are several reasons, which include, for example, the non-replacement of dismantled institutions, and the increased expense of participating in sports programmes. Recent studies report that some 20–30 per cent of young people are members of a sport club in the East, whereas current data for young people in western *Länder* indicate double the figure (Brettschneider and Sack 1996; Kurz and Tietjens 2000; Schmidt *et al.* 2000). The 'Golden plan for the East' to construct local sport facilities is laudable, but municipal authority and *Land* financial investment is required. Furthermore, with the necessity these days of economic public–private investment partnerships to create modern-styled sport facilities, it will take several decades before the standards set in the West can be realised.

In physical education in schools, the early post-reunification years were marked by irritation and uncertainty about whether everything from the past should be disowned, and the extent to which the new West German approaches of the 1980s should be incorporated (Naul 1992b). Confusion and reluctance over old and new methods and curriculum content were much in evidence, and were openly discussed both in the West and the East. After observing lessons in West German schools, some prominent former GDR physical educationalists expressed doubts as to whether the prevailing ideas on 'student-centred teaching', 'deconstructing the structure of sports' and 'alternative body experiences' should form the basis of a renewal of physical education (Porschütz 1991). With the establishment of new education authorities in the eastern *Länder*, curriculum development in physical education began to progress (Helmke 1995). Partnerships between East and West German *Länder* were developed (e.g. North Rhine-Westphalia and Brandenburg; Hesse and Thuringia; Bavaria and Saxony amongst others). Within the new curricula, a mixture of former West German approaches, in particular *Handlungsfähigkeit* and 'body experiences', can be identified, as well as some relics of the past which were combined with more recently popular kinds of physical activities like aerobics and floor ball, etc. Content of some curricula in the new eastern *Länder* outmoded those of the West in the late 1990s. The philosophy and principles underpinning the last GDR physical education curriculum of 1989, which was introduced just prior to the demise of the GDR, were revised by Hummel (1994; 1997) and others. Subsequently, this latest modified East German approach influenced physical education curriculum development in Saxony and Thuringia. The essence of the approach was 'general motor-skill-ability education'; its focus was on a range of physical abilities as a foundation for the acquisition of physical skills and techniques to be applied to a spread of physical activities and sports.

In the western part of Germany, four main tendencies in physical education became visible in the 1990s. First, the re-establishment of the educational purpose of physical education as a compulsory part of general education frequently featured in academic discussion and support (Stibbe 1992; Prohl 1993; Schierz 1997); it was also linked with critical evaluation of the *Handlungsfähigkeit* approach, because of its exclusion of character-building. The re-enhancement of the educational purposes of physical education with new normative standards was also demanded as an important integral part in the new legitimation of school physical education (Scherler 1995). Others have argued that the re-enhancement of the educational purpose in physical education is closely linked with the basic physical activities of the 'body experiences' approach but not with typical sport activities. Currently, such sport pedagogues prefer the term 'movement education' to 'sport education' (Moegling 1999). A general problem in the legitimatisation of physical education occurred with the progressive decrease in school physical education lessons in the 1990s. This decrease reflected financial constraints and insufficient numbers of replacements for retired physical education teachers.

The second trend is mirrored in the global picture of a perceived crisis in school physical education reported by Hardman and Marshall (2000).

Since the early 1990s, despite doubts cast by some *Länder* authorities, physical education has been declining in many German schools. Today, governments' decentralisation policies devolve powers to schools and so provide them with greater autonomy for programmes and syllabi, with consequent opportunities to reduce and/or increase the amount of time allocated to selected subjects. Each school in North Rhine-Westphalia, for example, can now add or subtract one hour per week to or from certain curriculum subjects. For physical education, this flexibility devolved to local school boards has produced a decrease of physical education time from 3 to 2 hours per week in over 95 per cent of schools. Generally throughout Germany today, the devolved powers in schools and increased flexibility have meant the greater engagement of physical educators, in incorporating into school programme guidelines measures which contribute to the strengthening of ties with other social and sport institutions within the local community (Stibbe 1998).

The decline of physical education in schools across Germany is not only related to decentralisation policy. Some politicians and head teachers, the grammar school teachers' association, and in some cases also parents, have serious doubts as to whether it is necessary to have physical education in the school curriculum because so many boys and girls are physically active outside school. Indeed, some education experts share these doubts (Lenzen 2000). For some, it seems that the 1980s physical education teaching approach, *Handlungsfähigkeit* (an outcome of which is to prepare children for involvement in organised sport programmes) has become so successful that further physical activities at school are no longer necessary. A new legitimation of physical education by emphasising its former contribution to educating young people not only in physical terms, is currently under discussion; this development underpins the traditional and re-discovered role of physical education as 'educational physical education' (Balz and Neumann 1997; Aschebrock 2000). The new physical education curricula of North Rhine-Westphalia reveal modifications in the *Handlungsfähigkeit* approach towards a multi-perspective teaching approach (Kurz 1995; 2000; 2001) to stress the importance of education within physical education. The development is closely linked with the objectives of the 'body education' concept, because some physical educators doubt whether education in physical education can be achieved in the context of sports activities and in the spirit of competition (Beckers 2000). It has to be pointed out, however, that Beckers and 'body education' protagonists have overlooked the fact that the spirit of competition did not develop in the context of modern sports; rather, it developed first of all as an educational goal when sport did not feature in physical education programmes (Naul 2000).

A third strand in German physical education of the 1990s is the focus on health education within the subject, to include not only the physical aspect but also the broader context of individual and social well-being (Küpper and Kottmann 1993; Balz 1995). In the 1990s, the *Land* Ministry of Education's official policy on physical education curricula in North Rhine-Westphalia was to focus on the health education aspect. The Ministry endorsed new school-based health programmes at all levels, and was supported by life insurance companies (Pack and Becker 1995). However, the orientation of health education in German physical education curricula is more related to a psycho-social well-being approach than with a real physical impact on the cardiovascular system, as in Scandinavian or North American school health education programmes. At the present time, the renewal of physical education in vocational schools in North Rhine-Westphalia is focusing more on the health impact, testimony to which is a change of subject name to 'sport/health promotion' (Naul 1999).

School physical education in the 1990s was under pressure from two major developments, which also presented an obstacle for the process of reconstruction of physical education in the East. Just as the late 1960s physical education curriculum was challenged by out-of-school developments, so the mid-1990s was affected by the external sport movement initiatives of the 1980s. This represents the fourth strand in German physical education in the 1990s. American imports of aerobics, baseball, skateboarding, skating and mountain biking were well received by children and adolescents outside the school system in their informal settings (Schwier 1998). Traditional school sports like basketball and soccer were re-shaped by sporting goods companies such as Adidas and Puma, which since 1992 have sponsored PR-events in rule-, space- and equipment-modified small-sided games and versions of basketball ('street ball') and soccer ('street soccer'). In general, these so-called 'trend and street sports' are challenging the canon of school-based physical education in discussions on curricular developments (Balz *et al.* 1994; Schulz 1994). Meanwhile, some late 1990s curricula in East and West have already incorporated some of these new or newly styled physical activities.

The rigorous support of co-education in physical education in the 1970s and 1980s for children aged 10–16 (secondary I schools), when girls were taught soccer and boys dance in co-educational classes, has been subjected to a critical evaluation of whether girls (and boys) really benefited from co-educational classes. A more reflective practice is now encouraged. In grades 7–8 for instance, the motivation and socialisation into physical activities attitudes of boys and girls at that time of personal development, are thought to be sufficiently different to warrant the division of physical education lessons into single-sex classes (LSW NRW 1998a; 1998b). Nevertheless, the 1990s phenomenon of 'anything goes' persists in terms of physical education concepts at school, but increasing numbers of physical educators and scholars have become aware of critical issues in physical education in schools in more recent years. There are some collaborative institutional initiatives, involving the DSB, the federal Physical Education Teacher Association (DSLV) and others, to re-establish the lost third hour of physical education in order to enhance its educational remit, and to re-shape the physical impact of physical education to provide more support in the development of children's lost basic physical abilities, and to promote healthy lifestyles amongst young people. It is in such a context that the 'new physical education' is also assessed (hitherto mainly by commentators outside of the physical education and sport system) for its role as an antidote to increases in physical and social aggression and violence in daily school life.

Finally, sport and physical education in Germany in the decade since re-unification has not only been influenced by re-unification policies and characterised by reconstruction issues and postmodern trends. The Maastricht Treaty of 1991 signalled further European harmonisation, which has become an important issue in Germany. Cross-cultural studies in physical education, sport for all, youth sports, women in sport, etc. have become popular areas of study in recent years, and have led to reflection on the German system and structure of sport and physical education within the broader European context.

With re-unification, the former GDR was divided into five *Länder*. The previous education system was largely dismantled and the new *Länder* embarked on the course of devising curricula and guidelines modelled on (some would argue imposed by) those of 'partner' *Länder* in the West. Thus a process of revision and reconstruction occured in the name of rede-velopment. Ironically, these sweeping changes came at a time when some of the West German curriculum models were themselves in need of revi-sion, and scientific and didactic standards in need of examination. The dominant role of the former West German state caused some physical educationists (Helmke *et al.* 1991) to comment that positive elements from the former GDR school sport system were totally ignored, as were their own ideas of democratic renewal. The 'open' strategies and 'fun'-orientated teaching methods introduced by some West Germans as 'missionaries of democracy', produced some understandable doubts amongst some East German physical educators and sport pedagogues about the value of innovative teaching approaches when discipline and performance were neglected (Porschutz 1991), and when they observed the teaching of some West Germans.

Re-unification presented an opportunity for rethinking in physical education. Many West German sport pedagogues have overlooked the curriculum reforms undertaken by the GDR authorities in the late 1980s. In the new *Länder*, physical education has been seen as a socialist relic of the former GDR's competitive sport system: physical education is now regarded as 'less important and having only minor significance in school education like it is more or less in West Germany' (Naul 1992b: 18); the trend of the early 1990s was to replace specialist teachers dismissed for economic reasons by non-specialists; discipline, order and performance largely disappeared from the teaching situation; the status of physical education changed to relative inferiority, with the result that many teachers let pupils do what they want, rather than intervening, for fear of 'accusation of being an authoritarian ex-socialist' (Naul 1992b: 18); the 'open instructional methods' introduced produced conflicts and chaos, with teacher confusion on methods and pupils faced with unfamiliar lesson formats. In adopting former West German values and norms, the 'baby was thrown out with the bathwater', for whilst there may have been negative features, and even some abuse, in the GDR delivery system, it also produced some positive results. However since tacit assimilation of West German concepts, change has been accomodated through revised curricula with accent on integration: chaos and conflict have been replaced by stability, conformity and progress.

References

Aschebrock, H. (ed.) (2000) *Erziehender Schulsport. Pädagogische Grundlagen der Curriculumrevision in Nordrhein-Westfalen*, Bönen: Kettler.

Balz, E. (1995) *Gesundheitserziehung im Schulsport*, Schorndorf: Hofmann.

Balz, E., Brinckhoff, K. P. and Wegner, U. (1994) 'Neue Sportarten in die Schule', *Sportpädagogik*, 18 (2) 17–24.

Balz, E. *et. al.* (1997) 'Schulsport – wohin? Sportpädagogische Grundfragen', in *Sportpädagogik*, 21 (1) 14–28.

Balz, E. and Neumann, P. (1997) *Wie pädagogisch soll der Schulsport sein?*, Schorndorf: Hofmann.

Baur, J., Koch, U. and Telchow, St. (1995) *Sportvereine im Übergang. Die Vereinsarbeit in Ostdeutschland*, Aachen: Meyer & Meyer.

Baur, J. and Burrmann, U. (2000) *Unerforschtes Land: Jugendsport in ländlichen Regionen*, Aachen: Meyer & Meyer.

Beckers, E. (2000) 'Grundlagen eines erziehenden Sportunterrichts', in Aschebrock, H. (ed.) *Erziehender Schulsport*, Bönen: Kettler, 86–97.

Brettschneider, W. D. and Klimek, G. (1998) *Sportbetonte Schulen*, Aachen: Meyer & Meyer.

Brettschneider, W. D. and Sack, G. (1996) 'Youth Sport in Europe – Germany', in de Knop, P., Engström, L. M., Skirstad, B. and Weiss, M. R. (eds) *Worldwide Trends in Youth Sport*, Champaign IL:: Human Kinetics, 139–151.

Digel, H. (1995) 'Sportentwicklung in Deutschland – Chancen und Risiken gesellschaftlicher Modernisierung', in Rode, J. and Philipp, H. (eds) *Sport in Schule, Verein und Betrieb*, St Augustin: Academia, 13–42.

Hardman, K. and Marshall, J. (2000) *World-wide Survey of the State and Status of School Physical Education. Final Report*, Manchester: University of Manchester.

Helmke, C. (1995) *Ziele, Inhalte und Organisation des Sportunterrichts in der gymnasialen Oberstufe. Eine Synopse aktueller LehrplanaussagenSportunterricht*, 44, 196–206.

Helmke, C., Naul, R. and Rhode J. (1991) 'Zur Lehrplanreform des Sportunterrichts in der ehemaligen DDR und in den neuen Bundesländern', *Sportunterricht*, 40 (10) 382–94.

Hummel, A. (1994) 'Die Konzeption der körperlich-sportlichen Grundlagenbildung – Weiterhin eine tragfähige Leitidee?', in Schierz, M., Hummel, A. and Balz, E. (eds) *Sportpädagogik. Orientierungen – Leitideen – Konzepte*, St Augustin: Academia, 133–53.

——(1997) 'Die Körperlich-Sportliche Grundlagenbildung – immer noch aktuell?', in Balz, E. and Neumann, P. (eds) *Wie pädagogisch soll der Schulsport sein?*, Schorndorf: Hofmann, 47–62.

Küpper, D. and Kottmann, L. (eds) (1993) *Sport und Gesundheit*, Schorndorf: Hofmann.

Kurz, D. (1995) 'Handlungsfähigkeit im Sport – Leitidee eines mehrperspektivischen Unterrichtskonzepts', in Zeuner, A. Senf, G., and Hofmann S. (eds) *Sport unterrichten – Anspruch und Wirklichkeit*, St Augstin: Academia, 41–8.

——(2000) 'Die pädagogische Grundlegung des Schulsports in Nordhein-Westfalen', in Aschebrock, H. (ed.) *Erziehenden Schulsport*, Bönen: Kettler, 9–55.

——(2001) 'Developing PE curricula in the Federal State of North Rhine-Westphalia: a chance for more autonomy for the individual school?', in EAdS (ed.) *Physical Education: From Central Governmental Regulation to Local School Autonomy*, Velen: EadS, 148–55.

Kurz, D. and Tietjens, M. (2000) 'Das Sport- und Vereinsengagement der Jugendlichen', *Sportwissenschaft*, 30, 384–407.

Lenzen, D. (2000) 'Sport, Bewegung oder was? Argumentationsrituale in der Sportpädagogik', *Sportunterricht*, 49, 77–80.

LSW NRW (1998a) *Sportunterricht ohne Grenzen. Beiträge des Faches Sport zum fächerübergreifenden Unterricht im Wahlpflichtbereich der Sekundarstufe I*, Bönen: Kettler.

——(1998b) *Mädchen und Jungen im Schulsport*, Bönen: Kettler.

Moegling, K. (1999) *Ganzheitliche Bewegungserziehung*, Butzbach-Griedel: Afra.

Naul, R. (1992a) 'Elite sport in Germany: the 1990s', *Journal of the International Council of Health, Physical Education and Recreation*, XXVIII (2) 17–22.

——(1992b) 'German unification: curriculum development and physical education at school in East Germany', *British Journal of Physical Education*, 23 (4) winter, 14–19.

——(1993) 'Neue Sportwissenschaft Ost-Akademischer Offenbarungseid der alten Sportwissenschaft West?', *dvs-Informationen*, 3, 15–19.

——(1994) 'German unification: decline or regeneration in physical education and sport sciences?', in Wilcox, R. C. (ed.) *Sport in the Global Village*, Morgantown: FIT, 281–8.

——(1999) 'Das Fach Sport im Berufskolleg – Ein Beitrag zur umfassenden beruflichen Handlungskompetenz', in Landesinstitut für Schule und Weiterbildung (ed.) *Sport im Berufskolleg. Werkstattberichte Curriculumrevision im Schulsport*, book 8. Soest: LSW, 14–30.

——(2000) 'Schoolsport and competition: sport pedagogy', *Perspectives. The Multidisciplinary Series of Physical Education and Sport Science*, vol. 1, 73–83.

Pack, R. and Becker, U. (1995) 'Umsetzungsstrategie für das "Handlungsprogramm zur Förderung der Gesundheitserziehung in der Schule durch Sport im Land

Nordrhein-Westfalen" ', in Kultusministerium Nordrhein-Westfalen (ed.) *Gesund-heitserziehung in der Schule durch Sport. Bilanz und Perspektiven*, Frechen: Ritterbach, 16–20.

Porschütz, W. (1991) 'Selbständigkeit, Leistungsstreben, Ordnung. Diskussion der notwendigen Komponenten im motorischen Lern- und Übungsprozess', *Sportunterricht*, 40, 377–81.

Prohl, R. (1993) 'Bildung durch Sport – ein überholter pädagogischer Anspruch?', *Sportunterricht*, 41, 454–62.

Scherler, K. H. (1995) 'Sport in der Schule', in Rode, J. and Philipp, H. (eds) *Sport in Schule. Verein und Betrieb*, St Augustin: Academia, 43–58.

Schierz, M. (1997) 'Sportunterricht und sein (möglicher) Beitrag zur Allgemeinbildung', *Pädagogik*, 5, 44–8.

Schmidt, W., Haupt, U. and Süssenbach, J. (2000) 'Bewegung, Spiel und Sport im Alltag ostdeutscher Kinder', *Sportunterricht*, 49, 116–21.

Schulz, N. (1994) 'Mit der Zeit gehen – zur Aktualisierung von Schulsportinhalten', *Sportunterricht*, 43, 429–503.

Schwier, J. (1998) *Spiele des Körpers. Jugendsport zwischen Cyberspace und Streetstyle*, Hamburg: Czwalina.

Stibbe, G. (1992) 'Brauchen wir eine Neuorientierung des Schulsports?', *Sportunterricht*, 41, 454–62.

Stibbe, G. (ed.) (1998) *Bewegung, Spiel und Sport als Elemente des Schulprogramms*, Baltmannsweiler: Schneider.

Chapter 5

Physical education in schools

Roland Naul

Introduction

At the present time there are differences in school physical education in the various types of school and at different levels (primary, secondary I and secondary II schools) from the concepts developed in the 1970s and 1980s. Unsurprisingly, delivery of physical education in primary schools has focal approaches which differ from those more frequently used in upper grades of the school system.

Primary schools

In Germany, non-selective (i.e. comprehensive) primary schools cater for children aged 6–10 (grades 1–4). In the early 1970s, teaching of sports motor skills and techniques was related to preparation for post-school leisure involvement or early elite sport development. Motor learning was regarded as a pre-requisite for successful teaching in primary schools. This 'sportification' of the physical education curriculum (see Diem and Kirsch 1975; Hecker 1977) was associated with the general shift from a physical education focus to a sport focus at that time (see Chapter 3 in this volume). A counter to this 'sportification' approach was an orientation to the social learning dimension of physical activities (Cachay and Kleindienst 1975). Discussion of other alternative approaches linking physical education with aesthetic education and Piagetian psycho-motor learning (see Bannmüller 1979; Scherler 1975) took place in the late 1970s; they largely excluded sports in early childhood. In many primary schools at the time, three lessons per week, taught by trained teachers, were allocated to physical education. Teachers organised their teaching on semester course bases and focused on gymnastics, athletics, swimming and mini-games, though emphasis on competition was much diminished. Swimming became the most important activity because of its propensity to avoid future risks.

Kretschmer (1981) developed a more balanced approach to sports instruction and physical education in the early 1980s. Kretschmer regarded sports as only one aspect of the complex personal, material and social environment of children's physical life experiences. The implication was that physical education should become child-centred, not sports-orientated, and embrace a broad range of opportunities and variety of physical activities, which children actually experience in different environments. Kretschmer proposed the all-encompassing term 'movement teaching' to describe the acquired learning of the physical, social and cognitive self through the comprehensive range of physical activities experienced, activities which are not specifically related to any kind of sport. However, it was Funke's 'body experience' approach (see Chapter 3 in this volume), which was popular in primary schools in the 1980s and early 1990s. Both Funke's 'body experience' concept and the so-called 'Frankfurt approach' of the 'de-construction of sports' excluded sport techniques teaching in the late 1980s.

This shift from 'sports instruction' for children to the emphasis on the concept of psycho-physical needs, which aimed to help rediscover the lost experiences in the physical world of children, became even more popular during the 1990s, when the under-developed basic motor abilities of children became increasingly visible in primary schools (Zimmer 1995). The alternative approaches of the 1980s transformed physical education in primary schools, for now the emphasis is on general movement and motor ability experiences, which have virtually replaced sports teaching in the day-to-day life of primary schools. This transformation has resulted in a change of subject name from 'sport education' to 'movement education' (see Grössing 1993; Moegling 1999), in which teaching strategies encompass the multi-purpose utilisation of apparatus and equipment in gymnasia and swimming pools, and cognitive processes in games instruction (Zimmer 1998). The primary school is the 'school of children', where basic forms of movement rather than teacher-directed sports instruction should be experienced individually (see Küpper 1997; 2000). The new physical education curriculum for primary schools in North Rhine-Westphalia (2000), for instance, focuses on this perspective with teaching principles and forty-seven special tasks in nine subject content areas of physical activity. Now the key tasks for physical education teaching in primary schools have become:

- individualisation of physical development and integration of children;
- child-centred learning and guidance of children;
- the practice of physical activity with application of motor abilities and experience; and
- reflection on a variety of movement tasks.

The sport activity approach has been abandoned.

The socialisation of children into sport and general life in society has recently come under scrutiny as technological developments, mass media consumption, the emphasis on competitive sport in clubs and decreases in school physical education timetable allocation (reduced from three to two lessons per week) have been linked with reduced participation in physical activity in childhood. Processes of individualisation have coincided with loss of neighbourhood spaces and places in urban development plans. Today young children spend more time on leisure activities at home than on physical activities in the wider community (see Dietrich and Landau 1990; Hildebrandt *et al.* 1994; Schmidt 1998). Within this context extra-curricular activities have taken on a new and important role. Breaks between lessons, for example, are used for physical exercise; ergonomically designed school furniture fosters correct postural sitting in classroom lessons; and school playgrounds accommodate a range of equipment for motor activities, etc. In several *Länder* there is a primary school-based campaign, 'Moving schools', to improve physical activity in the daily school life context (see Kottmann *et al.* 1997; Müller 1999). Less overt success, however, has come through restoring the lost third weekly physical education lesson, and in replacing retired physical-education-degree qualified primary school teachers with young qualified physical education teachers.

At the same time, 'movement education' is not without its critics. In the main, it is its educational concept and its inherent devaluation of sport which are problematic for some. Children's socialisation into sport and their associated physical, social and mental development (see Bräutigam 1997) are believed by many movement education protagonists to be suffering neglect. Some physical educators seriously doubt whether perceptions of modern childhood, with postmodern assumptions about children's resistance to sport, do actually coincide with children's perceptions of sport and their personal assessment of modern sport in the development of physical lifestyles (Schulz 1999).

Secondary I schools

The present system of secondary I schools (age 10–16, grades 5–10) was established in the education reform years of the late 1960s and early 1970s, when 'folk schools' became *Hauptschule* (main schools), and comprehensive schools (to provide an alternative form of school education) were introduced alongside the existing traditional types of schools. This stage of school education is diverse compared with primary, grammar, and vocational school education at secondary II level. Thus four types of school now form the lower secondary level of education for the 10–16 age group: the more practical and manual-orientated main school; the 'middle school' (or so-called *Realschule*), with a modern technical vocational-orientated curriculum for jobs in administration and industry; various types of comprehensive school, which includes all different school graduation levels up to grade 10; and the lower and middle school classes (up to grade 10) of the traditional grammar schools with a variety of special curriculum profiles (languages, sciences and humanities) embedded in the past.

After re-unification, the former two-tier GDR school system of 'all-through general polytechnic schools' (POS, grades 1–10) and the 'extended upper schools' (EOS, grades 11–12) of the polytechnic school were reconstructed on the West German school system model. However, in some Eastern *Länder*, the *Hauptschule* and *Realschule* have been integrated to leave only two types of secondary I schools (secondary and grammar schools).

Although there are common guidelines and regulations for physical education in secondary I schools, there are different traditions, social profiles and material resources, etc. Essentially, the key features of the physical education curriculum are co-educational classes (introduced in the 1970s), optional physical education specialisation in grades 9–10 (introduced in the 1980s) and a syllabus which bridges the subject content of primary and secondary II levels. This 'bridging' is seen both in the adoption in grades 5–6 (age 11–12) of the 'body experience' approach of primary schools and the opportunity for pupils to select physical education as a specialised subject in grades 9–10 (age 15–16). In the majority of *Länder*, physical education is divided into special teaching units of various types of sports. German gymnastics, gymnastics and dance, athletics and swimming are compulsory areas of activity in secondary I schools; a variety of games is optional within three compulsory groups of games (net games like racquet sports and volleyball; invasion games like football and field hockey; and target games like basketball and team handball). Teaching physical education in terms of special units of sport instruction occurred in the 1970s, when it was structured for the full range of school years (grades 5–10) into three types of physical performance levels: introduction to basic skills; advanced level skills training; expertise and competition. In the physical education curricula for secondary I schools in North Rhine-Westphalia (1973), three general targets were set: health promotion and well-being, motor and psycho-social learning to communicate with other people, and interaction with the complex environment, to be prepared for daily and lifelong participation in sport after school and in leisure time. Six aims were specified: learning to play, motor learning, participation in competition, movement expression, knowledge of sport, and evaluation of sport (KM NRW 1973: 10–11). Later in the 1980s, additional objectives were introduced through the *Sports Handlungsfähigkeit* approach. However, the teaching units remain structured as sports units. A special teaching unit on volleyball, for instance, featured in one or two grades (e.g. grades 5 and 6) and was divided into 'skills', 'tactics', 'physical peformance', 'knowledge' and 'organisation'; it prescribed precisely what should be achieved through teaching this particular kind of sport. Unfortunately, the aims and objectives of teaching in the context of sport activities are less integrated in the general educational context of subject aims and objectives; this is partly because of neglect in implementation within the structure of teaching sport. Teaching modifications to the structure of sport, which the most common *Handlungsfähigkeit* approach does include, have up till now been ignored in many secondary I schools' physical education curricula.

Attempts have been made by pedagogues, for example Brettschneider (1980; 1981), to extend the physical education curriculum beyond the traditional range of sports activities, by incorporating self-organised physical activities with modified rules to suit children's age and stage of development, to socialise children into physical activity and so place emphasis on the individual needs and interests within a relevant social and environmental context. However, the *Handlungsfähigkeit* approach supported by the DSB's second *Action Plan for School Sports* (1985) dominated curriculum development throughout the 1980s and into the 1990s (see Chapter 3 in this volume). In North Rhine-Westphalia, new pedagogical perspectives within the frame of 'multi-perspective teaching' brought an end to the dominance of *Handlungsfähigkeit* in the 1990s. The new focus highlighted the importance of the socio-cultural context of physical activity, perceptions and body experiences, including interaction of the body with social reality, reflection of physical activity and body appearance in social life, and social interaction and communication. The consequences of this reorientation are to be seen in the aims, which now have an extended pedagogical foundation to embrace social life, a broadening of activities included in the curriculum, and more active participation in the development of school programmes to achieve 'Moving schools' for the pupils. A preliminary draft of the new physical education curriculum for secondary I schools in North Rhine-Westphalia (LSW 1999) contains a broad view on young people's engagement in physical activity (including organised sport), their sporting lifestyles and body appearance in social life. Aims and objectives are focused on early, middle and upper stages (grades 5–6, 7–8, 9–10) and linked with special content areas. Content is no longer restricted to specific kinds of sport; there are opportunities to experience a variety of movement activities such as skating, climbing, acrobatic exercises, and traditional and new types of games, as well as thematic topics to be addressed: identity and social relations, ecology and the social world of sport, and health and well-being.

It is perhaps worth noting that the ideas of the late 1990s, and in particular the proposed new physical education curriculum for secondary I schools in North Rhine-Westphalia, are reminiscent of the early 1980s, when Brettschneider and others tried to supplement 'sports instruction' with their 'socialisation approach to physical activities' in order to underpin the necessity of considering the social context and daily life of children's physical activities in school physical education programmes.

Secondary II schools

The secondary II school system can be divided into two different school systems: the upper classes (in eastern *Länder*, grades 11–12; in western *Länder*, grades 11–13) of the traditional grammar schools in which matriculation (*Abitur*) leads to university-based studies; and the vocational school system with a variety of special schools. Vocational school attendance of between two and four years is obligatory for all students who leave a secondary I school after grade 10. The duration of vocational education depends on specific job preparation and the level of certification required. Most of the students in the age range 16–18 attend part-time vocational schools for one or two days per week, and usually follow curricula which are related to special professional fields of work in administration, industry and commerce. The status of physical education and its range of activities vary widely in secondary II schools, even within one *Land*. In the upper grades of the grammar schools for instance, physical education may be selected as a special subject with up to six lessons classtime per week to obtain credits for matriculation, whereas in some vocational schools only one physical education lesson is offered, and even this is under pressure and in some cases has already been omitted from the curriculum.

Grammar schools

The Cold War politics of 1960s West/East German relations, which resulted in a change from the traditional concept of physical education to 'sport' and the promotion of competitive sport, also prompted some West German politicians and sports leaders to seek the establishment of special sport schools along the lines of the GDR's KJS model. Some grammar schools established 'sport classes' in specific activities for gifted young people, to provide a better environment for combining academic learning with sports training and preparation for competition. However, many early attempts failed (see Bergner and Gabler 1976) and sport grammar schools in North Rhine-Westphalia, for example, were replaced by a new model of general grammar school education when the KMK agreed a complete new system of matriculation and teaching in grammar schools across all federal *Länder*.

The KMK agreement produced a fundamental shift in physical education in the upper grades of grammar schools. The shift began in 1972 when the Curriculum Reform Act changed teaching on a broad scale for grades 11–13 (KMK 1972). The Act ushered in flexible study courses involving individual student subject selection for five semesters. In addition to compulsory requirements in non-optional subjects (e.g. German, English, mathematics, etc.), students were given the opportunity to select two major subjects (each 5 or 6 'hours' per week; it depended on respective *Land* regulations) and two minor subjects (each 3 'hours' per week) to obtain credits for matriculation. Physical education became compulsory, with 2 'hours' per week, and was organised as a special course of instruction in one sport per semester, which students selected from a range of activity areas offered (e.g. athletics, swimming, basketball, etc.) according to their attained level of expertise in performance and personal interest.

In many grammar schools, students also had the option to choose physical education as a major or minor subject for matriculation. The KMK regulated matriculation for all subjects by laying down compulsory criteria to be achieved in examinations; some of these 'Common compulsory norms for matriculation examinations' (*Einheitliche Prüfungsanforderungen für die Abiturprüfung*) contradicted the new aims of physical education curriculum development. As a major subject, six 'hours' (in some *Länder* only five 'hours') per week were allocated. The six-hour course was organised in three sub-courses, each of two hours. Two courses (four hours), one a major sport (e.g. volleyball), the other alternating each semester; another sport, with a focus on practical learning and training (see Ziegler 1979; Quanz 1984). The third course focuses on theoretical and scientific aspects generally related to the practical courses. Compulsory homework and written examinations for matriculation were an integral part of the course. As a minor subject, physical education was allocated a three-'hours' practical course, with teaching on theoretical issues and a final oral examination for matriculation. In some *Länder* a one-hour lecture on theoretical principles was given in the last semester, as well as a two-hour practical course in two sports. The major/minor subject matriculation issue was a source of debate for over two decades. The main argument was around the practical *v.* theory issue, with *Länder* curricula variously placing more emphasis on one than the other (Schulz 1982). In North Rhine-Westphalia, for example, the dimension of social learning in sport received more attention than did science-related learning.

A further step in curriculum reform was taken in 1974 with the introduction at federal level of the comprehensive secondary II school, which would integrate the grammar school and all types of vocational school to form a 'college school' (Deutscher Bildungsrat 1974). Physical education as a subject in college schools was to become a compulsory part of matriculation if a student were to choose a vocational profile for employment in leisure and sport. The KMK reform, which made physical education a matriculation subject, and the idea of integrating academic and vocational training in physical education for the leisure and sport job market, markedly influenced physical education teaching in the 1970s and 1980s in secondary II schools.

In the mid-1990s, physical education at both major and minor matriculation subject level was widely criticised because of the high credit rates and grades awarded, far higher on average than for other school subjects with a greater homework study load. Additionally, some evaluation studies revealed doubts about levels of achievement in standards of theoretical instruction (preparation for scientific learning) and the outcome of cognitive learning (Naul 1988). Currently, there is an attempt to change the curriculum of the minor subject. An evaluation project involving twenty-five selected grammar schools in North Rhine-Westphalia is being carried out. Inclusion of the minor subject for matriculation has been shelved until the results of this project are known.

Vocational schools

Full- and part-time vocational schools play an important role within the education system. In some full-time schools, elements of physical education have long been an integral part of the courses leading to specific vocational qualifications, for instance as swimming instructors or kindergarten teachers. In some part-time schools, physical education curricula have been incorporated since the early 1970s in the 'general education' section of the syllabi for training in manual work. It is not unusual in these schools to find only one lesson per week, with content a mere imitation of grammar and secondary I schools' curricula.

Until the early 1970s, there had been minimal physical education curriculum development in vocational schools. Early developments focused on compensatory motor activity as a form of relaxation from the physical work of the job. In North Rhine-Westphalia, such an approach was supplemented with selected leisure sport activities such as badminton, ice-skating, canoeing, skiing, orienteering, etc., as preparation for participation in the new 'sport for all' movement in sports clubs. Similar developments occurred in other *Länder*. Noteworthy, however, is that some of these outdoor pursuits (e.g. canoeing and orienteering) were not included in the physical education curricula of other schools.

The rationale for introducing 16+ year olds to leisure-related activities was based on engagement attraction through motivation. Two other dimensions of the developments in physical education in vocational schools occurred in the 1980s: first, involvement of students in curriculum decision-making, particularly in activity preference choice; and second, promotion of 'open instruction' techniques with student-centred direction. As indicated in Chapter 3 above, the latter was a pervasive feature in German schools in the 1980s, as indeed was the *Handlungsfähigkeit* approach and the health focus, which also found their way into vocational schools (Hartmann 1983). The evolving physical education curriculum model showed other similarities with developments in secondary I schools in the advocacy (Bloss 1978) of the social and cognitive dimensions of sporting lifestyles promoted by Brettschneider in the 1980s. But curriculum delivery continued to suffer from inadequacies in time allocation and resources.

The physical education crisis extant in schools throughout Germany in the 1990s was especially acute in vocational schools to the extent that by the middle of the 1990s the subject was unofficially being excluded from the curriculum in several *Länder*. In the city *Land* of Hamburg, for instance, physical education was omitted from vocational schools, and students were given vouchers to attend sport-club based programmes during leisure time. But most of the students sold their vouchers instead of attending these club programmes free of charge. Contributory to the dire situation was the employment sector, which was critical of the levels of general education and qualifications attained, and which argued for an increase in teaching time for basic and new subjects (e.g. computing) in vocational training to meet the needs of changes in work practices and new technologies. Physical education was not viewed as necessary in 'general education' beyond the first ten years of compulsory schooling. Moreover, many students in vocational schools had no interest in compulsory physical activities such as gymnastics and athletics. In more recent times, evaluation of physical education in vocational schools has been undertaken. Schaefer (1995) criticised the leisure, health and *Handlungsfähigkeit* approaches, and suggested analysis of students' real social context of life and work and their interests in physical activities when entering vocational training after ten years of schooling. The reaction in one *Land*, North Rhine-Westphalia, was to remove physical education from general education and place it within the sphere of 'professional' training in preparation for jobs on the reformed model of the integrated 'vocational college' in 1998.

Physical education in the new vocational college schools has become part of a trans-disciplinary learning area, in which competences and qualifications are obtained to meet with the demands of particular job profiles (see Naul 1999). Health-related physical activity has replaced sports activities in programmes which are essentially concerned with a variety of professional qualifications and specific job-related situations in the workplace (see Gasse and Uhler-Derings 1999). Subsequently, this new form of physical education in vocational schools has been designated 'sport/health promotion'. The new term marks another step in the direction of health-related physical education in Germany.

Conclusion

In the early 1970s, the term 'physical education' was replaced by the term 'sport', thus signifying a change in concept. The change was entwined with the 'sportification' process in German society as a part of Cold War politics. As long as the 'sport' concept was applied in all types of schools at all levels, learning and improvement of motor skills and sport techniques formed the essential core purpose of physical education for everyone ('sport for all') and the athletically gifted (competitive sport). The 1970s was the 'golden decade' of physical education in Germany, not because of its conceptual merits but because of the manifold improvements and resources: facilities (gymnasia and swimming pools), increased numbers of qualified physical education teachers, and the allocation of three or four lessons per week. However, with the differentiation of approaches in the 1980s, physical education became more diversified in the various types of school. This differentiation coincided with the beginning of a crisis in school physical education directly linked with a substantial decrease in financial support, which produced high levels of unemployment of physical education teachers and less investment in school sports facilities, and reduced physical education timetable allocation. The situation deteriorated further in the 1990s, following politically inspired policies of devolution of powers and responsibilities to local levels, and an increase in individual school autonomy.

The 1990s witnessed a significant ideological and pedagogical shift in physical education in schools. Sport was devalued, and body experiences and motor abilities expanded beyond their presence in primary school curricula to the point that a terminological change to 'movement education' is now clearly on the agenda. Recently, young children's socialisation into physical activity has taken on a more ambivalent dimension, and is currently posing a challenge to physical education in schools: more children are less physically active, which causes deficiencies in their basic motor development; however, more young children are also more actively engaged in organised sport programmes than in any previous decade. The challenge is how best to reconcile the disparate needs through physical education in schools, and to bridge the gap between the socialisation of children and that of youth by diverse physical activities outside school. It is a challenge which may only be met by a multifaceted concept of physical education, one that is applied to the full range of abilities, needs and interests of children and young people.

References

Bannmüller, E. (1979) *Neuorientierung der Bewegungserziehung in der Grundschule*, Stuttgart: Klett.

Bergner, K. and Gabler, H. (1976) 'Modelle und Maßnahmen zur Förderung des Schul- und Leistungssports', in Gabler, H. (ed.) *Schulsportmodelle in Theorie und Praxis*, Schorndorf: Hofmann, 25–62.

Bloss, H. (1978) 'Sportunterricht an Berufsschulen – Überlegungen für ein Curriculum', in *Zeitschrift für Sportpädagogik*, 2, 138–47.

Bräutigam, M. (1997) 'Zur Sportartenorientierung von Jugendlichen', in Balz, E. and Neumann, P. (eds) *Wie pädagogisch soll der Schulsport sein? Auf der Suche nach fachdidaktischen Antworten*, Schorndorf: Hofmann, 203–18.

Brettschneider, W. D. (1980) 'Sport in der Sekundarstufe I – Stiefkind didaktischer Überlegungen', *Sportunterricht*, 29, 206–14.

——(ed.) (1981) *Sportunterricht 5–10*, Munich: Urban & Schwarzenbach.

Cachay, K. and Kleindienst, Ch. (1975) 'Soziales Lernen im Sportunterricht', *Sportwissenschaft*, 5, 339–67.

Deutscher Bildungsrat (1974) *Zur Neuordnung der Sekundarstufe II. Konzept für eine Verbindung von allgemeinem und beruflichem Lernen*, Bonn: Bundesdruckerei.

Diem, L. and Kirsch, A. (1975) *Lernziele und Lernprozesse im Sport der Grundschule*, Frankfurt am Main: Limpert.

Dietrich, K. and Landau, G. (1990) *Sportpädagogik: Grundlagen, Positionen, Tendenzen*, Reinbek: Rowohlt.

Gasse, M. and Uhler-Derings, H. G. (1999) *Sport im Berufskolleg. Diskussionspapier. Curriculumrevision im Schulsport*, book 4. Soest: LSW.

Grössing, S. (1993) *Bewegungskultur und Bewegungserziehung: Grundlagen einer sinnorientierten Bewegungspädagogik*, Schorndorf: Hofmann.

Hartmann, H. (ed.) (1983) *Sport in der Berufsschule. Didaktische Grundlagen*, Bad Homburg: Limpert.

Hecker, G. (1977) *Aufgabenkanon für 100 Sportstunden im 1. und 2. Schuljahr*, Schorndorf: Hofmann.

Hildebrandt, R., Landau, G. and Schmidt, W. (eds) (1994) *Kindliche Lebens- und Bewegungswelt im Umbruch*, Hamburg: Czwalina.

KMK (1972) *Vereinbarung zur Neugestaltung der gymnasialen Oberstufe in der Sekundarstufe II vom 7. Juli 1972*, Neuwied: Luchterhand.

KM NRW (1973) *Sekundarstufe I, Sport, Unterrichtsempfehlungen*, Ratingen/Kastellaun/ Düsseldorf.

Kottmann, L., Küpper, D. and Pack, R. (1997) *Bewegungsfreudige Schule. Band I: Grundlagen*, Munich: Baguv.

Kretschmer, J. (1981) 'Bewegungsunterricht – Aspekte einer kindorientierten Bewegungsdidaktik', in Kretschmer, J. (ed.) *Sport und Bewegungsunterricht, 1–4*, Munich: Urban & Schwarzenberg, 13–73.

Küpper, D. (1997) 'Die Richtlinien und Lehrpläne für den Sport an den Schulen im Land Nordrhein-Westfalen im Spiegel ausgewählter pädagogischer Leitideen, schulformspezifischer Richtlinien und Lehrpläne', in Schaller, H. J. and Pache, D. (eds) *Sport als Bildungschance und Lebensform*, Schorndorf: Hofmann, 79–88.

——(2000) 'Grundschulpädagogik und Schulsport auf gemeinsamen Weg', in Aschebrock, H. (ed.) *Erziehender Schulsport. Pädagogische Grundlagen der Curriculumrevision in Nordrhein-Westfalen*, Bönen: Kettler, 151–9.

LSW (1999) *Sport in der Sekundarstufe I. Diskussionspapier* (Curriculumrevision im Schulsport, book 5) Soest: LSW.

Moegling, K. (1999) *Ganzheitliche Bewegungserziehung. Pädagogische Bewegungslehre und Pädagogische Bewegungspraxis*, Butzbach-Griedel: Afra.

Müller, C. (1999) *Bewegte Grundschule. Aspekte einer Didaktik der Bewegungserziehung als umfassende Aufgabe der Grundschule*, St Augustin: Academia.

Naul, R. (1988) 'Learning about sports: a cognitve approach and its evaluation in the German grammar school physical education curriculum', *International Journal of Physical Education*, 25, 16–22.

——(1999) 'Das Fach Sport im Berufskolleg – Ein Beitrag zur umfassenden beruflichen Handlungskompetenz', in LSW (ed.) *Sport im Berufskolleg. Dokumentation einer Fachtagung* (*Curriculumrevision im Schulsport*, book 8) Soest: LSW, 14–30.

Quanz, D. (1984) 'Sportunterricht in der gymnasialen Oberstufe', in Carl, K. et al. (eds) *Handbuch Sport vol. 2*, Düsseldorf: Schwann, 701–36.

Schaefer, E. (1995) *Sport in der Berufsschule*, Hamburg: Czwalina.

Scherler, K. H. (1975) *Sensomotorische Entwicklung und materiale Erfahrung: Begründung einer vorschulischen Bewegungs- und Spielerziehung durch Piagets Theorie kognitiver Entwicklung*, Schorndorf: Hofmann.

Schmidt, W. (1998) *Sportpädagogik des Kindesalters*, Hamburg: Czwalina.

Schulz, N. (1982) 'Wissenschaftspropädeutik als didaktisches Prinzip im Sportunterricht der gymnasialen Oberstufe', *Sportwissenschaft*, 12, 152–73.

——(1999) 'Kindgemäßer Sportunterricht – Kritisch-konstruktive Anmerkungen zur sportbezogenen Grundschuldidaktik', in Kleine, W. and Schulz, N. (eds) *Modernisierte Kindheit – sportliche Kindheit?* (*Brennpunkte der Sportwissenschaft*, vol. 20) St Augustin: Academia, 183–201.

Ziegler, H. J. (1979) *Leistungsfach Sport. Aspekte der Entwicklung eines neuen Schulfaches*, Schorndorf: Hofmann.

Zimmer, R. (1995) *Handbuch der Bewegungserziehung*, 5th edn, Freiburg: Herder.

——(ed.) (1998) *Handbuch für Kinder- und Jugendarbeit im Sport*, Aachen: Meyer & Meyer.

Chapter 6

Physical education teacher training

Roland Naul

Historical antecedents of physical education teacher education

Physical education teacher education (PETE) is historically linked in Germany with 'Turnvater' Friedrich Ludwig Jahn and the sportsman Carl Diem, who respectively initiated important developments in the nineteenth and twentieth centuries. Jahn is unequivocally associated with the earliest attempts after 1810 to qualify students to organise and instruct their peers in German gymnastics on the outdoor gymnastic exercise areas (*Turnplätze*) in Berlin and other cities; Carl Diem is inextricably associated with the first institution of modern sport teacher training at university level, the Berlin College of Physical Exercise, founded in 1920. However, Jahn's work was terminated with the imposed 'Ban on *Turnen*' between 1820 and 1842 (see Chapter 2 in this volume) in Prussia; and Carl Diem's efforts in the early 1920s foundered because of lack of recognition of the Berlin College as an academic institution offering diplomas to certify teachers for state school employment.

When German gymnastics became an obligatory subject in state schools (e.g. Prussia, Saxony, Bavaria, etc.) after 1850, German gymnastics normal schools were established in each state capital (e.g. Berlin, Dresden, Munich and Stuttgart). Any young man skilled in German gymnastics could attend a half-year, later one-year, course offered by those training schools and receive on successful completion of examinations, a certificate as a gymnastic teacher. The certificate qualified the individual, even those who had not undergone any general training as a teacher, to teach physical education in schools. Between 1860 and 1900, teachers certificated for the lower folk schools (*Volksschule*) often attended an additional gymnastic teacher training course to gain teaching employment in the highly respected and better paid grammar schools, where in addition to physical education, they would spend two or three hours per week teaching 6–10 year old boys in reading and writing the German language. Thus gymnastics teachers in the nineteenth century acquired neither academic prestige because of their lack of academic study, nor were their training schools incorporated within the system of university departments for education (see Langenfeld 1985; Grossbröhmer 1994).

A silent revolution began in the 1920s when physical education became a part of the educational ideal of a healthy and well educated individual. German gymnastics changed in form and function to a more natural activity, and different types of sport were added to the physical education curriculum. Diem, as mentioned earlier, started a training course for sports teachers. But the most important reform from which physical education teacher training in Germany continues to benefit today was the establishment of university institutes for physical training, and the opportunity to select physical education as an academic subject for the teaching profession. After the late 1920s, physical education was recognised as an academic subject for students who wanted to become fully graduated grammar school teachers in the state of Prussia. Physical education was now accepted as one of the two possible academic subjects in the philological training of university students, supervised by state authorities, which certificated the university-based graduation with a state examination (see Mester 1931; Hibbeler 1988). At the same time, however, this government-regulated physical education teacher training, like philological training as a whole, was split into two phases. The first academic phase of training comprised practical and theoretical studies, and was followed by a second phase of teacher training in the school context of practical work. It can be argued that the academic upgrading of physical education teacher training within a university course of studies also brought about the dissolution of the older, integrated and practice-orientated gymnastic teacher training (Bernett 1989). This two-phase approach in physical education teacher training, with study of at least two subjects, remains the basis of the structure of physical education teacher training in Germany today.

Structure of physical education teacher training

After World War II and until the early 1970s, before educational reform acts led to integration of some schools to form secondary I schools, and teacher training colleges became part of universities in several *Länder* (see Baur 1981), physical education teacher training for middle and grammar schools was usually based (just as in the 1920s) at universities, for vocational schools at technical universities, and for primary (6–10 years) and traditional folk schools (10–14, later up to 16 years) at teacher training colleges (*Pädagogische Hochschulen*) as a minor subject. In the 1970s, there were some attempts at integrated (single-phase) and only university-based physical education teachers' training at a few newly established universities in West Germany (e.g. Bremen, Oldenburg). However, all attempts failed, either because of problems in financing longer university study periods, or because of legal problems over the recognition of the diploma for the integrated training courses for state employment of graduates. Furthermore, the directors of the teachers' seminars and the mentors in the second phase of training voiced doubts that the practice of physical education teaching at schools could be achieved at all, or in any adequately efficient way in a university-based course of training (Wiegand 1980).

Therefore, despite innovative ideas and experiments in the second half of the 1970s, the two-phase structure of academic qualification followed by pedagogical qualification continued to dominate the training of physical education teachers in West Germany, and has continued to do so in the re-unified Germany since 1990. In the former GDR, physical education teacher training was organised as a one-subject study course, with one phase of five years at a teacher training college (such as Potsdam or Zwickau) and the institute of sport science at a university (such as Rostock or Jena) (Brux 1980). It now consists of a six- or eight-semester academic course of studies (3–4 years), including some teaching studies, followed by a two-year practical and didactical teacher preparation course in physical education based outside the universities. This second phase is located at teachers' seminars integrated with the practical framework of daily physical education classes in schools, along similar lines to the former West German system.

Concepts of physical education teacher education

When physical education teacher training commenced in Germany within an academic framework, a well known educator and friend of Carl Diem, Eduard Spranger, described the profession of a physical education teacher in the late 1920s as akin to a well trained craftsman, who serves as a model for the students, who demonstrates all the skills needed to train and who should symbolise a private sporting lifestyle, which is consistent with the purpose of his education programme (Spranger 1928). This role model continued after World War II and until the mid-1960s. In the late 1960s and early 1970s, the school physical education curriculum changed, and the university institutes for PETE were re-organised. The development of sport science disciplines, as well as the greater impact on teaching of 'physical educator' training, led to some reduction in the traditional practical fields of studies (exercises and physical training) but sports like tennis and badminton were added to the course programme. In the early 1970s, many university departments began to restructure their training courses following a new ideal of the physical educator. At the same time, the DSB established a committee, which designed a training programme for physical education teachers (DSB 1975).

The modern physical education teacher is no longer perceived as a craftsperson only. Influenced by various sociological and educational theories, PETE now aims to develop four basic competences in the trainee: scientific action, political action, educational action and sporting action. In general a physical education teacher should not only know and practise what is necessary for the job, but also should be more skilful than is necessary for the job.

Many physical education departments accepted the DSB programme for a new teacher training programme in the mid-1970s. It still remains the basis for present course programmes in Germany. However, since the mid-1980s there has been another trend, which is re-focusing the issue of qualification. As a guideline for the teacher course programme, the Ministry of Education in North Rhine-Westphalia set the structure of the school physical education curriculum in 1985. The eight different sport groups studied by physical education students are identical to the school physical education curriculum reform of the late 1970s, and fields (bio-medical and psycho-social, including sport history and didactics) in sport science are used as the basis for theoretical lessons in PETE.

Today, each of the sixteen federal *Länder* in Germany has different examination guidelines for physical education teachers. Even within any one *Land*, each university has a different course programme for physical education teachers. Thus it is difficult to generalise about the training of physical education teachers. In order to be more specific about the different fields of training courses and the number of hours devoted to the different subjects of study, one exemplar, the Examination Act for Physical Education Teachers in North Rhine-Westphalia, has been chosen as an illustration of the official framework of a programme of study in the *Länder* (see Ministerium für Wissenschaft und Forschung NW 1986).

Sport-science based physical education teacher education

In North Rhine-Westphalia, the respective structures of the different school levels (elementary, secondary I and secondary II schools) and the study course are representative of a majority of *Länder*. A traditional credit point system, 'semester week hours' (SWS) prevails. Generally one course is limited to two SWS, that is a lecture is given two hours per week over fourteen weeks (summer semester, mid-April to mid-July) and up to eighteen weeks (winter semester, mid-October to mid-February). The load of contact hours for one course is on average 16 weeks $\times$ 2 SWS/week = 32 hours.

When a student wishes to study physical education he/she has to decide on a teaching degree for one of three bands: elementary school (6–10 year old children), secondary I level (10–16 year old boys and girls) or secondary II level (16–18 year old students in the grammar schools and the different vocational schools) (see Table 6.1).

Table 6.1   Structure of teacher training

Degree	Semesters	Age group
Elementary school teacher 120 SWS/approx. 1920h	6	6–10
Secondary I school teacher 120 SWS/approx. 1920h	6	10–16
Secondary II school teacher 160 SWS/approx. 2560h	8	16–18

A student in an elementary school study course, with physical education as one of the two possible main subjects, has to study for six semesters, which in North Rhine-Westphalia amounts to forty-five semester hours (in some *Länder* the number of hours is greater). In addition to this number of physical education lessons, the student takes a second and third subject, with around another 720 hours in total. As a third part of the teaching studies, general lessons in pedagogy, teaching techniques, sociology and psychology have to be attended with an average of thirty SWS (approximately 480 hours). The total number of contact 'hours' it is necessary to complete in order to become an elementary school teacher with a physical education degree, therefore, is about 1,920 (see Table 6.2).

The same structure and number of lessons in physical education and other subjects apply for for the secondary I level teaching degree. Students in the secondary II course have to study eight semesters physical education with a total number of sixty-four SWS in North Rhine-Westphalia (up to eighty semester hours in some other *Länder*), which means a total of about 1,024 hours. In addition the same load applies for the second academic subject and additional lessons in pedagogy, teaching, sociology and psychology. The total number of contact 'hours' it is necessary to complete in order to become a grammar school physical education teacher is approximately 2,560.

The physical education study course for elementary school teachers and secondary school teachers has an identical structure of four main fields. On average in Germany, more than 50 per cent of the entire course of study

Table 6.2   Structure of teacher training studies

Elementary school teachers		Secondary II school teachers	
German and mathematics	45 SWS approx. 720h	Biology	64 SWS approx. 1024h
Physical education	45 SWS approx. 720h	Physical education	64 SWS approx. 1024h
Pedagogy, psychology	30 SWS approx. 480h	Pedagogy, psychology	32 SWS approx. 512h

is devoted to skills training – including instruction in teaching techniques – in eight different sports. About 40 per cent of the course programme is devoted to scientific studies in natural and social sport sciences. Less than 10 per cent (in general only 5 per cent) of the course programme is taken up by school-based practical teaching studies, where the students can prepare for their future tasks by observing, analysing and planning phys- ical education lessons. As mentioned earlier, there are some differences in the teaching load for each main field between university departments. As an example, the numbers for Essen University appear in brackets beside the general average numbers (see Table 6.3).

At Essen University, all students following a secondary I physical educa- tion teaching degree have to study one 2-hour 'basic course' (BC) out of the eight different sports groups (sixteen SWS), and three additional 2- hour 'main courses' (MC) out of the eight groups of sports, chosen individually (six SWS) (see Table 6.4). For a secondary II (grammar school) teaching degree, every student has to undertake in addition to the eight 'basic courses', five 'main courses' (two more) out of the different groups, and at a third level of qualification, two other 'special courses' (SC) in two different sports, each of four semester hours (two hours practical lessons, two hours theoretical lessons). The total contact hours load for this part of the programme is approximately 480 hours (the additional study load for the secondary II level is placed in brackets in Table 6.4 and the following tables). There are no sex-related differences in studying the eight sport groups, that is, male students are obliged to study gymnastics/dance and female students must select football or field hockey. Studies in the field of sport science are divided into natural and social sciences/humanities.

Within six of the eight semesters, a student has to follow a two-hour BC course in each of the three fields, and a further two MC courses in two fields, and on a third level one 'special course' (SC), each course being of two hours. The student is free to specify within the natural sciences, which branch to follow after the basic courses (see Table 6.5). The same structure and obligations exist for studies in social sciences and the humanities in sports (see Table 6.6).

Teaching studies are the fourth part of the physical education study course (see Table 6.7).

Table 6.3   Structure of PE teacher studies

A	Motor skills training/basic methods of instruction	50%	(45%)
B	Natural sport sciences	20%	(17.5%)
C	Social sport sciences	20%	(17.5%)
D	Teaching studies	10%	(20%)

Table 6.4 Exercises and instruction in physical activities and sports

A	Motor skills training/basic methods of instruction	BC	MC	SC
	Each compulsory			
A1	Track and field	X	X	
A2	German gymnastics	X		
A3	Gymnastics/dance	X	(X)	(X)
A4	Swimming	X	X	
A5	*One compulsory*	X		
	Badminton, tennis, table-tennis, volleyball			
A6	*One compulsory*	X	X	
	Basketball, team-handball			
A7	*One compulsory*	X	(X)	(X)
	Football, field hockey			
A8	*One compulsory*	X		
	Outdoor leisure activities, e.g. skiing, canoeing, climbing, etc., or one more from A5–A7			

Table 6.5 Study of natural sciences

B	Natural sciences	BC	MC	SC
B1	Biological foundations of movement and performance (sport biology/sport medicine)	X		
B2	Movement, health, and injury and cardio-vascular disease prevention, therapy, rehabilitation (sport medicine/training science)	X	(X)	(X)
B3	Analysis and structure of movement and performance (biomechanics/training science)	X	X	

Table 6.6 Study of social sciences and humanities

C	Social sciences and humanities	BC	MC	SC
C1	Historical, anthropological and pedagogical foundations of movement, play and sport (sport pedagogy/sport history)	X	(X)	(X)
C2	Psychological foundations, development and learning in sport (sport psychology/motor behaviour)	X		
C3	Significance of sport for individuals, groups, and society (sport sociology/sport politics/sport history)	X	X	

Table 6.7   PE teaching studies

D	Teaching studies	BC	MC	SC
D1	Teaching methods and strategies of instruction (sport pedagogy/sport didactics)	X	X	X
			96h	
D2	Analysis, measurement and evaluation of PE (sport didactics)	X		X

Studies in didactics, teaching methods and strategies of instruction have the same structure as the studies in the natural and social sciences of sport. The 'main course' follows a two-'hours' 'basic course' in the first two or three semesters. Students in the secondary II school level study course have to attend the 'special course' to receive the certificate for this field of their studies.

As an example of this mandatory curriculum, the 'BC course' is entitled 'Introduction to sport didactics', which is open to all physical education students. The content is based on theories and different models of the physical education curriculum, as well as various teaching approaches, etc. The 'main course' is specifically related to the school level, in this case to the upper classes of the grammar school level, and the topic of the course is 'Teaching physical education at *Abitur* stage'. There are theoretical lessons with written and oral examinations in the physical education curriculum at the *Abitur* stage. The deeper cognitive approach in teaching sports, and learning about themes from sport science, is typical for this age group of school students. University students need to understand and be able to evaluate the different purposes of this specific curriculum. In the 'special course', entitled 'Analysing text books for physical education in the *Abitur* stage', students evaluate the content of textbooks available for teachers and students at the *Abitur* stage. Students learn how to prepare physical education lessons by using a variety of textbooks to attain the educational goals they have in regard to the curriculum.

For the second part, 'Analysis, measurement and evaluation of physical education lessons at school' (D 2), which 'bridges' the second training phase in the seminars, there are defined limits in some *Länder*. In North Rhine-Westphalia, one 2-'hour' course for one semester is the minimum, and four such courses, but within the three parts of the complete teacher training course, is the defined maximum.

Teaching studies in physical education teacher training

There is an essential problem with PETE in Germany. Many pedagogues in the field of PETE are unwilling to reduce their proportion of sport science studies in the study programme to release time for the benefit of teacher preparation. The two main arguments put forward are, first, that the natural and social sciences areas of the programme of study cannot be reduced, since there is already insufficient time for the range of disciplines in the sport sciences; and second, that teacher preparation is not the business of the university in the first place, and is seen to be the task of the second phase of physical education teacher training at school. The contrary position, represented mainly by sport pedagogues, calls for a maximisation of teacher preparation in the academic study phase at university, since the physical education teacher first and foremost has to apply scientific knowledge: the students aim to become physical education teachers and not sports scientists; their main task is teaching, not research. Teacher preparation in the university context, rather than supplanting the second phase, has a distinct goal of its own. While the second-phase emphasis is on class management, achievement of discipline and control in the classroom, and organisation and improvement of motor learning in physical education lessons, it scarcely leaves room for experimenting with a variety of teaching aims and tasks or with new methods of instruction. In the teacher preparation seminars, these opportunities often do not exist (see Altenberger 1984; Köppe 1993). As studies of the socialisation of physical education teachers show, they base their teaching concepts exclusively on what they have learned and practised at the university (see Bräutigam 1986; Treutlein et al. 1996).

In Germany, there are a number of university physical education departments offering only one theoretical course in teacher preparation for one semester, without analysis or evaluation of physical education lessons at schools. Others offer a two- or three-hour follow-up course, where students observe and analyse physical education lessons on videotape, or small groups evaluate lessons in schools. Sometimes students may be allowed to plan and teach one lesson. Generally these practical teacher preparation courses follow a tripartite structure over two or three consecutive semesters. These courses take up a total of 5–7 semester hours. At Essen University the school-based teacher preparation courses are structured as follows:

- an introduction to observation and analysis of physical education lessons at university, a two-hours-per-week course in one semester;
- a school-based practice in physical education, two hours of observation and analysis, perhaps taking over part of the lesson from the regular teacher, followed by one hour of discussion and evaluation, three hours per week as practice in school in a second semester;
- planning and practising physical education teaching on the basis of specific tasks (e.g. differentiation, group instruction, etc.), two hours

per week in a course at the university again, organised during a third semester.

Physical education teacher education: the teacher preparation seminar

After graduating from university, or gaining the so-called First State Diploma, the physical education student enters 'preparatory service', as it is officially known. Two or three days a week the trainee teacher attends courses for his or her two academic subjects as well as for pedagogy, didactics or instruction psychology. The courses cover teaching materials and planning of lessons, etc. (see Bauer 1975; Söll 1975). On the practical side, the trainee has to teach at least twelve hours per week, which includes the two academic subjects of study. A school mentor monitors and advises on lesson planning, and also reports on progress and achievements in these tasks. Some lessons are observed and graded by a subject representative from the seminar. At the end of the training, the trainee physical education teacher must write a thesis on a planned and conducted set of lessons about a specific topic of instruction over several weeks, e.g. 'Training a mixed grade-8 basketball class in zone defence'. The preparatory service ends with a final assessment of teaching by observation and an oral examination (see Wiegand 1980).

Sport Teacher Diploma training

Sport Teacher Diploma training began in Germany after World War II in the re-established *Deutsche Hochschule für Leibesübungen* (German College of Physical Training) in Cologne in 1947, under the direction of Carl, and later Lieselott, Diem. The new institution, the *Deutsche Sporthochschule* (DSHK), was only recognised as a full academic university institution in 1970, when entry level was officially limited to the *Abitur* certificate and additional doctoral studies were introduced. The Diploma course contains a study load of approximately 160 SWS over eight semesters, i.e. a total load which equates with that of the complete load of the university-based teacher training course at secondary II school level (two subjects and the additional studies in general education), but linked only with single subject-study in sport and related sport sciences. Other universities (Saarbrücken, Mainz and Munich) have also offered the Sport Teacher Diploma programme for many years. However, this single-sport study Diploma has not been widely accepted by *Länder* authorities across Germany for lifelong contractual employment as a physical education teacher. In the 1960s and 1970s, when there was a shortage of physical education teachers in schools, Diploma sport teachers were employed as physical education teachers on fixed-term contracts, but in the main, the qualification profile was associated more with instruction and coaching in recreational and competitive sport in sports clubs (see Tiegel 1984). As the sports sector became more diversified and differentiated in the 1980s, innovative courses were added to the Diploma course at the DSHK. Cologne graduates in the 1980s found employment in the health, recreation, rehabilitation and sports management sector outside the traditional sport club system (see Hartmann-Tews and Mrazek 1994). In 1992, a new compulsory framework of Sport Teacher Diploma examinations was agreed by the KMK at federal level. The new framework also saw a change in title of the award, from Sport Teacher Diploma to Sport Science Diploma.

Currently, Diploma sport studies at the DSHK are structured as follows: eighty-two SWS of 'basic studies', which includes two SWS introduction and orientation for the whole study programme; forty-six SWS theory and practice of sport and sport activities; and thirty-four SWS introduction to a range of sport sciences. Studies continue with sixty-two SWS of 'main studies'. These studies comprise a fourteen-SWS module of cross-specialisation studies, and another forty-eight-SWS module of specialisation. Five options form the basis of the specialisation studies module: training and performance; leisure and creativity; prevention and rehabilitation; economy and management; media and communication. For the third part of their studies (for which an additional award is granted), students must take an elective course module (sixteen SWS), one example of which is 'European sport studies'. Thus the total study load for the Sports Science Diploma is 160 SWS contact hours (see DSHS 2000).

Challenges for physical education teacher education

Because of the financial and organisational problems suffered by physical education since the mid-1980s, many teachers, particularly in primary schools, have been teaching physical education lessons without a physical education qualification. The early 1990s saw a reduction in time allocated to physical education in schools from three to two 'hours'. The reductions stemmed not from legislation but from *Land* policies devolving powers to local, school level, where greater autonomy provided more flexibility in control of the curriculum (Bildungskommission NRW 1995). Each school board is now empowered to increase or reduce weekly lessons for a subject. In the case of physical education, the result has been a significant decrease in the amount of lessons allocated. In more than 95 per cent of all schools in North Rhine-Westphalia it is down to two lessons per week. The physical education teachers of today have to work and lobby for their subject to become part of the official school programme (see Stibbe 1998). On the other hand, novel types of physical activity (e.g. skating, skate boarding, mountain biking, squash, floor ball, etc.) have become attractive to young boys and girls outside of schools in recent years, and these activities pose challenges, especially to older-generation physical educators, to modernise the content of the physical education curriculum. Recently, in the school year 1999–2000, a new syllabus for physical education in primary and secondary II schools has been implemented in North Rhine-Westphalia. The purpose and content of physical education are no longer restricted to rules and structures of competitive sports, but have been expanded by activities with non-competitive motives. Those trends in other *Länder* will have to be rethought to change and open up the traditional Physical Education Examination Act, as in 1985 in North Rhine-Westphalia.

A challenge for physical education teacher training is embedded in recent developments in teaching at different school levels (see Chapters 3 and 4 in this volume; Friedrich and Hildenbrandt 1997). In North Rhine-Westphalia, for example, the revision of physical education curricula with their links with redefined educational purposes, and extended non-competitive activities and movement experiences alongside the traditional forms of activity, have prompted innovations in ideas for the restructuring of PETE programmes as combined movement and sport studies (see LSW 1996). An overhaul of the traditional system of the separation of practical sport and sport-science based theoretical studies of the late 1970s and 1980s is overdue. One solution is their integration within specific modular units to fall into step with school physical education curriculum requirements, which place emphasis on cooperation, competition and communication (Beckers *et al.* 2000), albeit such a revision may not easily sit with the purpose of science-based graduation at a university level. Moreover, it does not take into account changes in the job market for teachers brought on by devolution policies.

Another challenge relates to the high rate of unemployment of physical education graduates (see Heinemann *et al.* 1990; Naul and Rodermund 1991). Different and alternative study profiles for physical education students who wish to teach and work outside the school system are now extant in many physical education departments. In addition, some university physical education departments have introduced master's degree (*Magister*) programmes. The KMK (1995) implemented an examination law for *Magister* studies in sport science, which reduced the amount of practical sport studies. Sport science can be studied either as one of two major subjects (seventy-two SWS) or one of two minor subjects (each thirty-six SWS). Whatever, sport science must be supplemented either by one other major subject (e.g. sociology, or a language) or by one more minor and one major subject. The traditional *Magister* is a long-term study course of 8–9 semesters with a total load of 144 SWS for graduation. However, this new type of master's degree in sport science is also under pressure from

Europeanisation processes (Petry and Jesse 2000). In 1998, the Federal Minister of Education and Research (BMBF) enacted a new federal state law for universities. It proposed the implementation of new consecutive degree profiles in accordance with the European model of bachelor's degree (three years) and master's degree (two years) after first graduation (see BMBF 1999). At present this new structure is under discussion in many physical education departments, and there is the possibility of a revision of PETE as well as the earlier model of master's degree (see Naul 2000). Whether the revision of PETE will become a part of undergraduate studies, or of a special master's course after B.A. graduation in sport science is as yet undecided. However, in North Rhine-Westphalia, the Ministry of Education and Science decided in 2000 not to implement a new European study programme, the European PE Master's Degree, developed by the PE Curriculum Development Committee of the European Network of Sport Science Institutes in Higher Education (ENSSHE). The ENSSHE initiative indicates that the European challenge in PETE has reached Germany, but the ministerial refutation suggests that it will be some time before international concepts of PETE are accepted.

References

Altenberger, H. (ed.) (1984) *Schulpraktische Studien – Modelle und ihre Verwirklichung*, Bad Homburg: Limpert.

Bauer, K. (1975) 'Die Ausbildung im sportpädagogischen Seminar an bayerischen Gymnasien', *Sportunterricht*, 24, 197–9.

Baur, J. (1981) *Zur beruflichen Sozialisation von Sportlehrern*, Schorndorf: Hofmann.

Beckers, E., Hercher, J. and Neuber, N. (eds) (2000) *Schulsport auf neuen Wegen. Herausforderungen für die Sportlehrerausbildung*, Butzbach-Griedel: AFRA.

Bernett, H. (1989) 'Der Dualismus von Wissen und Handeln in der Geschichte der deutschen Sportlehrerausbildung', *Sportunterricht*, 38, 168–83.

Bildungskommission NRW (1995) *Zukunft der Bildung – Schule der Zukunft*, Neuwied: Luchterhand.

BMBF (1999) *Hochschulrahmengesetz HRG*, Bonn: BMBF.

Bräutigam, M. (1986) *Unterrichtsplanung und Lehrplanrezeption von Sportlehrern*, Hamburg: Czwalina.

Brux, A. (1980) *Sportlehrer und Sportunterricht in der DDR*, Berlin/Munich/Frankfurt: Bartels & Wernitz.

Deutscher Sportbund (1975) *Sportlehrerausbildung. Analyse und Reform*, Frankfurt am Main: Hassmüller.

DSHS (2000) *Europäische Sportstudien. Das European Credit Transfer System*, Cologne: DSHS.

Friedrich, G. and Hildenbrandt, E. (eds) (1997) *Sportlehrer/in heute – Ausbildung und Beruf*, Hamburg: Czwalina.

Grossbröhmer, R. (1994) *Die Geschichte der preußischen Turnlehrer. Vom Vorturner zum staatlich geprüften Turnlehrer*, Aachen: Meyer & Meyer.

Hartmann-Tews, I. and Mrazek, J. (1994) *Der berufliche Werdegang von Diplom-Sportlehrinnen und Diplom-Sportlehrern*, Cologne: Strauss.

Heinemann, K., Dietrich, K. and Schubert, M. (1990) *Akademikerarbeitslosigkeit und neue Formen des Erwerbslebens*, Weinheim: Dt. Studienverlag.

Hibbeler, W. (1988) 'Zur Diskussion über die Neuordnung der Turnlehrerausbildung in Preußen bis 1929', in John, H. G. and Naul, R. (eds) *Jugendsport im ersten Drittel des 20. Jahrhunderts*, Clausthal-Zellerfeld: Greinert, 190–201.

KMK (1995) *Fachspezifische Bestimmungen für die Magisterprüfung – Sportwissenschaft*, Bonn: KMK.

Köppe, G. (1993) (ed.) *Theoriegeleitete Praxis in der Sportlehrerausbildung*, St Augustin: Academia.

Langenfeld, H. (1985) 'Die Entstehung der deutschen Turnlehrerschaft', in Naul, R. (ed.) *Körperlichkeit und Schulturnen im Kaiserreich*, Wuppertal: Putty, 164–201.

LSW (ed.) (1996) *Bewegungserziehung/Sport in der Lehreraus- und Lehrerfortbildung. Dokumentation 2. Schulsportsymposium NRW*, Bönen: Ketteler.

Mester, L. (1931) *Die Körpererziehung an den Universitäten*, Langensalza: Beltz.

Ministerium für Wissenschaft und Forschung NW (1986) *Lehrerausbildung in Nordrhein-Westfalen. Studium und Erste Staatsprüfungen für Lehrämter an Schulen*, Düsseldorf: Klüsener.

Naul, R. (2000) 'Flexibilisierung, Auslandsorientierung, Akkreditierung: Was kann die Sportwissenschaft aus der Studienreformdiskussion über Bachelor- und Master-Studiengänge lernen?', *dvs-Informationen*, 15 (3) 7–15.

Naul, R. and Rodermund, J. (1991) 'Unemployed PE teachers – their life cycle and job placement after graduation', *AIESEP Newsletter*, no. 34, 3–5.

Petry, K. and Jesse, B. (2000) 'Auf dem Weg nach Europa. Die Internationalisierung in der sportwissenschaftlichen Ausbildung', *dvs-Informationen*, 15 (3) 17–22.

Söll, W. (1975) 'Struktur und Aufgabe der Fachseminare', *Sportunterricht*, 24, 200–3.

Spranger, E. (1928) 'Die Persönlichkeit des Turnlehrers', *Die Leibesübungen*, 4, 511–13.

Stibbe, G. (ed.) (1998) *Bewegung, Spiel und Sport als Elemente des Schulprogramms: Grundlagen, Ansätze, Beispiele*, Baltmannsweiler: Schneider.

Tiegel, G. (1984) *Wie sind Diplom-Sportlehrer wirklich?*, Wuppertal: Putty.

Treutlein, G., Jalanik, H. and Hanke, U. (1996) *Wie Sportlehrer wahrnehmen, denken, fühlen und handeln*, 4th edn, Cologne: Strauss.

University of Essen (1988) *Studienordnung für das Unterrichtsfach Sport mit dem Abschluß Erste Staatsprüfung für das Lehramt für die Sekundarstufe I*, Essen: Selbstverlag.

Wiegand, M. (1980) 'Ziele Schulpraktischer Studien im Studiengang Sportwissenschaft', in Wiegand, M. (ed.) *Praxisbezug in der Sportlehrerausbildung*, Bad Homburg: Limpert, 41–52.

Chapter 7

Coach education and training

Arnd Krüger

Introduction

Germany's long tradition in the education of coaches (just as with teachers) has its antecedents in the early nineteenth century, when 'Turnvater' Jahn recommended that coaches be prepared for *Turnen* by the *Turner* organisations themselves. They were, and subsequently the national sports governing bodies have seen it as a duty to follow in the *Turners*' footsteps. The sport governing bodies were quicker to agree on basic terms for coaches in individual sports at a national level than were the state governments for physical education teachers. For the past 150 years the German physical education system has therefore had the problem that instructors of some sort were prepared by two separate sets of authorities, private and public, and that both sides diligently ensured that their boundaries were not infringed upon (Krüger 1980a). The right to educate teachers (and coaches), as shown in Chapter 6, is a right of the individual *Land*. The central government encourages coordination of some sort, but constitutionally it cannot enforce it.

As with any labour market, the laws of supply and demand have applied to the coaching profession. When the school physical education system was short of teachers, sports instructors and coaches with sport federation certification but without any academic training, were hired to fill the vacancies; when the universities prepared more physical education teachers than the school system could or would hire, many found employment within the system of sports clubs and federations, thus competing with coaches who were not academics but had been trained by their respective sport federation.

Although many coaches have a basic training in physical education, there are distinct differences between coaching and teaching. In this chapter the emphasis is on coaching aspects only. Coaching is understood here as the process of preparing athletes, especially high-performance athletes, to compete, and of supervising them during competition. In the German tradition, coaching is considered an educational process. The reality of the preparation of coaches is, however, that educational components are underdeveloped. The educational responsibility of the coach, therefore, is often a problem. A coach whose livelihood depends upon successful competitive performance will more often than not be predisposed to push the athlete to short-term success rather than address long-term issues that include the educational side of the athlete's personal and social development. The coach, however, does have a social responsibility, and not only to the athlete; nevertheless, those coaches who have the highest visible mass-media profile determine to a large extent the corporate culture of the elite sport system.

Coaching as a profession

Within the German employment system, it is possible to distinguish between a job with little if any systematic training, one with an apprenticeship of (generally in Germany today) three years, and a profession with a highly specialised, usually academic preparation. A profession such as dentistry has often developed from an occupation, but because of its importance for society, its prestige and autonomy, such a profession has had the authority to close its ranks and accept into it only those who are sufficiently academically qualified. A barber may pull teeth less painfully than an academically qualified dentist; a former athlete may be a more successful coach than an academically prepared one. This is the basic dilemma of coaching: that success seems to be measurable, a proper qualification is not a pre-requisite for success, and in many sports there is no real desire to exclude from coaching those who have had little formal preparation.

In the early twentieth century years of amateur sport, to coach for money was regarded with distrust (Hoole 1988). This changed when the national interest came into play. Preparing for the 1916 Olympics in Berlin, the German National Olympic Committee hired Alvin Kraenzlein (1878–1928), a former Princeton University coach, as national athletics coach. Kraenzlein, a former American Olympic champion of German descent, received a salary roughly equivalent to that of a university professor (Krüger 1995). At that time the American system of coaching appeared to be the most effective, since American athletes dominated the international sports scene. But what was overlooked was that many American sports coaches possessed both a university degree and a background in elite sports. Kraenzlein, for example, was a dentist who had won four Olympic gold medals (Krüger 1991). At that time professional coaches were prevalent in Germany in football, golf and horse racing. Kraenzlein was the first full-time national coach, and a role model for future development. The American influence on the education of coaches in Germany was stronger than that of any other country until Germany was divided after World War II, when there remained an American influence in the West and a new Soviet influence in the East (Krüger 1991).

After World War I, the National Sports Federation established its own college in Berlin with the financial backing of the Prussian state, the German Republic and industry. In two-year courses, students were prepared for a physical education diploma, which was accepted by the government as the equivalent to a teaching qualification. Although, theoretically, this *Reichshochschule für Leibesübungen* was preparing sport coaches for the club system, as long as there was a shortage of physical education teachers in the school system, many preferred stable employment in schools to an insecure job in a sport governing body or club. In addition, only a few sports, such as football and boxing, were able to pay salaries that could compete with the state system. Concurrently, the *Turner* Federation (DT) continued the preparation of its own club coaches in one-year courses. In many cases these were primary school teachers who took the one-year *Turner* course to become secondary school (grammar school) teachers, and thus also obtain a better paid job in the civil service; many also worked within the club system, either with a second job in the evening or exclusively for a club.

A coaching profession as such did not exist, although the number of people (mainly men) who were qualified for an occupation in a sports club was continuously increasing. When the National Socialists came to power in 1933, the number of full-time sport instructors for both the school and the club system was drastically increased. This increase reflected the high priority of sport on the Nazi agenda, testimony to which was a requirement for a daily physical education lesson. This meant, however, that there was a tendency for a shorter period of physical education teacher preparation, with a stronger emphasis on the practical at the expense of the educational and biological sides of sport, to meet the rapidly increasing demand. The Nazis ensured, however, that all paid coaches had some sort of certified qualification, even after a very short period of preparation of sometimes dubious quality. The Nazis also ensured that a certified coach who worked for a voluntary sports organisation did receive some form of remuneration. These subsidies were still being paid as late as spring 1945. The amount of research that went into coaching as a science was also continually increasing. Evident elements included: systematic anthropological measurement in talent selection; physiological research into the improvement of performance and medically orientated training; and biochemical research into doping.

As the ideology of 'strength' and 'vigour' was attractive to them, the Nazis had a disproportionate amount of physical educators in their ranks. An improvement in the status of the physical education and coaching profession was high on their agenda. For ideological reasons in the Nazi period, the athlete assumed a greater importance, as Germany wanted to demonstrate its racial superiority; and the more important the athlete, the more professional the coach needed to be. The importance of the athlete and the process of professionalisation appeared as a collective assertion of special social status and a collective process of upward social mobility. This process suggests that the model constituted by the first movements of professionalisation had become an ideology, and had changed from being a predominantly economic function, organising the links between education and the market place, to a function that was predominantly ideological. After the Second World War, in the Cold War era, the high status of the athlete was due to the struggle between the two opposing political and economic systems represented by the Federal Republic of (West) Germany and the (East) German Democratic Republic. Today, the athlete's importance is due more to economic reasons. A professional athlete also needs a professional coach, and in Germany as in many other countries, structures are in place to prepare coaches for positions at different levels within the sport performance continuum, from foundation to elite levels.

The German coaching qualifications

The year 1950 saw the foundation of the DSB in the Federal Republic and its equivalent in the GDR, which was later replaced by the DTSB in the German Democratic Republic. Both countries had a shortage of qualified coaches, and the two respective umbrella organisations started their own short training programmes to prepare individuals for coaching certification. Although there were some differences between the two countries in content and duration of courses for the first three levels of certification, and also between the different sports governing bodies, the basic West German structure was acceptable to most:

(i)   120 hours training (C-licence – level 1)
(ii) an additional 40 (later 80) hours training (B-licence – level 2)
(iii) an additional 120 (later 100) hours training (A-licence – level 3)(Kreiss 1995; 1999).

In German terminology, somebody working at level 1 is often referred to as *Übungsleiter* (instructor), while from level 2 on, the term *Trainer* (coach) is used. The GDR had a 'pre-certification' of only half of the first level to encourage young people into the coaching ranks. In most sports, the first level of certification is undertaken locally, the second at state level and the third at national level. Between each certification level, a year's practical experience is required. The extent to which national sport governing bodies try to influence coach education at local and regional levels differs considerably. In some sports like athletics, team handball or basketball, the national body produces learning materials suitable for coach education and expects coaches to be familiar with such material. In others, like rowing and canoeing, with fewer centres in which elite sport is practised, the national coaches personally provide coach education down to the local centre level (Fritsch 1995).

The main problems here are in the selection process and in the levels of standardisation or equivalence. As the sports governing body is responsible for the admission of candidates into the certification process, it can control access to the coaching ranks on grounds other than quality. A university degree in physical education, even where the emphasis is placed on coaching a particular sport, is generally only accepted by the sports governing bodies as equivalent to a level 1 coach. Until 1980, this was never much of a problem, as the educational system was in dire need of physical education teachers and often even hired club coaches to do the job. In the early 1980s, the market completely changed. The school system was replete with teachers and many physical educators were trying to obtain jobs in the club system. It became obvious that organising the link between education and the market place on a predominantly ideological basis was to be the norm. This was already visible in 1974 when the German Coaching Academy was founded in Cologne. It was here that level 4 coaches were educated in courses that at first lasted eighteen months. Although this was the highest DSB coaching qualification, in terms of the school system, the graduates had less than a high school diploma in their hand when they finished at the Academy, because as candidates the entrance requirement to the course was only ten years of schooling. Although some coaches used the Academy as part of their graduate or postgraduate study, status was defined by the general entrance requirement – and that was low for ideological reasons. No connection to a university was sought, as the DSB and the separate sports governing bodies were distrustful of academic freedom. It was also a time of discussions within the universities about the social justification of the privileges of elite sport; the DSB, therefore, wanted to have its own institution. Only coaches with a level 3 qualification, or elite athletes at the end of their careers, were admitted. In all cases a recommendation from the governing body of the respective sport was mandatory.

Some sports like tennis, skiing and figure skating, which traditionally had their own level 4 courses in Munich, continued with their own preparation programmes. The Munich-based Academy is different in that it places far more emphasis on the actual coaching process, and on teaching supervised by a 'master coach'. Whereas at the Cologne Academy learning is more theory-based in a standard seminar fashion with only limited practical work, the Munich coaches must have a 'master coach' as their tutor for long periods of time away from Munich. There are weeks with seminars in Munich alternating with weeks acquiring experience as an 'apprentice' of an acknowledged 'master coach', who is actually supervising the work of the 'apprentice coach'. This type of learning is similar to the dual educational system of the vocational schools, where there is alternation between classroom work and workplace experience. In horse riding, the apprenticeship situation is a real one: the future coach has to learn with a certified 'master coach' for three years to pass the examination, work as a coach for at least another four years, and then take more courses and an examination before finally being acknowledged as a 'master coach'. Here, the education is fully in the hands of the Chambers of Commerce, just as in the case of all other apprenticeships.

In football there are different arrangements. Courses at level 3 are regionally administered, and only level 4 courses are organised at national level. Unlike the courses at the Cologne Academy, they are only six-month courses, and Bundesliga (federal league) players of a certain calibre may receive a reduction even on the six-month programme. Football was, however, the first sports governing body to go one step further than other sports in terms of 'professionalisation'. Only coaches with a level 4 qualification (*Fussballlehrer*) are permitted to coach professional (leagues 1–3) football (Bisanz 1995). An increasing number of sports governing bodies, like handball and basketball, etc., are following suit for their premier division teams. The problem remains, however, that 'national coaches' are still chosen by the sports governing bodies for reasons other than their level of certification, and in many cases they do not possess the same 'paper' qualification as the coaches to whom they are supposed to be superior. The best known coaches are the premier league football coaches, i.e. level 4 coaches who often have only six months of formal preparation for their job.

The GDR tradition of coach preparation

On 18 January 1950, the SED Central Committee passed a resolution entitled 'The free course of youth' to develop the sports school in Leipzig into a central institute for physical exercises and sport. Following Soviet Union experience and practice, a 'coaching faculty' was opened at the newly founded German College of Physical Culture (DHfK) in Leipzig as early as 1951. This was the direct result of a government decree in March 1951 that the GDR should catch up in sports with West Germany to demonstrate the superiority of socialism over capitalism. The DHfK was charged with:

- training sports teachers and coaches for all fields of physical culture, particularly the competitive sports movement;
- training sports scientists, university teachers and sports leaders;
- conducting research;
- developing a range of teaching materials – publications, visual aids;

- introducing the results of research into the lifestyles of the general public.

The Leipzig Institute came to be recognised as one of the world's leading academic institutions in physical education and sport. In its heyday, the DHfK had a staff of 440 teachers and more than 2,000 full-time and extra-mural students from the GDR and other countries.

Initially, five-month courses led to fully qualified coach status, but it was not long before this was doubled to ten months. For many, the duration of the training course was regarded as inadequate, and so the coaches organised themselves in study and discussion groups to obtain coaching literature from other eastern European countries. Further education of coaches was initiated by the coaches themselves, and remained an integral part of the system (Röder 1961). The duration of the course was soon extended, at first to two years, then to three years and eventually to four years. In addition to those (often young) students that actually went to Leipzig to study, a distance-learning course was introduced to enable coaches already working to qualify for the profession without interruption of their actual work. As early as 1956, the term 'coach' became a special category in the educational field and was included in trade union contracts with the government (this inclusion was completed in 1960). From then on it was established that a coach had to work twenty-four contact hours a week with athletes (the same as a high school teacher), and that during the rest of the working week, the coach had to prepare for actual coaching, including service in Party organisations and personal further education. To include the coach as a basic category in the national education pay scale had an advantage, one that was typical for the GDR. The GDR had an unemployment rate of zero per cent. Everybody not only had the right to work, but also the obligation. An unsuccessful coach could not be sacked and unemployed, but could be transferred into a different hierarchical coaching position. All coaches received a basic level of pay that was similar to that of a teacher with the same length of preparation and the same length of service, plus various additional premiums according to the actual position and the actual degree of success. Such a high degree of job stability ensured in the long run that GDR coaches did not need any rapid success with young talented athletes, but could bide their time and wait their turn.

To enter the coaching profession, students needed ten years of school (or less and a qualified apprenticeship) and a recommendation from their sports governing body. As of 1976, two years after the opening of a similar institution in Cologne, the GDR gave up this pre-academic training of coaches. In 1974, the DHfK began a fully fledged course of academic training for coaches, allowing it to abandon the old form of preparation. These academically trained coaches became the backbone of the most successful elite sport system in the world (in terms of success *per capita*). Already in 1955, the DHfK had introduced distance-learning courses for their physical educators, so to extend this to coaches was not difficult. What made these courses so attractive was the fact that anybody in the civil service (including coaches) could have as many as forty-eight days per year paid leave of absence for further education, and that the coaches would receive a better paid position on attainment of a higher qualification. The higher qualification also had advantages in terms of retirement benefits, which were calculated on basic salary and not pay-plus-premiums.

With the inception of the full academic training course came higher-level entry qualifications. Candidates (male and female) were required to have completed twelve years of formal schooling and graduated with the *Abitur*. Applicants who had achieved 'Master of sport' (international status) in the ranking system could apply with less than the minimum qualifications. They also took a wide-ranging practical test, which included athletics, swimming, gymnastics and games. As an illustration, the following standards were expected:

100 metres	Males 12.8sec	Females 15.2sec
Long jump	Males 5.0m	Females 3.8m
Shot put	Males 8.5m	Females 7.5m

For swimming, all candidates had to demonstrate the ability to swim crawl and breast stroke, but not against the clock. In gymnastics, all candidates had to perform one exercise or combination on each of floor, parallel bars and vaulting box (males longways, females crossways). In the area of games, all male candidates had to play two games to a good standard. It was advantageous if a prospective student could demonstrate prior involvement in sport as a competitor, official or voluntary leader with an approved qualification.

For distance-learning courses, there were DHfK distance-learning centres in each district, usually attached to the elite sport training centres. To attend a distance-learning course, the coach had to spend two weeks each year in Leipzig and one day a week in a regional centre. Thus the participants could continue to coach their athletes. Most of the instructors were employed on a part-time basis, which meant a relatively inexpensive but high-quality form of coach education could be provided.

In 1958 all previous coaching licences were cancelled and new ones supplied. The occasion was also used to check whether the 'new' coach was politically suitable, as coaching science increasingly became secretive. In addition to the openly published *Theorie und Praxis der Körperkultur* ('Theory and Practice of Physical Culture'), a new journal for coaches was published – *Theorie und Praxis des Leistungssport* ('Theory and Practice of High Performance Sport'). The latter journal, in which papers of high quality on elite sports were published, was essentially for their further education. The coaches were allowed to read it on signature and return it; moreover, issues raised were not to be discussed with people who had no reading privileges. The secret monthly journal was published until the very end of the GDR but even this journal did not publish anything on the official GDR doping practices (Spitzer 1998). However, it has to be stated that the GDR's sports successes were not entirely due to performance-enhancing drugs. Until the Olympic Games of 1972, steroids were legal and their use was widespread. In spite of this, the GDR was already achieving superior results over the Federal Republic. Much of its success can be traced to the large numbers and quality of professional coaches. While the Federal Republic had about 400 professional coaches who were paid by federal or state governments of some sort (excluding club coaches), the GDR had 1,555 (including club coaches) in 1972, a figure that gradually increased until it reached 4,745 at the time of the demise of the GDR (Teichler and Richartz 1999: 297). It can be safely assumed that the GDR had about four times as many full-time coaches as the Federal Republic, or on a *per capita* basis, twelve times as many. After 1989 most coaches ceased to practise; they sought and found employment in physical education teaching, mainly in high schools. As indicated earlier in this volume (Chapter 3) when discussing school physical education in the GDR, out-of-school sports activity had a significant presence, a presence which was organised by (often professional) coaches. Others competed with West German coaches for the highly paid jobs in clubs and federations, and yet others looked for jobs abroad.

The importance of well qualified coaches to the elite sports system has been shown in the above analysis, but this is no less true of mass sport. Factories or places of work sponsored voluntary sports clubs and they relied on a reservoir of voluntary coaches, almost all of whom had taken a qualifying course. Less than 10 per cent of such coaches were unqualified, and most of this number gained experience before attending a course. They were recruited from all walks of life, but very often they were former active athletes wishing to put back into sport some of their experience. Many embarked on coaching as a hobby before retiring from active sport. The minimum age to begin training as a coach was sixteen, with the additional requirement that all candidates complete the ten-year polytechnical education.

These lower-level coaching courses, whatever the sport, were comparable, based on a unified syllabus set out by the State Secretariat in consultation with the DHfK. The various national sports associations in membership of the DTSB, e.g. swimming, soccer and athletics, set out the technical, sporting aspects of the course. Coaches could qualify at three levels. For grades I–III inclusive, a total time of 105 sessions of 45 minutes. Grade I: 25 lessons; grade II: 40 lessons; grade III: 40 lessons. The length of each course was regarded as the minimum necessary to supply the information required by a coach without previous technical knowledge.

Whatever the sport, each training course included, within the 105 sessions, twelve on civics and twenty-five on fundamental issues in sports science; this section being identical to all courses. The remainder of the sessions was spent on the techniques and coaching methods of the sport concerned. Seven sessions were reserved for examinations. In general, before coaches could qualify at one level and progress to the next, they had to serve at least one year's practical experience working in a sports club. In theory, this implied a period of at least five years to qualify at grade III level. In practice, few coaches progressed beyond grade II, losing interest or succumbing to domestic or professional pressures. This was a matter of some concern, and great efforts were made to encourage coaches to take grade III and remain in coaching. Grade III coaches were required to take a refresher course every three years. At this level coaches could work in junior sections of elite sports clubs, for which a modest fee was payable.

The training of both voluntary and professional coaches was treated meticulously. The course content, no matter what the sport, was centrally controlled with an input from the governing bodies of sport. Uniform standards of assessment applied to all sports. The placement of professional coaches was in the hands of a central sports body, which regulated promotion and appointment to posts at regional and national level. Graduates from Leipzig were allocated posts within the sports system and employed by the DTSB. They were expected to continue in a post for a minimum of three years before applying for a move. Since almost all posts in sport and physical culture came under the auspices of the DTSB, it was unlikely that a coach could work without the approval of the DTSB. Outstanding students, particularly those with international competitive experience, were usually placed in specialist sports clubs.

Coach education programmes in the two Germanies

Curriculum evaluation and revision were constant features of coach education programmes in both countries. Whilst the last curriculum of the DHfK in the GDR that was valid at the time of the nation's demise was that of 1981, essentially and apart from minor revisions, it comprised details set out in 1975. The 1975 curriculum served as the basis for a comparison between the GDR and the other eastern European countries. For the German Coaching Academy, the most recent curriculum (2000) is considered, as it shows how the impact of the GDR has influenced developments there.

As indicated above, the GDR coaching preparation course contained four years' full-time university education on the basis of twelve years of schooling and graduation from high school, and some background in elite sport, but no previous coaching licence or experience was necessary. Usually the number of students accepted was restricted to the number of vacancies existing in the sports movement at the time of graduation, between 100 and 120 per year. The *Studienplan, Sportwissenschaft*, published in 1981 by the State Secretariat for Physical Culture and Sport on behalf of the DHfK, set the aims of courses to train coaches and specialist sports teachers in both general and specific terms.

General outcomes comprised:

- Sports officials prepared to fulfil the tasks of physical culture and sport in developing a socialist society. For this the students were trained and educated so as to be able to direct the political education and sports training of those in their care. Thus there was a strong political bias to all training.
- The display of outstanding physical and athletic skills and the personal adoption of a healthy lifestyle.
- The ability to direct training for, and organise, competitions in one particular sport.
- The guidance of their athletes' activities, morally and politically as well as in sport.
- The ability to work in close cooperation with officials, other coaches, scientists, sports medicine practitioners and physical education teachers.
- Coaches who will apply the results of their experience and, through further training, improve the performance in their sport.

Each academic year was divided into two semesters, one in the autumn and one in the spring. Teaching took place on six days per week, sessions lasting forty-five minutes. The working week was long, with an estimated thirty sessions of contact, twenty-four sessions of personal study, and between two and six sessions of personal sport participation. Coaching experience was acquired through periods of practice, varying in length according to the study year, but with at least one period per year. Students were continually assessed in physical performance, practical coaching, teaching, and by written assignments. There was a one-week examination period at the end of each year and a four-week examination period at the end of the final (fourth) year. The final examination included the presentation and defence of a thesis, for which six weeks of preparation were allocated; this carried 25 per cent of the final marks. Areas of study comprised: Marxism-Leninism; logic; teaching method; psychology; history of sport; politics of sport; socialist physical culture; cybernetics (higher mathematics, basic concepts of statistics and their practical application, the requirements of automated information processing for sport);

fundamentals of natural sciences; sports medicine; bio-mechanics; theory and method of sports training (coaching); basic course (athletics, swimming, apparatus gymnastics, handball, football, volleyball, skiing, water sports, outdoor pursuits, combat sports and minor games, and theory and practice of coaching, organisation and administration of competition, direction and planning of the coaching process); special courses, including theory and methodology of coaching, and practice of coaching of one selected sport, including participation in that sport throughout the course for training and regular competition; teaching and coaching practice; foreign languages (in Russian, students had to achieve good proficiency and acquire a technical vocabulary in a second foreign language); and public speaking. Students also gained valuable experience working as assistants at major sports festivals, and events at local level, where they assisted in administration or officiation. Table 7.1 details programme content and allocated hours.

The 750 hours of general sport preparation in ten different sports ensured that a coach could also be placed into the physical education school system. A basic requirement for teachers was 156 hours of Marxist theory. The GDR Labour Regulation Law of 28 June 1956 placed coaches within the Teachers' Union; the Law ruled that a coach was a teacher, that a teacher was supposed to spend twenty-four hours a week in direct teaching contact, whilst the rest of the time the coach was either preparing for the job or doing paid overtime.

Several factors stand out from a study of the course syllabus. The first is the comprehensive nature of the course, covering almost every eventuality in the coaching environment. Since it was almost impossible to be employed in the GDR as a coach in competitive sport without a qualification from the DHfK, this meant that not only did all coaches have an academic training, they all underwent the same training. Thus athletes as they progressed through the system and passed from coach to coach, experienced minimal, if any, conflict, either of techniques taught or training methods used. A second point to note is that because of the DHfK's commitment to research, theoretical training throughout the course was well founded and constantly updated by a group of specialists who, in close association, one with another, took an integrated and balanced view of sports development.

Each coach had to specialise in a specific sport, but in addition was taught about the 'group' in which this sport was placed. For example, a long-distance running coach learned about other endurance sports; a boxing coach learned about other forms of fighting. In this way, expertise in one sport was transferred to similar sports. These were elements that were absent from the Coaching Academy in Cologne. To enter the Coaching Academy, either a level 3 coaching licence, on the basis of a minimum total of 270 hours' previous coaching education and at least three years' experience as a coach, or experience as an elite athlete (plus

Table 7.1   DHfK coach education programme

Semesters 1–4	hours
Marxist theory	156
Logic and dialectics	66
Maths and statistics	60
Speech	12
Basic natural sciences	120
Sports medicine	12
Biomechanics	36
Sport pedagogy	72
Sport psychology	96
Coaching science	96
Special theory of selected sport and its 'group'	136
total hours	850
Theory and practice of ten different sports (athletics, swimming, gymnastics with apparatus, gymnastics, combat sport, football, volleyball, team handball, basketball, small games)	
total hours	750
Additionally	
2 courses of skiing (11 days each)	
1 course water sport (rowing, canoeing)	
Internship I (56h)	
2 foreign languages (Russian plus elective)	
training camp (5 weeks)	
total hours	1600

Semesters 5–8:	
Marxist theory	96
Sport pedagogy	36
History of physical education and sport	36
Leadership	60
Mathematics and statistics	48
Sports medicine	74
total hours	350
Specialisation	
Theory and Methods of the specialised sport	356
Theory and Methods of the sports 'group'	52
Internship II	186
Internship III	600
Diploma thesis	240
Additional participation in training and competition of the specialised sport	
total hours	1784

Source: Krüger 1980b

the recommendation of the sports governing body in both cases) was required. As only ten years of schooling are necessary, the Academy has the status of a specialised trade school and not that of a college. In essence, it is a two-year intensive training programme, which includes 960 hours of general theory, 520 hours of theory in a particular sport (4×100 hours with a master coach of the federation, plus 4×30 hours in the Coaching Academy): a total of 1,480 hours of class work. The 960 hours are divided into 480 hours of discipline-related work in the first year, and 480 hours topic-related interdisciplinary work in the second year. Just like the DHfK format, a distance-learning course is also offered with only a limited amount of direct teaching and examination hours. Whereas in Leipzig the four-year course was stretched to five years, the Cologne two-year course is stretched to three years in the distance-learning programme. Tables 7.2 and 7.3 respectively highlight the theory courses' and interdisciplinary courses' programme contents and allocated hours at the Cologne Academy.

Table 7.2   Theory courses at the Coaches' Academy, Cologne

	hours
General coaching theory	60
Sport pedagogy/sport sociology	60
Biomechanics/movement theory	60
Sports medicine	60
Sport psychology	60
Sport management	60
Current sports affairs	30
Information technology	30
Statistics	30
Time management	30
total hours	480

Source: Kreiss 1999

Table 7.3   Interdisciplinary courses at the Coaches' Academy, Cologne

	hours
The coaching of juniors	60
Social competence of the coach	60
Management of the training process	60
Tests and measurements	60
Coaching and public relations	60
Rehabilitation	60
Nutrition	60
Current sports affairs	60
total hours	480

Source: Kreiss 1999

While most of the inter-disciplinary courses are taught from a disciplinary point of view, additional aspects such as sport ethics, sport politics and sports journalism are added to enable graduates to handle everyday situations. The work with the 'master coach' emphasises the inter-disciplinary nature of the course work. There is no final thesis, but there is a comprehensive final examination.

Comparison of the two reveals that the GDR coach had a broader base as a physical education teacher, while the West German coach has a broader understanding as coach, including management functions. The latter were not seen to be the business of the GDR coach, who could concentrate on the actual coaching process and had experts in other fields to do the rest. In the case of the GDR, there were more sessions relating to the actual culture of the sport, for example sport history, a contrast with West Germany, where there was, and is, minimal concern for sports-related traditions. A weakness of the Cologne system is the blatant disregard of the general education of the coach. It is highly unlikely that two years of education on a basis of ten years of schooling can result in the same level of understanding as four years on a basis of twelve.

Application of European rules for coaches

According to the rules of the European Community, there is a free exchange of trade and services, in other words a coaching qualification in any one European Union (EU) country is supposed to be accepted in any other. Under European rules, there is also a level 5 in the hierarchy of coaching qualifications; coaching on the basis of university-level study of at least four years (level 4) is, however, the highest recognised qualification under DSB rules. The paradox of the situation is visible when looking at the situation of the former GDR. In 1976, it forewent recruitment to a short pre-academic coaching qualification similar to that of the Cologne Academy, and provided for certification at the highest level only for individuals with at least four years of university study at the DHfK in Leipzig (Hoffmann 1995). From 1978 until the collapse of the GDR, these qualified coaches numbered about one hundred per year for all major sports combined, i.e. about twice the number of the then much more populous Federal Republic.

Former GDR coaches are a sought-after commodity, for their qualifications are among the best in the world. Under DSB regulations the qualifications were, however, only accepted as level 3, an anomaly, which made sure that graduates of the Cologne Academy had a higher level of certification. It remains to be seen whether this system will stand legal tests in the European Court, but for the time being the sport governing bodies are using their monopoly for certification to demonstrate what former GDR sport officials call a 'victors' mentality'. Nevertheless, it should also not be overlooked that the situation varies from sport to sport. Football readily accepts the highest coaching qualification of the other EU countries and Switzerland as equivalent. After the 'Bosman case' in the European Court (and in the future with the 'Perugia case'), the German Football Federation is fully aware that limiting the free exchange of services would be costly. Other sport governing bodies still have to endure similar experiences.

Working conditions for coaches in the 'new' Germany

Working conditions for coaches today in the new unified Germany resemble more the conditions of the 'old' Federal Republic than anything in the former GDR. There is no serious level 5 coaching education left (Thierer 1999). The Cologne Academy has managed to require that former top-level GDR coaches take additional courses in Cologne to be recognised as level 4 coaches. Germany has made surprisingly little use of the skills of the former GDR coaches, as the fear of becoming involved in the GDR doping system was considerable (Krüger 2000). German conditions are, therefore, quite distinct from those in other leading countries in the field of elite sport, and are also distinct from sport to sport. One of the main characteristics is the varied amounts of money available for sports through government agencies, spectators and sponsors. At the top end of the spectrum of professionalisation there is football and tennis, while at the bottom end there are such successful sports as field hockey. Working conditions are equally complicated: internal competition for the few top jobs, high external control and little security with top athletes (Bette 1984). In very few cases has a leading coach a chance against a leading athlete, or group of athletes. On the whole it is easier to find a new coach than to find new athletes, and coaching contracts do not provide job stability. A professional coach, although theoretically at the centre of the training process, may be considered as an outsider by the training group and the sports governing body (Hagedorn 1991). This has made coaching such a difficult task in times of cultural revolution. In the late 1960s, students, and among them many athletes, rebelled against the authoritarian structure of their sports governing bodies in the Federal Republic of Germany. In recent years, coaches from the former GDR have experienced similar problems, as the GDR structure was far more authoritarian than that of elite sport in West Germany.

While sports governing bodies down to county level have now hired professionals as administrators and often as educators for coaches, only very large clubs, or those that are engaged in sport in the top leagues and divisions, are as yet part of the professionalisation process. This has much to do with the amateur ideology of sport, which is still persistent at grassroots level in many sports, and regards professional occupations with a certain degree of contempt and distrust. This is similarly the case in most German non-profit organisations. In this respect Germany is somewhat different from the rest of Europe, as can be seen in the high numbers of voluntary/honorary unpaid jobs in the service sector, and the relatively small number of paid occupations (Meyer and Ahlert 2000). Although the regional sports governing bodies and the DSB as the umbrella federal sports organisation have launched an initiative to increase the number of full-time staff members, it does not look as if this initiative will really make much of a difference in the coaching field.

From 1984 to 2000 a voluntary association of coaches existed in Germany (the VDDT). Initially the organisation of the graduates of the Cologne Academy, it later opened its doors to all professional coaches. It closed down because it could not materialise its aims. The DSB neglected the workers' rights of coaches. The status enjoyed by GDR coaches as early as 1960 was never achieved in western Germany. Neither have the rights that the Dutch *sportwerkers* have in their trade union contracts been attained.

If there is a problem at the top of the coaching pyramid, what of the base? Groth (1993) looked at working conditions in rhythmical gymnastics in three western Federal Republic *Länder*. This may not be a typical sport, as the percentage of female coaches is much greater than in most other sports, but it has the advantage of being an example of an Olympic sport far removed from the privileges of football. Rhythmical gymnastics is a relatively small sport in terms of numbers of participants, in which 169 coaches were identified. Of those, around 45 per cent had finished university-level studies and all held a coaching licence (4 per cent level 3; 15 per cent level 4; and 81 per cent level 5), yet only five were full-time professional coaches; the others were voluntary coaches. Of the latter some 85 per cent were, however, paid by the hour for their job, and about 61 per cent of these were content, if not happy, with the amount of money received. Yet (excluding the professional coaches) on average, they were receiving only DM12.47 (about $6) an hour, or about the same amount they would earn as house cleaners or less as office cleaners. Generally, the relatively low income earned from coaching commitments was felt to be more than compensated for by the pleasure of coaching individuals and improving performances, but significantly also by teaching the young girls independence, solidarity and fairness. In short, these particular coaches love their occupation, although for most it will never become a profession.

It is precisely this pyramid structure of coaches at club, regional and national level, that is the backbone of the German elite sport system. As long as this system works, even a lowly coach has the opportunity to work his/her way to the top. The system of twenty Olympic training centres does not infringe upon the pyramid structure in most sports, as traditionally the stronger clubs have attracted the better athletes. At present, federal monies to provide professional coaching go to the stronger clubs. The high level of coaching skill at the top, but also in many sports all the way to the very bottom, in formal and informal education, has been the backbone of German coaching education. It needs to be seen whether this system can maintain its high standard in the face of increasing individualism and a reduced degree of willingness for low-paid, long-term volunteer work. But the example of rhythmical gymnastics shows that there is a high degree of dedication still present at all levels of the sport.

References

Bette, K-H. (1984) *Die Trainerrolle im Hochleistungssport*, St Augustin, Academia.

Bisanz, G. (1995) 'Trainerausbildung im Deutschen Fussballbund', in J. Kozel (ed.) *Trainerakademie Köln e.V. 20 Jahre Trainerakademie. Internationales Trainer-symposium*, Cologne: Sport und Buch, 148–57.

Fritsch, W. (1995) ' "Zentralisierung oder Vielfalt" – Aspekte der Ausbildung von Trainern für den Vereins- und Verbandsbereich des Deutschen Ruderverbandes', in Kozel, J. (ed.) *Trainerakademie Köln e.V. 20 Jahre Trainerakademie. Internationales Trainersymposium*, Cologne: Sport und Buch, 228–33.

Groth, U. (1993) 'Zur Situation der Übungsleiterin/Trainerin für Rhythmische Sportgymnastik in der Bundesrepublik Deutschland', unpublished M.A. thesis, Göttingen: Göttingen University.

Hagedorn, G. (1991) 'Die Rolle des Trainers – eine soziale Rolle?', *Leistungssport*, 21 (4) 16–9.

Hoffmann, B. (1995) 'Leipziger Konzept der universitären Ausbildung im Diplom-studiengang Sportwissenschaft Studienschwerpunkt Leistungssport', in Kozel, J. (ed.) *Trainerakademie Cologne e.V. 20 Jahre Trainerakademie. Internationales Trainersymposium*, Cologne: Sport und Buch, 358–65.

Hoole, H. (1988) *The Science and Art of Training. A Handbook for Athletes*, London: Truber.

Kreiss, F. (1999) 'Das (ausser-)verbandliche Qualifizierungswesen des deutschen Sports – ein Weg zur Professionalisierung?', in Hartmann-Tews, I. (ed.) *Professionalisierung und Sport*, Hamburg: Czwalina, 55–8.

Krüger, A. (1980a) *Das Berufsbild des Trainers im Sport. International vergleichende Studie und Perspektiven der Traineraus- und weiterbildung in der Bundesrepublik Deutschland*, Schorndorf: Hofmann.

——(1980b) 'The preparation of coaches in East and West Germany – science vs. art', *Newsletter of the International Committee on Comparative Physical Education and Sport*, 2 (3) 7–15.

——(1991) ' "We are sure to have found the true reasons for the American superiority in sports". The reciprocal relationship between the United States and Germany in physical culture and sport', in R. Naul (ed.) Turnen *and Sport. The Cross-Cultural Exchange*, Münster: Waxmann, 51–82.

——(1995) ' "Buying victories is positively degrading". The European origins of government pursuit of national prestige through sports', *International Journal of the History of Sport*, 12 (2) 201–18.

——(2000) 'Die Paradoxien des Dopings – ein Überblick', in Gamper, M., Mühlethaler, J. and Reidhaar, F. (eds) *Doping – Spitzensport als gesellschaftliches Problem*, Zurich: NZZ Verlag, 11–33.

Meyer, B. and Ahlert, G. (2000) *Die ökonomischen Perspektiven des Sports. Eine empirische Analyse für die Bundesrepublik Deutschland*, Schorndorf: Hofmann.

Röder, H. (1961) 'Der Trainer als Erziehungspersönlichkeit im Leistungssport der DDR', dissertation, Leipzig: DHfK Leipzig.

Spitzer, G. (1998) *Doping in der DDR. Ein historischer Überblick zu einer konspirativen Praxis*, Cologne: Sport und Buch.

Teichler, H. J. and Richartz, K. (1999) *Das Leistungssportsystem der DDR in den 80er Jahren und im Prozeß der Wende*, Schorndorf: Hofmann.

Thierer, R. (1999) 'Studiengänge/Ausbildungsgänge im Berufsfeld Sport/-Sportwissenschaft', *dvs-Informationen*, 14 (1) 18–21.

Chapter 8

Elite sport

Martin-Peter Büch[1]

The elite sport system in West Germany (up to 1990) is an example of the development of high-performance competitive sport in a highly developed industrial and service economy country, in which the sport sector contributes over 1.4 per cent of gross domestic product, that is more than either agriculture or iron and steel production in Germany.

The rebirth of elite sport after the Second World War

Soon after the end of the war in 1945, sporting life in Germany began to show signs of a revival. The occupying powers had done all they could to eliminate sporting organisations, since they could not be sure to what extent the latter's representatives were still charged with the unacceptable ideas that prevailed under the National Socialists. For the people in the different occupied zones, however, the urge to participate in sport and competition was so strong that very soon there were, albeit modest, club-based competitive events. Soccer, in particular, began in divided Germany with zonal championships and received a great deal of spectator interest. These championships were approached pragmatically: technical organisation was of primary significance; the important thing was that the sport centre was available and functioning on the day of the event and that people had the opportunity to spectate (DSB 1990).

A model of how sport and its organisation might be arranged in future years was to be found, if anywhere, in the imaginations of just a few leading minds. Only one thing was certain: the basis of mass and top-class performance sport in the Federal Republic of Germany was to be the clubs, organisations that people came together to found, which then brought those people together to engage in sport on a voluntary basis. Elsewhere, after an interim phase, the alternative that was preferred in the Soviet-occupied zone (the later GDR) was for sport to be regimented and governed centrally by the state: initially from 1948, by associating it with the political organisation, the FDJ; and then, finally, following the second party conference of the SED in 1952, with the structure that was to continue (Wonneberger 2001). In contrast, in the West German *Länder*, sport and the state, the self-administration of sport and the state administrative machine were to remain separate, largely as a result of people's experience during the Third Reich between 1933 and 1945, when sport, and particularly Olympic competitive sport, had been instrumentalised and misused for political ends.

For top-performance sport this had the effect that athletes trained in clubs with long traditions, particularly performance-orientated clubs, which attempted to use the reputation acquired from successes in competitive sport to attract other athletes, particularly the young and talented. Opportunities were provided here for young people to gain access to international championships and the Olympic Games, and also to demonstrate their high level of achievement. The athletes in these clubs worked with highly motivated coaches, most of whom had learned their craft as teachers and gained experience as athletes. In general their work had no scientific basis, nor did they receive any assistance from sport science.

Initially, it was quite possible to achieve international success on the basis of this approach. However, by the mid-1960s, after the Olympic Games in Tokyo and Mexico City, it could be seen that these handed-down structures were no longer adequate for international competitive sport. Conversely, in several sports, but more notably soccer, which is extremely important in Germany, there had been attempts to employ new organisational structures to lay the foundation for enhanced performance. A number of individual associations had already formulated regulations which stipulated that only particularly well qualified coaches were to be employed in their clubs. Individual federal sports leagues were also created, in an attempt to unite the athletes participating in individual sports so that they could be trained, by engaging in competitions, to a higher standard.

Competitive sport in the inter-sytems conflict

During the 1960s, international competitive sport was increasingly at the forefront of the conflict between the political systems of the East and the West. In the early 1950s, after the founding of the GDR, sport had already been conscripted to the service of the socialist government. At home, international success was to indicate the superiority of the socialist system, giving the people a reason to identify themselves with their state, i.e. a national consciousness. To outsiders it was to underline the superiority of socialist systems and provide an international representation of a separate, communist, part of Germany. This contrast between 'capitalist' and 'socialist' competitive sport was becoming apparent and fully impacting on the political systems by 1964, when, for the last time prior to the re-unification of Germany in 1990, a joint German team participated in the Olympic Games in Tokyo.

In both the German Democratic Republic and the Federal Republic of Germany, there was consideration of how competitive sport could be organised more effectively. In the GDR, it was regimented after 1961 (the year of the Berlin Wall's construction) in a way that was not possible within a free, federal system of government. The promotion of high-performance Olympic sport in all its aspects was treated with absolute priority. Both the organisers and those responsible for providing resources did everything in their power to support competitive sport and to fulfil all the necessary conditions for international success (Krüger 1997).

In the FRG, changes were naturally rather more difficult to accomplish. It was recognised that it was no longer feasible for the hobbyist or amateur to compete successfully at top-class level, that there was a shortage of well trained coaches, that there were insufficient training centres, and that there was no central advisory body to deal with competitive sport. Hence change became inevitable. It commenced with the establishment of the German Sports Aid Foundation, to provide material support to athletes for better management of training and competition. In the late 1960s, when the Olympic Games were awarded to Munich in 1966, in response to this catalogue of inadequacies and the challenge of hosting the Games in 1972, a competitive sport section was established at the DSB and 'federal achievement centres' were set up as centralised locations for training purposes. The Federal Committee for Competitive Sport, which was set up in 1970 within the DSB on the initiative of the top-ranking sports clubs, was intended to provide support for federal specialist clubs performing their original tasks within competitive sport, organising sport-medical care, dealing with the advanced training of coaches, and providing the clubs with comprehensive information and services (Andresen 1988).

Eventually this approach was modified in view of athletes' negative responses to the centralisation measures. Wherever possible, bases were set up close to residential areas, allowing athletes to work with coaches who had a proper scientific training. In 1974, as a necessary consequence of these considerations, a coaches' academy was founded in Cologne. This was particularly necessary because the alternative training centres in universities did not want to meet or failed to fulfil the requirements of elite sport, namely to furnish coaches for competitive sport – a failure that is entirely understandable in view of the *Zeitgeist* that followed the 1968 upheavals in many German universities. There was a clear shift in the early 1970s from the American, university-based model for elite sport to a new independent DSB 'elite sport system', inaugurated using techniques from Eastern Bloc countries.

Sports events continued against a backdrop of competing political systems. The highest possible performance (and nothing less could hope to prevail at the Olympic Games and other international championships) called for a new breadth of training. Continually increasing demands were made on the quality of this training, and for more and better care and support for athletes, but it was just this level of support that could no longer be offered in the numerous sport bases that had been set up locally in residential areas.

Once the GDR had discovered and coached its talented and aspiring elite athletes in training centres, the armed- and security forces and the factory-based clubs largely became the centralised locations for the country's athletes, offering everything from training to elaborate precautionary health-care services. This was the type of system that, after the 1984 Los Angeles Olympic Games, inspired the FRG to set up an organisational structure to concentrate services in so-called 'Olympic centres', as a way of offering high-quality services to athletes alongside their training and care without this being an inefficient use of resources. The plan was to develop Olympic centres as basic training centres to cover all types of sport. On offer was full scientific support and care: training science, performance diagnostics, sport medicine, psychological and pedagogical measures, as well as sport-medical care of injuries and measures for rehabilitation. Before this process of setting up and developing the Olympic centres could be completed on a broad scale, the re-unification of Germany had introduced additional factors into the development of elite sport and its associated structures. Nonetheless, the system of Olympic centres was retained, albeit with modifications (Büch 1994).

Changes in the elite sport system in the 1970s and 1980s

When trying to systematise the previously described relationships in competitive sport in Germany, it has to be noted that clubs still constitute the basis for high-performance sport, no less today than in the 1950s and 1960s. They take in the children and young people who approach them, introduce them to sport, and look out for particular talent that they then pass on to specialist regional associations. These associations, which are generally responsible for the C and D youth squads, train these young athletes until they are taken over by the corresponding specialist federal associations in the high-performance A and B squads. This traditional system of competitive sport in the Federal Republic of Germany remains, as it was then, the responsibility of the appropriate federal specialist association.

The creation and consolidation of a number of support systems during the 1970s and 1980s introduced no real significant changes to this system. To be sure, the German *Länder* employ a variety of support and sponsorship measures for seeking out, identifying and developing talent. Such measures are agreed and financed jointly by the state government and the regional sports associations. The regional committees for competitive sport set the criteria for sponsoring young athletes, and the specialist regional associations can rely on assistance from the training centres of the regional performance centres. Responsibility for education and training remains with the specialist regional associations.

The setting-up of federal performance centres and training centres, expansion of sport science institutes at universities, and the simultaneous establishment of the Federal Institute for Sport Science as a central organisation for the promotion of research, considerably increased the range of assistance available for competitive sport, both quantitatively and qualitatively. From the outset of its establishment in 1970, the DSB's Federal Committee for Competitive Sport performed an essentially consultatory function, advising the federal government on public funding grants for setting up individual organisations and promoting specialist federal associations. Little was changed regarding the structure of responsibility, and this also applied to the setting-up of Olympic centres as service centres, incorporating the former GDR elite sports organisations as specified in the Unification Treaty (see below).

Figure 8.1 provides an overview of the organisation of competitive sport in Germany. All the services provided by the various institutes are to be understood as 'on offer'. Under this system, the specialist regional and federal associations are free to decide to what extent they wish to avail themselves of these services, because it is they who will finally carry the responsibility for the successes and failures of their associations.

Individual developments, particularly in the scientific field, are considered in more detail below. There is no question that, albeit through a protracted diffusion process via the education, training and advisory services provided to trainers and coaches, knowledge about – and new developments in – performance diagnostics, training management, injury prevention and rehabilitation were incorporated into athletes' training programmes and reflected in their competitive performance.

The GDR's integrated elite sport system was highly sophisticated in its structural organisation and administration. In the third year of school, all children underwent tests, the results of which were analysed by the DTSB in East Berlin. The so-called Grade 3 Performance Control Spreadsheet (*Leistungskontrollbogen Klasse 3*) recorded details of each pupil's name, month and year of birth, sex, demographic details, weight, height and results of tests in the 60 metres sprint, long jump, triple jump, endurance run, rounders ball throw, push ups, shot put, and a mark for performance in apparatus gymnastics and a game, as well as for participation in extra-curricular sport and motivation in sport. This was one device for identifying and screening children and young people in schools (and kindergartens) and clubs for promising talent. In training centres, these talented youngsters came under further scrutiny and the most talented then attended a KJS and/or sports club, and later transferred to high-performance groups within the elite clubs. During this process, the ruling

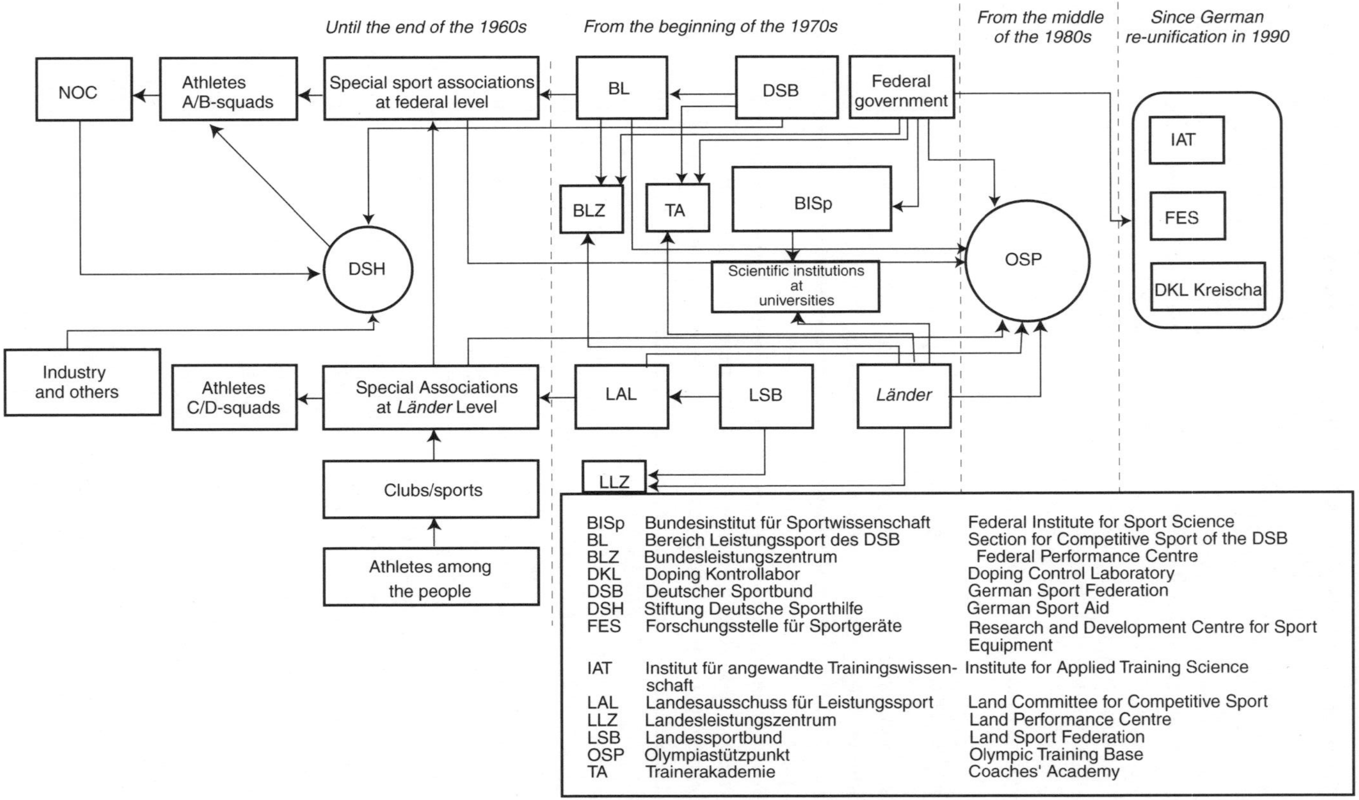
Until the end of the 1960s
From the beginning of the 1970s
From the middle of the 1980s
Since German re-unification in 1990
NOC
Athletes A/B-squads
Special sport associations at federal level
BL
DSB
Federal government
IAT
FES
DKL Kreischa
BLZ
TA
BISp
OSP
DSH
Scientific institutions at universities
Industry and others
Athletes C/D-squads
Special Associations at *Länder* Level
LAL
LSB
Länder
LLZ
Clubs/sports
Athletes among the people
BISp Bundesinstitut für Sportwissenschaft Federal Institute for Sport Science
BL Bereich Leistungssport des DSB Section for Competitive Sport of the DSB
BLZ Bundesleistungszentrum Federal Performance Centre
DKL Doping Kontrollabor Doping Control Laboratory
DSB Deutscher Sportbund German Sport Federation
DSH Stiftung Deutsche Sporthilfe German Sport Aid
FES Forschungsstelle für Sportgeräte Research and Development Centre for Sport Equipment
IAT Institut für angewandte Trainingswissen-schaft Institute for Applied Training Science
LAL Landesausschuss für Leistungssport Land Committee for Competitive Sport
LLZ Landesleistungszentrum Land Performance Centre
LSB Landessportbund Land Sport Federation
OSP Olympiastützpunkt Olympic Training Base
TA Trainerakademie Coaches' Academy

Figure 8.1 Structural relationships between athletes, associations and specific competitive sport institutions

SED and the state, through the DTSB, maintained controlling influence on KJSs and sports clubs, just as they did on the scientific institutions, i.e. the Research Institute for Physical Culture and Sport (FKS), the Research and Development Centre for Sporting Equipment (FES), the German college for Physical Culture and Sport (DHfK), and the Sports Medicine Service (SMD). The specialist sports associations and scientific centres directed the attention of the scientific institutions towards those problems that were to be the topic of scientific study. In this way, these scientific institutions were subject to a rigidly supervised and controlled application-orientated utility research for sport – from questions of performance diagnostics to matters of doping, the magnitude of which was not fully comprehended in the Federal Republic until the early 1990s, after re-unification (see Figure 8.2).

Early scientific concomitants of sport

It has become a truism that sport, and particularly competitive sport, can no longer get by without scientific assistance, although this was not openly accepted during the first twenty years that constituted the initial period of the post-war development of elite sport in Germany. At that time there were no widespread overtures from the field of sport science. Contacts between practising sportsmen and women (coaches and athletes) and scientists were more likely to be based on chance meetings and personal interests. 'Sport science' as an academic area of study (e.g. for coaches) did not exist until the mid-1970s in West Germany, and coaches, as previously mentioned, acquired their knowledge from practical experience and example. The development was gradual and came through individual scientists' research findings that seemed likely to be useful for the purposes of sport, and particularly competitive sport. These scientists had an affinity with sport, either from previous experience as competitive athletes or from personal inclination, and they applied the methods of their own scientific discipline to deal with sporting questions within that discipline.

Sport pedagogy, as a subject for study at teacher training colleges and to a lesser extent at universities, had no part to play in day-to-day research during the early post-war years. So it was a significant development when, in 1955, the Committee for Sports Medicine Research, under the chairmanship of the DSB President, was founded for the purpose of advising the federal government on the suitability of research projects for funding. At that time, the country's limited competence in sport at federal level was already significant. For this reason, only proposals relating to competitive sport could be considered, because competitive sport (so the argument ran) is by its very nature a federal matter, and the federal *Länder*, which were responsible for any sport-related questions calling for government intervention, left its furtherance to the central government.

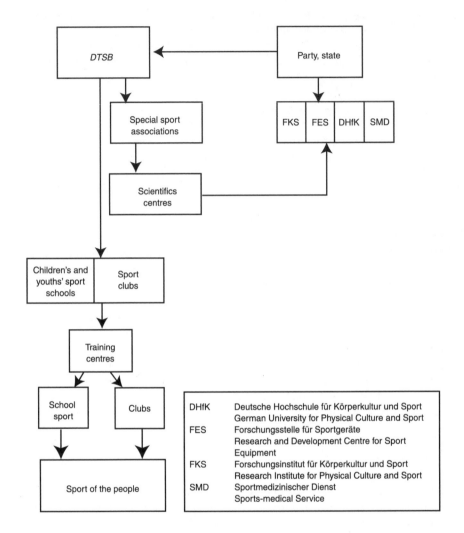

Figure 8.2 System and structure of competitive sport in the former GDR

The development of sport science as a scientific adjunct of sport is nothing short of remarkable. When it was founded, in Hanover in 1950, the DSB undertook to promote sport science. No doubt it was expected that the work of this umbrella organisation and its member associations would receive assistance, advice and recommendations from the scientific world. Such expectations, along with the increasing need of the clubs engaging in competitive sport for scientific support, may have played a considerable part in sport science beginning to 'get itself organised', because this development also makes it clear that (in part due to the dichotomy between self-governing organisations and public sports administration) public funds would have to be called on if results were to be obtained from research. Naturally, the DSB's 'organisational responsibility' for sport science also increased science's influence on the development of sport, and particularly competitive sport. Although initially the breadth of sport science findings was not quantitatively great, there was in time a noticeable tendency for scientists to do more for sport. Further initiatives can also be recognised at universities and in the area of research grants.

The tasks of the Committee for Sports Medicine Research were extended to cover training science, and psychological, pedagogical and sociological topics. In 1963 it was renamed the Central Committee for Research into Sport Science. The funds provided to the Committee by the federal government were increasingly stepped up; whereas in 1961 only DM153,000 had been available, in 1970 a total of DM1,421,000 was granted for research into sport medicine and sport pedagogy, the latter term being used to cover all those topics that did not fall under sport medicine (Federal Institute for Sport Science 1973).

The increasing volume of funding for research, which was marked by a further differentiation of the various fields to be addressed by scientific research, clearly indicated the way in which requirements were increasing, particularly from high-performance sport, but also demonstrated to the scientists serving as honorary officials on the Central Committee that only better scientific results could enable top-class sport to achieve further gains and a more pronounced professionalisation. The search, the demand, for scientific findings in the field of competitive sport, as well as the characteristically inherent dynamism of the young scientist, led to the setting-up and enlargement of sport science faculties at universities and, at the same time, the creation of professorships and qualification centres for young scientists. Increasingly, research centres were being set up, initially in the field of medicine. Separate departments came into being in those university faculties that looked at sport from a scientific point of view. More and more it was publicly admitted that elite sport was in need of public assistance, and that the funds made available by the federal government represented a contribution to the fulfilment of a task that was in the interests of the country as a whole.

During the run-up to the Olympic Games in Mexico City, sports medicine expertise had been much in demand due to the exigencies of altitude, and it had become clear that elite sport could no longer be a matter that was left to individual clubs, however excellent their performance. It was, therefore, directly after these Games, and certainly prior to the Olympic Games in Munich, that plans were mooted to create a central, federally funded, scientifically operating institute for the advancement of high-performance sport. In the end, the Federal Minister of the Interior and the German Sport Federation decided, by setting up the Federal Institute for Sport Science (BISp), to transfer the patronage of sport that had previously rested with the Central Committee for Research into Sport Science to this central body. This Federal Institute for Sport Science was also to administer research funding, oversee the projects that were to be sponsored, maintain contact with the scientific community and individual scientists, provide them with additional information, help them to obtain literature, and make sure that research was not being duplicated. Another important task was to translate new findings into sporting practice, to make it easier for practical training to make progress, to address new questions, and most particularly to promote interdisciplinary cooperation. The foundation of the Federal Institute for Sport Science on 10 October 1970 was thus the response to a challenge in high-performance sport, which skilfully exploited the favourable sport-political situation prior to the Olympic Games of 1972, and simultaneously provided a new basis for sport science that had previously been a mere adjunct of sport.

In the GDR, the response to the increasing demands of high-performance sport was somewhat similar, although more centralist and systematic as dictated by the different political system: the Research Institute for Physical Culture and Sport had been set up in Leipzig prior to the Olympic Games in Munich. Its specific approach was geared to making available to high-performance sport scientific findings for specific sports that could be directly applied to practical training. For its sophistication, from the selection of athletes, through training and sport-medical care, to job security at the end of the individual's sporting career, this integrated system could scarcely be surpassed.[2]

At the end of the 1980s, prior to the re-unification of Germany, it could be seen that, as regards achievement, the GDR had evidently been more successful in exploiting its sporting potential. Treatises on sport-scientific topics from both East and West were highly regarded in scholarly circles, although papers from the GDR were not always available, but in implementing these findings the GDR's system was clearly superior to that of the Federal Republic.

System and development after re-unification – accent on the scientific support of elite sport

When the re-unification of Germany occurred on 3 October 1990, it ushered in a new context for German high-performance sport and the sport science that supported it. Two very different systems of sport and science needed to be brought together, whereby the former GDR sports and science institutions were to be adapted to conform to the democratic and federal structures of the Federal Republic of Germany. In doing so, the state was also to accommodate the concerns of German sport, namely to adopt and integrate the GDR's sport science facilities. Thus, while the competency of university research in the former GDR was to be the responsibility of the newly created *Länder*, the wishes of the sporting organisations were to be fulfilled. Specifically, the former Research Institute for Physical Culture and Sport in Leipzig (FKS), the Research and Development Centre for Sports Equipment in Berlin (FES) and the doping test laboratory in Kreischa (near Dresden) would, where necessary, be allowed to continue in whatever legal form was appropriate, or affiliated with existing institutions. In taking over these institutions, the sporting interests were aiming to incorporate those former GDR institutions that were considered responsible for the outstanding performance of the GDR's athletes in international competition, including the associated scientific systems, into the elite sport system of the FRG. The Federal Institute for Sport Science was to continue to fulfil its existing tasks, now extending to the new German *Länder*, but using its matured and proven principles, regulations and methods (Büch 1996). For example, the Federal Institute for Sport Science was asked to collaborate with the Federal Minister of the Interior with responsibility for sport and the Free State of Saxony, to wind up the former Research Institute for Physical Culture and Sport in Leipzig and set up in its place an Institute for Applied Training Science. In 1992 this work finally began under a legally constituted 'registered association', which clearly labels it as an institute of German sport. To underline its connection with the sport science research promoted by the federal government, the Director of the Federal Institute for Sport Science took on the chairmanship of the scientific advisory board of the Institute for Applied Training Science and the Institute for Research and Development of Sports Equipment, which was not wound up but remained essentially the responsibility of a private sports association. At the same time, with the support of the Federal Minister of the Interior and under the leadership of the Director of the Federal Institute for Sport Science, the doping test laboratory in Kreischa was wound up and re-established as the Institute for Doping Analysis and Sport Biochemistry, and re-accredited as an institute recognised by the International Olympic Committee (IOC). This had the desired effect that Germany now possessed two IOC-recognised doping test laboratories.

The process of integrating the sport science of the two Germanies did not pass without difficulty. Revelations of large-scale doping with the connivance of the all-controlling, all-powerful and all-suppressing state security apparatus of the GDR had provoked widespread public discussion about the negative aspects of state sport. It became increasingly clear that the sporting superiority of the GDR had come at a high price: it was evident that maintaining the organisations and institutions in and around high-performance sport in the GDR had consumed a very high level of resources (Teichler and Reinartz 1998). Additionally, sport scientists from the Federal Republic of Germany voiced reservations regarding former GDR scientific practices. Initially this had the effect of distancing the two sides. The general opinion was that preserving the former GDR's sport scientists' expertise ought not to be the only criterion for accepting these scientists into the new bodies. In the interests of minimising conflict, those former GDR scientists, who were to be employed in the new scientific institutes, were subjected to a test of their technical and political integrity. This in turn had the effect that noted sport scientists who had identified themselves too strongly with the GDR political system left Germany to make their services available to high-performance sport elsewhere.

The process of integrating sport science facilities also had the effect of inflaming the competition for research funding for individual sport science institutes at universities. Here again there were two opposing opinions: on the one hand, that research appertaining to the department included applied basic research too, and on the other, that research sponsored by the federal government primarily had to be relevant to the practice of high-performance sport. The Federal Institute for Sport Science eventually managed to achieve a compromise between these opposing interests. Indeed, the Institute intervened to ensure that the existing sport science expertise in the new Länder would be developed for German sport, and that sport science research, therefore, would be fostered without disadvantaging the proven institutions in the old West German Länder. Of course, the sport science institutions in the new German Länder, that is, in the former GDR, had to become accustomed to open scientific and pluralistic discourse and to the federal structures that also applied to research rivalry and the presentation of research plans seeking public funding. Conversely, the sport science institutes at the universities in the old West German Länder increasingly had to learn that their findings were expected to prove themselves in the day-to-day advancement of sport (Büch 1997).

The integration process affecting the sciences ancillary to sport progressed rather better than similar processes in other areas following German re-unification, because attempts were also made to take on the new German Länder sport science institutes' employees into the sport science bodies of the old German Länder and the Federal Institute for Sport Science. Gradually a basis was achieved for fruitful cooperation. A further element of this integration was, so far as possible, to secure and write up in suitable form those previously existing collated former-GDR research findings that had remained unpublished because of excessively stringent secrecy regulations, and to make these findings available to sport. Analysis of documentation and compilation of information on pedagogical research dealing with school children, young people and young athletes was achieved, with some difficulty (Büch 1996).

Current sport science for elite sport

The early work conducted in the field of sport science consisted primarily of sports medicine investigations, which aimed to obtain results that could be directly applied to practical work with the training of athletes, as comprehensively and quickly as possible. At first, therefore, the focus was on medical investigations for the purposes of training. At the same time, there was recognition of the responsibility of sport science to provide assistance for sport. Scientifically based guidelines were developed for non-manipulative high-performance sport. These were aimed at avoiding physical, psychological and social injury to high-performance sportsmen and women. In addition, very soon there were research projects on the prevention of drug abuse in sport.

It was seen as important to break new ground in the development of sports equipment and, increasingly, training equipment. This included the identification of suitable materials for the safety of athletes in training and competition. It also became clear that, with the broadening of the system of elite sport, it would be necessary to procure suitable facilities for training and competition. It was necessary to have such facilities designed with due regard to economic and ecological aspects, in order to provide athletes with appropriate facilities in their residential neighbourhoods. In recent years, the development of elite sport and its professionalisation and commercialisation has had a decisive influence on the structure of sports clubs and associations; they have made sport into an important part of the national economy, and have produced side effects that also received scholarly attention during the process of developing design recommendations.

Over the last decade or so, a number of scientific issues related to elite sport have been addressed. These are discussed below.

Science and training

Studies on training for competition and actual competition events, further developments in measurement techniques, and models for evaluating sporting performance and performance conditions, were initially to the fore. After all, the intention was to determine the requirements for, and the effects of, sporting activities in order to derive recommendations for such activities. Hence investigations were carried out into means of controlling and regulating training for high-performance sport, with the aim of improving the monitoring and evaluation of training and competitions; in this area increasing use was made of computer-supported systems. Projects were developed for improving performance diagnostics in endurance disciplines; studies dealing with the hormonal effects of stress and training on women athletes helped considerably to improve methods of training. Other basic research plans were promoted regarding training for combat sports and weightlifting and the like, which established numerous pointers that could be implemented in practical training, and to explain the processes of fatigue and regeneration. In the last ten years, training science has increasingly been devoted to sport for those with disabilities, and a series of investigations has been commissioned specifically related to competitive sport for disabled people (Hartmann 2000).

Sport science in the service of elite sport

Elite sport can have a humanitarian side, in the sense of respecting human dignity, considering people's independence, and minimising potentially harmful risks, but only if those responsible for the sport make it humane! Such 'humane' sport must take place without pharmacological and other forms of manipulation, and must refrain from taking unreasonable risks with the health and well-being of its athletes. A number of pioneering research projects dealing with this question have been initiated in Germany over the last few years, in an attempt to minimise the risks involved in high-performance sport. These include collaborative (sport medicine practitioners, bio-mechanists, psychologists and pedagogues) pioneering research into stress and risks in women's gymnastics, which resulted in the International Gymnastics Federation (*Fédération Internationale de Gymnastique* or FIG) modifying its regulations and prescribing additional soft landing surfaces in order to reduce the risk of injury to athletes dismounting from the equipment; additionally, it has raised the minimum competition entry age for female gymnasts. The same research also produced a number of indicators for reorganising the training of young female gymnasts.

Projects on accident prevention have served to reduce risks in sport. Studies have been carried out into muscle development imbalance, questions relating to regeneration and prevention of injuries, the prevention of accidents and consequently on safety in sport. The findings have assisted in remodelling training and competition processes in a variety of ways, and they have helped the need for accident prevention in sport to be fulfilled more effectively. Research projects on competitive sport for children and the problem of talent have also influenced ways of controlling the stress placed on children and young people. Longitudinal studies have investigated the effects of competitive sport on children from psychological angles, and have provided a scientific basis for ways of recognising and encouraging talent.

Sport science in the service of anti-doping research

In the Federal Republic of Germany attention was paid to anti-doping research quite early on, and doping analysis facilities were already being set up prior to the Olympic Games in Munich. The Federal Institute for

Sport Science, whose function consisted essentially of the promotion of research related to high-performance sport, was soon involved with supporting doping analysis, and indeed did so during the Munich Games. The Institute for Biochemistry, which was set up in 1976 at the German Sport University in Cologne, was another body that was essentially devoted to doping analysis; this was financed through the BISp. Whereas the task of doping analysis was initially to detect stimulants and narcotics, it was not too long before anabolic steroids and related substances became the centre of attention.

The discovery of the comprehensive state-sanctioned doping practised in the former GDR, and a number of individual doping violations in the old German *Länder*, made it clear that the doping control system in German competitive sport would have to be more effectively handled. Following publication of the Reiter Commission Report in 1991, comprehensive testing was introduced for athletes in training, and the number of tests was increased by way of setting an example in the fight against doping. Implementation was possible because of the availability since the early 1990s of the two doping control laboratories with the necessary analytic capacity. Additional research enabled German doping analysis to extend significantly the limits of detectability for drug use, even of the minutest quantities of doping substances. Application of findings from other research projects inhibits tampering with, for example, urine samples; hair analysis prolongs the detection period for consumption of illegal substances; and the reliable detection of anabolic steroids and administered growth hormone (rhGH) has been enabled.

Scientific support for doping analysis has led to high standards at the two German doping control laboratories, and their regulations for the standardisation of analytical procedures and quality assurance for doping analysis laboratories have been adopted by the IOC Medical Commission. The role of German scientists in the fight against drug abuse in sport is also underlined by the fact that the delegate for doping analysis at the Federal Institute for Sport Science, who is simultaneously head of the Institute for Doping Analysis and Sport Biochemistry in Kreischa, also chairs the scientific workgroup of the Council of Europe's monitoring subcommittee for combating drug abuse in sport.

Development of sports equipment in the service of competitive sport

Since the foundation of the Federal Institute for Sport Science at the beginning of the 1970s, there has been an increase in the number of sponsored projects relating to the development of equipment, particularly in those forms of high-performance sport that are highly equipment-dependent, such as bobsled, sailing, rowing, canoeing and cycling. There has been some research emphasis on safe and properly functioning equipment, and there has been close cooperation between sport and science in standardisation committees at national and international level, to ensure elite athletes train and compete in safe environments. The Federal Institute for Sport Science has collaborated directly with sports clubs. The German Cycling Federation has participated in discussions about on-cycle controls for mobile training; the German Association for Bobsled and Luge Sport has been involved with the development of complex diagnostic and training equipment for optimising start and run performance in tobogganing; the German Skating Union took part in the development of a figure skate with improved provision in the ankle for jumping without endangering stability; the German Canoe Union was involved with setting up a biomechanical measurement system for flat water diagnostics in canoe slalom; the German Rowing Association has made recommendations for the measurement and output of sport-physiological parameters in a movement-specific training and diagnostic system based on the rowing action; the German Triathletic Union has been involved with the development of sport-related software for analysing skill structures; and the German Gymnastic Federation has cooperated in an investigation into the ageing of gymnastic landing surfaces. The German Rowing Association has also been involved with investigating questions relating to the hydrodynamic effect of oar blades.

Research projects have been initiated and carried out in the field of sport safety. A 'Safety in fencing' project was carried out under the auspices of the Federal Institute for Sport Science and in collaboration with representatives from the German Fencing Federation, the German Sports Federation and the Federal Minister of the Interior. The aim of this project was to increase both active and passive safety in fencing. The incentive for the project on improved safety was a fatal accident to a Russian fencer at the 1982 World Championships in Rome. The search for greater safety resulted in the development of a new type of steel for fencing foils, equipment for detecting pre-damaged blades, and use of specific materials to improve the clothing worn by fencers.

Research into basic planning issues relating to sports facilities

Systematic work on fundamental planning issues for functional sports facilities started as far back as the 1950s, and was part of the intention to build sports grounds and facilities in the Federal Republic of Germany in accordance with the latest scientific findings and with the basic principles of economic efficiency and functionality. The results of research into sports facilities were incorporated directly into new planning guidelines. This research, which was principally carried out by the Federal Institute for Sport Science, led to a considerable improvement in the economy, usefulness, technical facilities and equipment of sports complexes.

Further research projects facilitated test procedures for the evaluation of purpose-built sports floors, and these results have proved significant for purposes of standardisation. Other research projects developed criteria for user-friendly sports grounds, sports facilities for disabled people, and a combined swimming pool and ice rink conceived as a way of designing sports facilities with an eye to economic efficiency; yet other research topics relating to sports facilities intended for competitions addressed questions of environment protection, safety, accident prevention, and emissions of noise and light. Under the direction of the Federal Institute for Sport Science it was possible to compile a set of guidelines for the developmental planning of sports facilities in Germany, incorporating a number of significant research results.

The Federal Institute for Sport Science also participated in developing the 'Golden plan' for the former East Germany (see Roskam, Chapter 11 in this volume). After re-unification in 1990, it was found that the sports facilities in the new *Länder*, including those used for elite sport, were in a poor state as regards both quantity and quality. It became clear that elite athletes in the former GDR had had to make do with sports grounds, some of which were in exceedingly bad condition, and that the infrastructure of sports facilities was seriously in need of refurbishment. A further research project, again by the Federal Institute for Sport Science, also developed a set of guidelines for the renovation and redevelopment of sports facilities in the new German *Länder*. The outcome will be sports facilities which will enable elite and other athletes to train and compete more effectively.

Developments in elite sport and their scientific assimilation

Elite sport, particularly after the late 1970s, has become increasingly professionalised and to some extent commercialised. It is a trend which has led to developments in research in, and appliance of, sports science. Training for young athletes, for example, has been the subject of a growing number of studies into specific aims both within and outside of the sport's environment, examples of which are seen in work undertaken on issues related to training and competition from a social environment perspective. Other areas under investigation have addressed not only children and young people in high-performance sport, but also questions relating to vocational training and sport and post-school careers, violence in sport, women in sport, the dropout problem amongst athletes, the influence of the media on competitive sport, and the social competence of trainers and sport leaders (Strähl and Anders 1993).

In recent years there has been further emphasis on sport as an important economic factor. The commercial significance of sport has been emphasised, and studies have been carried out using simulation models to examine the effects of public sponsorship of sport. Large sporting events are an obvious area for future study in terms of impacts, costs and benefits from an economic perspective.

Since the end of the 1970s, the Federal Institute for Sport Science has underlined its responsibility for sport science by carrying out a number of high-profile investigations. Activities have been initiated on the basis of studies and projects on ethics in sport, and fair play in training and competition. The Federal Institute for Sport Science has also been involved in reformulating the 'Declaration of fair play' by the Council for Sport Science and Physical Education, and at the end of the 1990s was able to produce a lexicon of ethics in sport. The representation of the ethical and moral basis of sport makes it a significant help for all those who carry responsibility in and around sports – in particular in the field of elite sport.

Elite sport: another challenge for sport science?

In a cautionary summary of the activities carried out in sport science in the advancement of elite sport, it is apparent that sport science, which has been developing more rigorously since the end of the 1960s, has provided elite sport with an expanded spectrum of knowledge. It is this knowledge that has made it possible to explain a number of problems and influences in the field of elite sport. Sport and its agents have not always made use of this knowledge; they have not always been able to do so. This might well be regretted; however, the situation of people who are engaging competitively in sport has to be borne in mind. For such people it will always be easier to implement findings from sport science that promise higher, faster and further, than to take cognisance of organisational suggestions for improving individual sporting processes (Schmidtbleicher 1991).

At the beginning of the twenty-first century, new questions are emerging for elite sport to ask of its supporting science: training models do need to be evaluated, new findings on regeneration and the study of learning processes can help athletes and coaches, but it is also important to consider how future knowledge can be more effectively integrated into the training process. Furthermore, there is an increasing number of issues relating to suitable forms of organisation in elite sport, from talent-spotting right through to post-sport careers. Responsible science will not run short of challenges.

Financial resources for elite sport

It is tacitly agreed that elite sport occupies a singular position in the German sporting landscape, and because of this position many in Germany have helped provide it with the resources it needs for its development. First, the clubs and associations themselves, who through their own efforts help athletes develop their skills by means of training and competition. Second, the substantial assistance given to athletes by their families, friends and acquaintances should not be ignored. Third, a major group of supporters of elite sport are the various public bodies (federations, *Länder* and communities) and private commercial organisations. Without public support, and without the now-customary sponsors, much of elite sport could no longer be financed. Unfortunately, there are at present no meaningful estimates of just how costly elite sport is. Reliable figures exist for only a few sub-fields.

In order to illustrate the extent to which elite sport research funding is supported, some figures for the sponsorship of scientific research by the Federal Institute for Sport Science are provided here. From 1971 to 1999, the Federal Institute provided an average of around DM2.6 million annually for the sponsorship of scientific research. To begin with, the annual total was less than DM1 million but this has increased over the years, reaching about DM3.5 million in 1999. Such funding has made it possible to advance the projects listed above. It must be remembered here that the Federal Institute for Sport Science grants its research funding in accordance with the principle of subsidiarity, which implies that considerable sums will also have been received from scientific institutions. If it is assumed that for every Deutschmark of research grant the sponsored institute contributes another, then elite sport has essentially received funding of the order of about DM6 million annually. Including transfer payments, publications, events and the like (and bearing in mind that the expenditure on doping analysis doubles this amount), this adds up to some 12 million Deutschmarks during the 1990s, which facilitated significant results in elite sport. If the reckoning is extended to include the value of the additional scientific and auxiliary services provided annually since the 1990s by the Institute for Applied Training Science and the Institute for Research and Development of Sports Equipment, together of the order of DM12 million, we can see just what volume of scientific services is devoted to elite sport.

Prospects

While elite sport was being dragged further and further into the political conflict between East and West as a way of comparing the two systems, more and more effort was being spent exhausting all possible means, including those with a sound scientific basis, in order to gain advantages from this meta-contest. As shown, the influence exerted by sport science increased during this period. Now that the 'war of the systems' is over, elite sport increasingly has to consider a new and significant issue: the issue of the total commercialisation of sport.

This commercialisation, which is the counterpart of the desired professionalisation of sport, could lead to a schism among athletes: here, professional, high-performance sport in all its aspects and with commercialisation as a source of finance; or there, thoroughly professional high-performance sport funded largely from the public purse. Whatever, sport science will be needed. However much the findings of training science facilitate 'faster, higher and further', anthropological findings will be needed in order to establish a balance between the technically still possible and the ethically still responsible. Elite sport, founded on the Olympic ideal, challenges sport science. Moreover, at the same time, the development of elite sport is a challenge for all – even in Germany.

Notes

1 Appreciation is extended to Jürgen Schiffer for assistance with the English version of this chapter.
2 Hinsching (1996: 16) has pointed out that sport science in the GDR was divided into two parts. This division came from the theses assigned to competitive sport: whereas research into high-performance sport followed the command structures of the state and kept its findings secret, research into mass sport was able to develop more or less transparently.

References

Andresen, R. (1988) 'Der Spitzensport im Umbruch (High-performance sport in upheaval)', *Sportphysiotherapie Aktuell*, 9 (5) 314–16.
Büch, M.-P. (1994) 'Olympiastützpunkte – ökonomisch betrachtet (Olympia bases – viewed economically)', *Olympische Jugend*, 6, 8–9.
——(1996) 'Das Bundesinstitut für Sportwissenschaft (BISp) in den Jahren 1991–1994 (The Federal Institute for Sport Science [BISp] in the years 1991–4)', *Sportwissenschaft*, 26, 74–91.
——(1997) 'Bundesinstitut für Sportwissenschaft, Jahresbericht 1995', *Sportwissenschaft*, 27, 173–9.
Deutscher Sportbund (ed.) (1990) *Die Gründerjahre des Deutschen Sportbundes: Wege aus der Not zur Einheit (The Early Years of the German Sport Federation: The Paths from Crisis to Unity)*, Schorndorf: Hoffman.
Hartmann, W. (2000) 'Schwerpunkte der Forschungsförderung und Beratungsleistungen des Bundesinstituts für Sportwissenschaft über fast drei Jahrzehnte (Priorities of research funding and counselling services of the Federal Institute for Sport Science over almost three decades)', in Federal Institute for Sport Science (ed.) *BISp-Jahrbuch 1999*, Cologne: BISp, 15–26.
Hinsching, J. (1996) 'Ostdeutsche Sportwissenschaft vor und nach 1990 (East German sport science before and after 1990)', *dvs-Informationen*, 4, 15–25.
Krüger, M. (1997) 'Olympische Spiele in Deutschland: ausgefallen, mißbraucht, überschattet, gescheitert (Olympic Games in Germany: cancelled, misused, overshadowed, foundered)', in Grupe, O. (ed.) *Olympischer Sport. Rückblick und Perspektiven*, Schorndorf: Hofmann, 71–84.

Schmidtbleicher, D. (1991) 'Der Sportwissenschaftler zwischen den Erwartungen des Leistungssports und den Möglichkeiten, Problemen und Grenzen wissenschaftlicher Beratung (Sport scientists between the expectations of competitive sport and the possibilities, problems and limitations of scientific counselling)', in Bührle, M. and Schnur, M. (eds) *Leistungssport: Herausforderung für die Sportwissenschaft. Bericht über den 9. Sportwissenschaftlichen Hochschultag der Deutschen Vereinigung für Sportwissenschaft*, vol. 72, Schorndorf: Hofmann, 47–57.

Strähl, E. and Anders, G. (eds) (1993) *Spitzensportler – Helden und Opfer. Bericht zum 31. Magglinger Symposium vom 28–30 Mai 1992*, Magglingen: Eidgenössischen Sportschule Magglingen.

Teichler, J. and Reinartz, K. (1998) *Das Leistungssportsystem der DDR in den 80er Jahren und im Prozeß der Wende (The System of Competitive Sport in the GDR in the 1980s and During the Changeover Process)*, The Federal Institute for Sport Science, vol. 96, Schorndorf: Hofmann.

Wonneberger, G. (2001) 'Studie zur Struktur und Leitung der Sportbewegung in der SBZ/DDR (1945–1961) mit Skizzen, Diagrammen und Dokumenten (Study on the structure and management of the sport movement in the Soviet-occupied Zone/GDR (1945–61) with sketches, diagrams and documents)', in Buss, W. and Becker, C., *Der Sport in der SBZ und frühen DDR (Sport in the Soviet-occupied zone and early GDR)*, Schorndorf: Hofmann, 167–247, documents pp. 576–586.

Chapter 9

Sport for all

System and policy

Ilse Hartmann-Tews

Roots of the German sports system

The sports system in Germany is characterised by a strong voluntary sector that consists of numerous clubs and federations. The foundation of these so-called non-profit organisations can be traced back to the beginning of the nineteenth century. As described in Chapters 1 and 2 of this volume, gymnastics were popularised through the work of GutsMuths and Jahn and their colleagues. This initial form of gymnastics included throwing, jumping and 'formal' physical exercises, but was extended after the publication of a jointly written book, *Die deutsche Turnkunst* (*Manual of German Gymnastics*) by Jahn and Eiselen (1813), which aimed at improving physical health, shaping and strengthening the body, improving dexterity as well as courage, and stimulating intellectual and moral growth. The extended range of activities incorporated climbing, running and wrestling. Jahn and Eiselen invented a variety of apparatus such as parallel bars, and with the establishment of outdoor public gymnastics areas and gymnastics halls there was soon an increase in interest and involvement in physical exercise.

The second half of the nineteenth century saw the founding of numerous clubs in general and gymnastics clubs in particular. The character of these clubs was multi-functional. Their central aim was to provide the material basis for gymnastics and to enable interested people (predominantly young men) to do physical exercises. Apart from this main objective, gymnastics became a means to educate young men, and the clubs became a place to celebrate community and convey social responsibility, solidarity and patriotism, the latter having particular resonance in fostering the idea of German unity. The founding of these gymnastics clubs and social clubs in general can be interpreted as an effect of rapid economic and social change and a reaction to diminishing social integration, loss of traditional values, and social hardship stemming from the disruptive consequences of industrialisation and urbanisation. The creation of clubs, communities and societies offered opportunities to like-minded people to come together to share common interests, community and solidarity, and to discuss cultural and political issues. As political participation by the middle class was still illegal, the character of these clubs and societies had to be free of any political involvement.

As gymnastics clubs were often multi-functional clubs, with a variety of cultural and leisure activities offered in addition to gymnastics, they were closely monitored by state officials and were forbidden for a period of time. A critical stage of this development arose in 1863, when the Prussian government removed from schools parallel bars and other pieces of apparatus integral to Jahn's form of gymnastics in an attempt to placate government critics (Hartmann-Tews 1996).

At the beginning of the twentieth century, a new and different form of physical exercise increasingly influenced the development of gymnastics and clubs: English sport. Although the first rowing club modelled on the English example had already been founded in Hamburg in 1836, English sport started to spread throughout Germany towards the end of the nineteenth century, when commercial relations with England intensified. The Prussian government at that time was involved in a modernisation policy, and was impressed by progressive development of industrialised England. This in turn led to political support of the concept of sport, and merchants who imported and promoted English sports were encouraged to found sports clubs in the English style. At first these sports clubs were established in bigger cities only, offering golf, horse riding, rowing, sailing and fencing. Different from gymnastics clubs, their membership was exclusive, recruiting mainly aristocratic and upper-class people. Their ideals were based in competition and striving for excellence, whereas gymnastics was characterised as the form of exercise of the masses, closely connected with ideals of patriotism as well as middle-class values.

However, the central idea and reference point of gymnastics *and* of sport has been the communication of physical ability and improvement in performance. Irrespective of differences between German gymnastics and English sports, co-existence developed. Gymnastics was 'sportified' by setting up championships and offering new disciplines, and gymnastics clubs often changed their name and turned into *Turn- und Sportverein* (gymnastics and sports clubs). Competition, performance and improvement increasingly became the general orientation of action, and can be seen as the driving force in codifying sporting activity, establishing rules of competition, creating clubs and associations, and integrating these into national federations. At the end of the nineteenth and beginning of the twentieth centuries, gymnastics and sports began to take the clear shape of a social system, with its characteristic social and material structures. Voluntary organisations were the trailblazers of this complex socio-structural development.

Before 1933 the sports system was characterised by a multitude of organisations and independence from government. Clubs and federations were organised along political, religious and philosophical lines, so as to allow a huge variety of thousands of clubs to co-exist, but without obligation to cooperate. This structure changed radically along with the new National Socialist regime. Clubs and federations were brought into line and integrated into a united sports association (*Nationalsozialistischer Reichsbund für Leibesübungen*). Clubs and federations lost their democratic legitimacy as their personnel were no longer elected by the membership but delegated by the state; and a variety of sports organisations were banned (e.g. denominational organisations). Along with this policy of conformity, clubs became cells of political indoctrination, and were assigned the important function of improving the population's capacity for work and strength (Bernett 1992). In brief, between 1933 and 1945 the German sports system was subjected to fascist sports policies.

General features of the German sports system

Reaction to the experience of the instrumentalisation of sport later determined the establishment of a new sports system and influenced its policies. In accordance with the constitutional maxim that the interests and rights of the individual are to be exercised and fostered in free, autonomous organisations, German sports policies have since been based on the principle that independence and self-responsibility are fundamental features – thus sports organisations control their domains autonomously.

The federal structure of Germany, consisting of sixteen constituent *Länder*, is reflected by the structure, organisation and division of responsibilities in the field of sport (see Figure 9.1).

Government spheres of responsibility

The Federal Government, the *Länder* and local authorities provide the legal and material basis for the development of sport. They support the activities of sports organisations in those cases where the latter's staffing and financial resources are inadequate. All public promotion is in accordance with this principle of subsidiarity. The autonomy of sport with regard to governmental policy is well reflected by the fact that the constitution in Germany does not explicitly assign responsibility for sport to the federal government, and there is no federal Ministry of Sport authorised to control matters of sport and implement a general sports policy. Instead, both at federal and *Land* level, there are departments within ministries that are responsible for fulfilling a supportive action (Bundesminister des Innern 1998).

Within this division of labour at federal level, a central function is located within the Ministry of the Interior with responsibility for elite sport only. Additional responsibilities and competencies are located in the

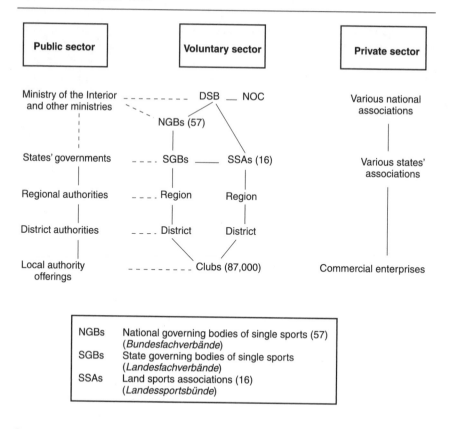

Figure 9.1 Structure of the sports system in Germany

ministries of Defence and International Affairs. Federal government support includes the building of sports facilities in those cases where nation-wide initiatives are concerned, especially for Federal Performance Centres or Olympic Training Centres, and funds for programmes intended to assist top-level sport in general and athletes in particular. This function is closely connected with the so-called voluntary sector of non-profit sports organisations.

In accordance with the constitution, most aspects of sport are the sole responsibility of the sixteen constituent *Länder* of Germany, as they hold supremacy in cultural affairs and sport is understood to be part of culture. At *Land* level, sport is most often located within the ministries of culture, but also with the ministry for schools and education, or urban development, depending on the policy of the respective *Land*. The *Länder*'s foremost tasks are to promote sports especially at school, which includes teacher training and education at universities. Although elite-level sport is supported in a number of ways, the promotion of recreational sports is prioritised.

Voluntary, public and private sector sports provision

The structural features of the sports system in Germany are characterised by a highly organised voluntary sector. The DSB is the umbrella organisation of approximately 87,000 voluntary associations at grassroots level, comprising a membership of 27 million people. It was founded in 1950, when there was still a strong mistrust of organised interests (a legacy of the Nazi era). The DSB's aim has been to coordinate all necessary joint measures for the promotion of sport and physical recreation, and to represent the mutual interests of its member organisations at all governmental levels and to the general public. The National Olympic Committee (NOC) for Germany is an independent and autonomous non-governmental sports organisation. It promotes the Olympic ideal and carries out the tasks entrusted by the IOC to NOCs.

Public sector sport comprises provisions that are predominantly financed by municipalities, churches, unions and charities and organised by their institutions of further education. They offer a variety of recreational sports and physical activities mainly intended to support health and well-being.

Private sector sport is characterised by a variety of commercial institutions. Research on the development of the commercial sector suggests that this sector is an amorphous category of a sparkling range of various contents and forms of supply, as well as of different types of organisation. There is a large number of small firms, usually single-activity enterprises, as well as multipurpose centres. Amongst the sports activities on offer, fitness-related activities are dominant (comprising up to two thirds of registered institutions) followed by squash and martial arts. The increase of these fitness and health-related commercial enterprises is remarkable: at the end of the 1980s there existed some 2,000 fitness centres, with a total membership of around 750,000 customers; ten years later, surveys suggest that there are currently about 6,000 fitness studios, with a total membership of 2.5 million (Velten 1995).

Structural and organisational features of the voluntary sector

The DSB represents five groups of members:

- Fifty-seven national governing bodies for single sports (*Bundes-, Spitzenverbände*) such as the German Football Federation, the National Federation of German Weightlifters, the German Rowing Federation or the German Athletics Federation
- Sixteen sports confederations of the constituent states (*Landessportbünde*), the Sports Confederation of North Rhine-Westphalia

being the largest and the Sports Confederation of Mecklenburg-Vorpommern being the smallest
- Twelve federations with particular tasks and responsibilities, including the Students' Sports Association (*Allgemeiner Deutscher Hochschulsportverband*), the German Police Sport Consortium (*Deutsches Polizeisportkonsortium*), and the German Industrial Sport Association (*Deutscher Betriebssportverband*)
- Six federations of science and education, including the German Association of Sport Science (*Deutsche Vereinigung für Sportwissenschaft*), the German Association of Physical Education Teachers (*Deutscher Sportlehrerverband*) and the Sports Commission of the Union of Education and Science (*Gewerkschaft Erziehung und Wissenschaft-Sportkommission*)
- Two promoting federations, the German Olympic Society (*Deutsche Olympische Gesellschaft*), and the Foundation for Safety in Sport (*Stiftung Sicherheit im Sport*)

In contrast to the sports structures extant at the end of the nineteenth century, the DSB represents a unitary sports movement, regardless of social, professional or religious affiliation. It claims to represent sport in general – encompassing competitive sports and 'sport for all'. All members are independent as far as their organisation, finance and activities are concerned and the DSB has no right of interference in these matters. However, the DSB represents their interests as regards sports development in general, and plays a lobbying role at national and regional (European) level. In doing so, the DSB is bound to maintain a neutral stance in party politics. Because of its various functions and responsibilities, the DSB has established different departments that are run by volunteers and assisted by paid staff. These departments are:

- Top-level sport
- Sport for all
- Youth sport
- Women and sport
- Finance, law and taxes
- Staff development and training
- Environment and playing fields

(DSB 1999)

The national governing bodies represent and organise the activities of their respective sports and have subdivisions at *Land* level (governing bodies of the *Länder*) and at regional and district levels. They are responsible for the coaching and care of their top-level athletes, organising championships and selecting teams for participation in international competitions.

To pursue these tasks, they have federal training centres (*Bundesleis-tungszentren*) at their disposal as well as federal coaches (*Bundestrainer*) employed by the DSB. The five biggest governing bodies of the DSB are those for football (6.3 million members), gymnastics (4.8 million), tennis (2.1 million), rifle shooting (1.6 million) and track-and-field (0.8 million). Each of the sixteen *Länder* has established a sports confederation which represents the interests of all clubs at *Land* level. Their main characteristic is that they represent gymnastics and sports clubs beyond the interests of individual disciplines, and therefore serve different purposes as the governing bodies of sport. Their activities in the area of top-level sport and the development of mass sport are multifarious. They have responsibilities similar to those of the DSB, but only with regard to their respective *Land*: they represent the interests of the sports clubs at *Land* level and promote recreational, competitive and elite sport. As the *Länder* are relatively autonomous, sports development varies between them, as well as do the sports policies of the respective sports confederations. Compared with population figures, the largest percentage of sport practitioners is recorded in the former West German *Länder* (e.g. Saarland, 40 per cent, and Rhineland-Palatinate, 36 per cent), whereas the new eastern *Länder* still have fewer sports practitioners (e.g. Brandenburg and Thuringia, 12 per cent, and Saxony-Anhalt, 11 per cent).

At grassroots level, 87,000 gymnastics and sports clubs provide the material and social resources for participation in sports. The majority of sports clubs are small in size. Two thirds of all clubs have less than 300 members, and one third have less than 100. Only 6 per cent of all clubs have a membership of more than 1,000 people. Although these large clubs are in a minority, their membership amounts to 30 per cent of total membership of the DSB (Heinemann and Schubert 1994). Surveys among sports clubs indicate that they offer various forms of physical exercise and 240 different sports, but at the same time data suggest that most of the clubs offer one sport only, and 10 per cent provide more than four sports. Those sports and kinds of physical exercise most often offered in sports clubs all over Germany, irrespective of their size, are gymnastics/physical exercise/dance, soccer, table tennis, tennis, shooting and volleyball (Heinemann 1996).

The voluntary sector of sport is financed from various sources. These comprise:

- Subscriptions and donations from members (at club, federation and confederation level)
- Public subsidies that are granted at all administrative levels
- Proceeds of the national lottery (*Glücksspirale*) of which 17.5 per cent is donated to the sports bodies

- Indirect financial support by the state via tax relief and building programmes
- Sponsorship and catering trade profits at club level

At club-level membership, fees are the most import source of revenue and make up to 55 per cent of total income. Commercial income, i.e. catering and trade profits, amount to 25 per cent; subsidies and grants amount to about 20 per cent (Heinemann and Schubert 1994). The data do not take into account indirect state subsidies that derive from recognition of the charitable status of all clubs affiliated to the DSB. This recognition allows for tax relief for sports clubs, i.e. they pay no taxes and moreover, donors are entitled to claim income tax relief for their donation. In addition, this includes low, or even no charges for the use of public sports facilities. Generally speaking the German sports associations are dependent on the support of the federal and *Land* governments.

Sport for all policy

Competition, performance and improvement are traditional values and orientations of the sports system in general and sports clubs in particular. These values and ideals have been the central reference points for action of the German sports system. One implication of this value system is a limited inclusivity, as these ideals have particularly attracted young, male, middle-class people. This is well reflected in DSB membership figures, which indicate for the 1950s a male proportion of membership of 90 per cent and an approximate 70 per cent dominance of young people (see Table 9.1 below).

In spite of this tradition, the DSB adopted an active 'sport for all' policy right from the beginning in the mid-1950s. A central driving force for this strategy can be identified in the fact that after World War II, organised sport in Germany had to regain recognition and acceptance. The former ideal of 'train the fittest', which prepared young males for military service, could no longer be the frame of reference. Hence the foundation of the DSB was celebrated as a new beginning with new organisational structures, which in turn became a breeding ground for the development of 'sport for all' initiatives. The challenge was to open clubs for all sections of the population, to introduce people to all forms of physical recreation, and to convince the public of the benefits of physical activities.

The two pillars of organised sport, the national governing bodies and the sports confederations at *Land* level, represent a division of labour: the governing bodies, responsible for their respective sports, concentrate on competitive and elite sport, whereas the sports confederations, representing the interests of the clubs beyond their activities, devote more attention to the promotion of recreational physical activities for all. They have often been labelled as a 'steering machine' in promoting 'sport for all', i.e. in providing courses and facilities for recreational physical activities and sport for everyone.

In 1959 the DSB began a campaign to promote the idea of recreational sport. Its motto, 'second way' (to sport) was chosen to indicate that beside the traditional understanding of sport, i.e. competitive and elite sport, new models and methods were to be developed in order to broaden the definition of sport by encompassing recreational sport for all (*Freizeitsport*). This policy was designed to attract different 'audiences': it had to convince the political system that sport and physical activities could support the public welfare, and it had to convince the sports clubs and associations that the inclusion of many more people with a variety of skills and motivations could be an opportunity to regain social recognition and credit. Thus the strategy was manifold.

The heart of the policy was the elaboration of the central positive effects of participation. These are, first, educational values and the contribution of sport to a person's moral development; second, positive health-related effects such as the improvement of health and the consequent financial savings to be made within health budgets; and third, benefits for social integration with respect to the reduction of youth delinquency. Another central aspect of the strategy was to lobby at government level and to convince federal politicians and civil servants of the relevance and positive effects of physical recreation and sport for the social system as a whole. The aim of this lobbying strategy was to gain direct and indirect financial support for the activities of the clubs and to initiate building programmes.

The structural base for this policy was provided by a professionalisation of internal structures. In the mid-1970s, the DSB established specialised committees and working groups for 'sport for all' at national level and made it clear that it would expect its member federations to restructure themselves in the same way. Gradually, these working units became 'think tanks' in a double sense. On the one hand they developed an enormous range of public campaigns to attract people who had not (regularly) taken part in sport (adults, women, older people) and convince them of the benefits of taking part in physical activities; on the other hand, they developed tools for their clubs that would enable them to cater for a broader range of physical activities and to prepare for a new clientele. With this manifold strategy, the DSB not only attracted millions of people, especially adults, but also gained state support on the basis of being recognised as a relevant part of society, and its clubs as proactive organisations for the public welfare. This support includes a variety of federal building programmes for playing fields, and a range of tax relief packages for its member organisations on the basis of undertaking public tasks. These positive effects naturally helped the DSB to convince clubs to foster 'sport for all' and to implement leisure sport activities and physical recreation right alongside the traditional structures of performance and elite sport.

Structural changes

The success story of the DSB is based mainly on the fact that it succeeded in attracting a growing number of members (see Table 9.1). Membership grew from 3.2 million in 1950 to 10.1 million in 1970 and 26.8 million in 2000. DSB statistics generally include figures referring to the percentage of total population included in sport, indicating that in 1950, 6.7 per cent of the total population was in membership of a sports club, and in 2000, 28.5 per cent. Some critics contended that these figures are exaggerated, as they are calculated on the basis of membership data without reflecting multi-membership and the real number of members (individuals). Young people in particular tend to join several clubs and are registered several times, thus inflating the DSB statistics.

During the 1960s and 1970s, membership increased to a greater extent than the number of clubs. Clubs attracted more people than in previous years, and the average size of a sports club increased from 160 members in 1950 to 320 members in 1980. In the late 1980s and 1990s, we see a different trend. Increase in membership slowed down, but the increase in the number of clubs was significant. There were two reasons for this trend. First, the re-unification of the two Germanies brought together two different systems of sport – the former GDR was characterised by a state controlled sports system which strongly supported elite sport and had only a few, small, voluntary sports clubs. Second, during the past decade there has been a wave of new small-scale clubs in western Germany. Some of these clubs were brand new and usually devoted to fun- and recreational sports; some were established as semi-autonomous branches of existing, larger clubs.

Table 9.1   Increase of membership, clubs and proportion of females within the German Sports Federation 1950–2000

Year	Membership	Proportion of population (%)	Proportion of women (%)	Clubs
1950	3,204,005	6.7	10.1	19,874
1960	5,267,627	9.5	21.0	29,486
1970	10,121,546	16.7	26.8	39,201
1980	16,924,027	27.6	34.1	53,451
1990	23,777,378	30.7	36.5	67,984
2000	26,815,717	28.5	38.6	87,052

Source: DSB 1990; 2000

Membership of sports clubs has always been characterised by social stratification. Sports clubs have tended to attract the young rather than the elderly; boys and young men rather than girls and women; and the middle and upper classes rather than the working class. But this typical feature of the traditional sports club has been changing constantly over the past fifty years. Growing numbers of adults and senior citizens, as well as girls and women, are joining sports clubs. The number of female members has increased constantly in this period. The proportion of female members has risen from 10.1 per cent in 1950 to almost 39 per cent in 2000. This constant increase is mainly related to the broader variety of sports and physical activities on offer, as women are more attracted by leisure and recreational sport than by competitive sports.

Children and adolescents have always formed bulk of sports club membership. However, from the 1970s onwards, there has been a significant change in the age stratification of the membership, due to an influx of very young children (under six years of age) on the one hand, and adults on the other hand. This development has changed the structure of membership significantly. Whereas the proportion of children and adolescents was 52 per cent in the 1970s, this fell to 34 per cent at the beginning of the 1990s (Hartmann-Tews 1996). This development is partly due to demographic changes, as the proportion of senior citizens is constantly growing, but it is also partly due to the sport for all policy of the voluntary sector. Nevertheless, young people, children and adolescents remain the most sport-active age group of the total population.

Concluding comment

Germany's sports system is characterised by the marked autonomy of the so-called voluntary, non-profit sector of organised sport. The DSB has increasingly managed to empower its associations to provide a wide range of sports and physical activities, and subsequently gained recognition as an important agency for public welfare. Its active role in fostering 'sport for all' is an important feature of the German sports system, and has been continually strengthened by annual sporting events in major cities, and by various successful campaigns to attract more people to participate in sport and volunteer work.

References

Bernett, H. (1992) 'Sport and National Socialism: a focus on contemporary history', in Haag, H., Grupe, O. and Kirsch, A. (eds) *Sport Science in Germany*, Berlin: Springer, 439–61.

Bundesminister des Innern (ed.) (1998) *Neunter Sportbericht der Bundesregierung 1994–1997*, Bonn: BMI.

Deutscher Sportbund (1990) *Deutscher Sportbund 1986–90. Bericht des Präsidiums*, Frankfurt am Main: Limpert.

——(1999) *Jahrbuch des Sports 1999*, Frankfurt am Main: Limpert.

——(2000) *Bestandserhebung 2000*, Frankfurt am Main: DSB.

Hartmann-Tews, I. (1996) *Sport für alle!? Strukturwandel europäischer Sportsysteme im Vergleich*, Schorndorf: Hofmann.

Heinemann, K. (1996) 'Sports policy in Germany', in Chalip, L., Johnson, A. and Stachura, L. (eds) *National Sports Policies*, London: Greenwood Press, 161–86.

Heinemann, K. and Schubert, M. (1994) *Der Sportverein: Ergebnisse einer repräsentativen Untersuchung*, Schorndorf: Hofmann.

Jahn, F. L. and Eiselen, E. (1996) [1813] *Die deutsche Turnkunst zur Einrichtung der Turnplätze*, Zurich: Kohler.

Velten, C. (1995) 'Strukturanalyse des kommerziellen Sportangebots in der Stadt Köln', unpublished diploma thesis, 2 vols, Cologne: DSHS.

Chapter 10

Sport for women

Gertrud Pfister

German women in sport and physical education: from exclusion to integration

The Middle Ages and early modern times

Scholars have only recently begun to write the history of women, and in order to gather evidence of ancient and medieval women's sports, it is often necessary to glean the historical field after conventional historians have finished their harvest. Hence the picture of pre-industrial body and movement culture is far from complete. Nevertheless, it is clear that in the various periods of German history, as in many other cultures and societies, numerous and various physical activities existed, ranging from the tournaments of knights to the folk games of farmers and the archery and fencing of the inhabitants of towns and cities. However, physical activities were restricted to certain social groups, and they had specific functions and meanings, such as preparation for war, religious or mystical aims, or as part of a festival.

In the Middle Ages and in early modern times, German women appear to have played a marginal role in society as well as in physical activity and sport. Nonetheless, and despite the predominance of male power, some women did achieve privileged status at court or in a convent; indeed, some of these privileged women rode horseback and enjoyed the sport of falconry or simple ball games. Aristocratic women also played an ancillary role at the medieval tournaments that were an important aspect of the life of a medieval knight. Tournaments served not only to harden the warrior's body and prepare it for battle, but also were vivid symbolic demonstrations of social order. It was important that women be present to admire and encourage the combatants and to acknowledge the right of men to rule.

In medieval towns, the most popular sports (archery, wrestling and fencing) were also related to the exigencies of warfare. This generally meant the exclusion of women from the archery guilds that were a prominent part of urban life. Archery contests throughout Europe were important social events that would have been painfully incomplete had admiring female spectators been excluded. Among the peasantry, women were so essential in the struggle for mere survival that it seemed only natural for them to share in many of the sporting activities of their fathers, husbands and sons. They appear in paintings not only as dancers but also as participants in the widely popular (and wildly chaotic) game of folk football. In Germany, as in other European countries, girls and women ran races for smocks and similar prizes.

The eighteenth and nineteenth centuries

In Germany, the first systematic concept of physical education to be applied in schools was that of the Philanthropists. In accordance with the ideals of this more enlightened age, the pedagogues of the Philanthropist movement, among them Johann Friedrich GutsMuths, developed a concept which included physical education as a pre-condition for mental development and intellectual learning. The gymnastics of the Philanthropists aimed at the education of 'useful' citizens, but they were focused on boys and excluded girls and women. It was only in the second edition of his seminal text *Gymnastics for Youth* (1804) that GutsMuths even mentioned girls' education, when he categorically stated that there should be 'No formal gymnastics for girls' (Pfister 1998a: 68).

At the beginning of the nineteenth century, 'Turnvater' Friedrich Ludwig Jahn developed German *Turnen* as an expression of patriotism and a means to overcome the feudal order that had divided Germany into a patchwork of different states. Jahn's movement was also aimed at the expulsion of the French, whom Napoleon, in the wake of the French revolution, had led to a series of military victories over the divided German states. Given his patriotic goals and emphasis on military preparedness, Jahn saw no reason to include women in his programme. The exclusion of women from the ranks of the *Turner* seemed so self-evident that Jahn and his followers never bothered to explain or justify it (Pfister 1996).

In the course of the nineteenth century, however, there was increasing concern about the health of the 'weaker sex' and a lively debate ensued over the physical education of girls. Among the first to champion physical exercise for girls were Phokion Heinrich Clias (1782–1854) and Johann Adolf Ludwig Werner (1794–1866). Their work found adherents because, among other reasons, they emphasised exercises for health, beauty and grace, which reproduced the feminine ideals of the time. After the 1830s, some physical educators offered gymnastic courses for girls which promised to prevent or heal the typical illnesses of the female sex, which included spinal curvatures and anaemia. It is unlikely, however, that many girls benefited from these opportunities, and most who did came from affluent middle-class homes.

By 1850 a number of gymnastic clubs (*Turnvereine*) were organising physical education for girls. Physical education for girls in schools was only gradually introduced (mostly in private schools) in the latter half of the nineteenth century. It did not become a compulsory subject for girls until the end of the nineteenth century, initially in higher education (in Prussia in 1894), and only after the turn of the century in elementary schools. The activities were restricted to freestanding exercises (callisthenics), drills, dancing and simple movements on apparatus such as hanging from a bar. To preserve health and decorum, girls were not allowed to perform exercises that required strength or endurance or which forced them to spread their legs or to lift them above the waist. The strict rule was: heads up, legs down and closed (Pfister and Langenfeld 1980). In spite of the moderate level of exercise, fierce resistance based on moral, medical, and aesthetic arguments emerged against the physical education of females. The fear of endangering the health of girls and reducing their capacity to later give birth to strong children, as well as the fear of changing the female body shape and masculinising women, were important obstacles to the promotion of girls' physical activities (Pfister 1990).

The upturn in women's Turnen and sport

Women's roles changed rapidly with the industrialisation and modernisation of society at the end of the nineteenth century. Universities began to open their doors to female students and educated women began to enter the professions. In Prussia, for example, women were allowed to enter universities in 1908 (Frevert 1986). These social changes influenced discussions about the physical education of girls and the physical activities of grown women. In particular, the effects of industrialisation and urbanisation on girls' and women's health on the one hand, and rising nationalism on the other, seemed to require that something be done. Thus the way was open for the integration of physical education in girls' schools and for the participation of grown-up women in physical activities. After the 1880s, when increasing numbers of women participated in *Turnen*, women's sections of men's gymnastics clubs were formed and independent gymnastics and sports clubs for women were founded.

In the twentieth century, modern sport began its triumphal march in Germany. Courageous women participated in many of the new types of English sports, but not without facing resistance. The concern for preserving health, beauty and morals set limits for the sports activities of women, who were especially restricted by their clothing. Shortly before the First World War, knee-length trousers and sweaters replaced corsets, long skirts and narrow blouses. At that time, women were accepted only in 'feminine' or upper-class types of sport like swimming (segregated from men) or tennis. Participation in tournaments or competitive and aggressive sports like track and field and soccer (association football) were taboo for the 'weaker sex' (Pfister and Langenfeld 1980).

Whereas the economic costs of tennis, golf and rowing tended to restrict participation in these sports to the affluent, there was also a movement for workers' sports which had two major aims: first, to support socialist politics; and second, to give working people the chance to take part in physical activities and in healthy recreation. The German Federation for Workers' Sports, founded in 1893, attracted a number of female members who had full membership rights. Using the motto 'make yourself free', the proletarian gymnasts and athletes fought for the liberation of the body and for the liberation of women. However, the hard lives of proletarian women kept the number of female members in the proletarian sports movement rather low.

World War I and its aftermath brought profound political, economic and social change, including changes in gender relationships. In 1919 women won the right to vote and hold office, but they were still regarded as 'the second sex'. A woman who chose to embark on a professional career suffered from various discriminatory practices, such as having to acknowledge her husband as head of the household if she chose domesticity. According to family law, it was the husband who made decisions on all major domestic issues; a woman had to have the approval of her husband if she wanted to go out to work. Nevertheless, conspicuous changes were occurring in the ideals of femininity and in the everyday lives of women. Among other things, fashion had freed women from many restrictions: there was more freedom of movement as ankle-length dresses and tight corsets were discarded; and a new, more athletic ideal of femininity was proclaimed with short hair, a tanned body, and narrow hips being thought to be fashionably 'modern'. However, these new freedoms had to be paid for by the pressure to be slim, with an internalisation of body ideals and a high amount of body control.

Although few people doubted that girls and women should be physically active for the sake of their health, their participation in highly competitive sports led to fierce controversy. The core debate was over the compatibility of competition and motherhood. The weightiest arguments against strenuous sports came from medical experts, especially gynaecologists, who inveighed against competition and against participation in 'manly' sports such as soccer. The danger was that a female might be 'masculinised'. Time and again, the 'Cassandras' of the medical profession complained about the female athlete's diminished fertility and her disinclination to bear children.

In spite of these barriers, increasing numbers of German women participated in sports contests, including those in track and field that had earlier been considered 'unwomanly'. In 1919 the German Sports Authority called upon its member clubs to create sections for female athletes, and in

1920 the first German championships for female athletes were organised in Dresden. But many sports, from ski jumping to soccer, remained taboo. With few exceptions, German sports organisations were sexually integrated, a feature which placed women under men's supervision, while the tendency in some other countries (e.g. France and Great Britain) was for women to form their own organisations. Towards the end of the 1920s, the mass media regularly began to celebrate the achievements of female athletes. Among the early idols was the German airplane pilot Elli Beinhorn, who made headlines not only with her round-the-world flights but also by her marriage to a famous racing driver. While the achievements of female track-and-field athletes continued to be met with a mixture of fascination and disgust, rhythmical gymnastics were gradually transformed into an almost entirely female domain.

In Germany, as well as throughout Europe, a variety of systems and schools propagated different types of gymnastics, some emphasising health and hygiene, some more intent on the aesthetics of human movement. Strongly criticising modern sports and their obsession with quantified achievement, the proponents of gymnastics were concerned principally with the quality of the movement experience, the form and shape of the body, and the harmonious development of the whole person. Common also was a tendency to cultural criticism; gymnastics were affirmed as a 'natural' contrast to the mad pace and artificiality of modern civilisation. Although the gymnastics movement portrayed a rather traditional image of womanhood, it appealed to many who believed that it offered an essentially feminine movement culture that was free from men's interference and control.

Women's sports and National Socialism

In National Socialist ideology, biological and racist ideas were fostered in order to restructure the gender order and to recast masculinity and femininity as the polar opposites they were thought to be in the nineteenth century. With varying degrees of success, ideologues sought to limit women, once again, to their wifely and maternal roles. The fecund female body and the hardened male body were icons of Hitler's 'racial hygiene'. Physical education was a central pillar in the structure of the Nazi state. It was supposed to prepare men for their pre-determined biological role as fighters, and women for theirs as mothers. In Nazi discourse and in the medical literature influenced by it, discussions of women's sport centred on two questions: what enhances and what diminishes a woman's reproductive function? By providing 'healthy' and 'appropriate' exercises, organisations like the *Bund Deutscher Mädel* (BDM – 'Federation of German Maidens') tried to institutionalise the goals of motherhood and the health of the community. However, the everyday practice in the BDM groups varied greatly, depending on the available sport facilities and the attitudes and competencies of the leaders, as well as on the interests of the girls. Although National Socialist ideology had originally been opposed to sports competition for women, Hitler realised the propaganda advantages that were sure to accompany demonstrations of physical superiority. Accordingly, his regime supported female athletes in a number of ways, and the 1936 Olympic Games in Berlin seemed to prove him right. Although the Games were staged to demonstrate to the point of absurdity the cult of masculinity, Germany fielded the most successful team of female athletes.

Developments after World War II

After the devastation and deprivations of World War II, the German population turned quickly to sport, in part because it represented a more attractive world than the ubiquitous ruins of the post-war environment. With the gradual return of ordinary life came a call for women to resume the domestic roles they had been obliged to abandon by the exigencies of war. The 1950s were a decade that emphasised traditional ideals of home and hearth. Despite this emphasis, women's sports became increasingly important within the context of the Cold War. Sport was used as a weapon in the political struggle, and the then German Democratic Republic in particular, and the Eastern Bloc countries in general, invested huge material and personal resources in the sporting success of their female athletes.

The astonishing success of East Germany's female athletes was the result of a number of inter-related factors: the centralised search for athletic talent which began with the systematic recruitment of children; scientific research designed to maximise performance; the concentration of financial resources on sport; the high prestige, social security and other material rewards (such as trips abroad) granted to successful athletes; and medical manipulation through drugs. This concentration on elite athletics came at the expense of recreational sports. Among other things, facilities available to ordinary citizens were few and of poor quality. Although propagandists proclaimed the contrary, women in the GDR were far less likely than those in West Germany to be involved in recreational sports.

In the West, the debate over femininity and sports was resumed. When athletes from the so-called 'socialist bloc' introduced new acrobatic movements into women's gymnastics, the German Gymnastics Federation (*Deutscher Turnerbund*) found the contortions ugly and unfeminine and withdrew from international competition for a number of years. In other sports, women had to face similar resistance and restrictions: for example, women were discouraged from playing soccer, which was still deemed unfeminine as late as 1955. The German Football Association decided then that clubs should not be allowed to let women's teams use the football pitches. It was not until the 1970s that the Association reversed its decision and began to accept and later support women's soccer.

Women and sport in East Germany

A scientific analysis of women's sport in the GDR has yet to be undertaken. Here it is intended to provide further support for previously mentioned relationships between sport and politics and so place them in a wider context.

Various gender order studies in the GDR have concluded that the ideals and roles of GDR women and men have developed in a specific way, particularly in broader societal values, norms and interpretation patterns, and that in many respects these have differed from commonly held perceptions of images, characterisations and representations in the West. However, even in the GDR, a hierarchy of the sexes can be seen. The reasons for the typical arrangement of the sexes in the GDR can be found in the everyday life-shaping image of the duality of the sexes, which is symbolically conveyed and is sex-specific in the division of labour. Furthermore, in the GDR, despite the high employment rate amongst women, the truism held that the higher the position, the lower the proportion of women. Additionally, work production and reproduction of society only worked because women took on unpaid housework and above all were responsible for raising children, which could only be partly integrated into society. Moreover, at an individual level, and as clearly seen in association with homosexuality, a 'doing gender' orientated to the duality of the sexes was in place (Diemer 1994).

The process of restructuring society in the GDR brought a redefinition not only of sex roles but also of sport. In the light of discussions on the system and the Cold War, sport was given central, political tasks: principally to oppose the single representative claim of the Federal Republic and to support GDR integration into international committees; to prepare the way for state recognition of the GDR in the sporting world; and to strengthen its influence on sport- and world politics. Key personnel, institutions and organisations in sport, as well as practitioners linked with sport, were directed to these tasks and subjected to political stipulation. Responsibility and administration in sport were anchored in the Socialist Unity Party and state committees, as well as in the umbrella organisation of sport, the German Federation for Gymnastics and Sport.

The central direction and administrative control of sport contributed considerably to the successes of elite sport. The sports system was differentiated, but at the same time was tied into the total system as a consequence of anti-differentiation processes and central direction and control. As shown in earlier chapters of this volume, the GDR had a centrally organised sports system, in which the development and realisation of numerous strategies to increase performance and its promotion, the search for talent up to medical manipulation, and concentration of measures and means, were combined to guarantee GDR sporting success.

In accordance with the expectation that the equality of the sexes in GDR society be achieved, the view was held that women in the world of sport had the same chances as men. The sporting successes of female athletes seem to prove this. Above all it was the top performances achieved by women, 'the diplomats in tracksuits', that brought to the GDR the prestige of a world-class sports nation and world-wide recognition in areas outside of sport. For example, women won almost 40 per cent of all GDR world and European championship titles from 1953 to 1982. Furthermore, the great boom in GDR women's sport can be seen in women's participation and successes in the Olympic Games. The increase in numbers of participants in the Olympic Games between 1956 and 1988 reveals that the number of female athletes performing for the GDR was above average for all women participants, and proportionately higher than that of West German female athletes. The number of medals won in the Summer Olympic Games clearly shows that GDR female athletes were far more successful than their male counterparts. In 1980, the proportion of women in the GDR team was, for example, 36 per cent, and yet they won 47 per cent of medals won by GDR athletes (Pfister 2001b). The reasons for the 'Miss GDR miracle' lie on the one hand in the previously mentioned system of sport and its associated measures like talent identification, and on the other hand, the targeted promotion of female athletes without regard for medical and aesthetic dogma. Additionally, there was, from end of the 1960s, the systematic use of drugs, which were more effective at performance-enhancement amongst women than amongst men (Spitzer 1998).

The successes in elite sport in the GDR came at the expense of recreational and leisure sports. Care needs to be taken in interpretation of general population participation data in the GDR. Strikingly, in the 1980s only some 20 per cent of the population participated in organised sport. By way of comparison, in the Federal Republic about 34 per cent were members of the DSB (Baur et al. 1997). In the GDR, women were substantially less interested than men in sport, accounting for around 27 per cent of membership of DTSB organisations. According to an investigation in the GDR, 56 per cent of the male population, but only 37 per cent of females, engaged in sport at the beginning of the 1980s. With increasing age, the proportion of girls and women participating in sport steadily decreased, but already amongst young people sex-stereotypical differences in sporting engagement were demonstrated. Bierstedt (1981) found that amongst young people, it appeared that more boys than girls took part in sporting activity during leisure time, and that a growing proportion of women amongst the sports-active decreased with rising intensity of engagement as well as increasing orientation to performance. Other investigations in the GDR showed that men preferred types of sport that are competitively orientated, entail a degree of risk, and require strength and endurance. In contrast, aesthetic and less physically demanding types of sport dominated women's preferences.

Preferences and sports activities correlate highly, as seen in membership figures for different DTSB sports. Women dominated in gymnastics clubs; men in combat, strength and team sport, but above all in football (Wonneberger 1983). The interests of women and men also differed in informal recreational sport. For example, many more men than women were engaged in running activities. In contrast, women exclusively were enthusiastically interested in pop-gymnastics, an imitation of aerobics popular in the West which was offered in groups organised by the GDR Federation for Women. Various ways of increasing participation in sport in the GDR were tried. Thus, for example, a competition for families (multi-discipline and long-distance events) was organised from 1967 on by the women's magazine *For You*, which attracted more than 36,000 families in 1976.

All in all it was aimed to integrate informal sports activities into an organisation. Sport societies attached to firms, educational institutions or to residential areas assisted in working to achieve this. This link, as well as the integration into the DTSB and its organisations, provided opportunities for state influence and control, but also created opportunities for the formation of programmes and activities through the 'collective' (Baur *et al.* 1997). A big advantage was the resources, which were made available by the factories. Case studies show that factory sports societies were organised similarly to clubs. This also signifies that they were not particularly more appealing to women than traditional clubs. The types of sport practised and the extra-sporting 'trappings' were frequently determined by men's preferences and their 'time-budget'. Hence the motivational nature of what sports activities were on offer for women was minimal.

Sports provision in residential areas (in the 1980s, estates of pre-fabricated buildings) was, as the DTSB frequently lamented, scarcely in demand. Why women were not motivated by such provision and why they were not attracted to sport is puzzling, the more so as the neighbourhood provision met with repeated requests to organise sport for women on an almost daily routine basis. It must be assumed (and in part gathered from time-budget investigations) that the threefold burden of work, family and social activity cost so much time and energy that engagement in sport was hardly possible. Additionally, there are numerous findings about lack of, and inadequate, sports facilities; there were too few sports halls and swimming pools were a scarce commodity (Teichler 1997). A survey carried out in 1977, in which 2,500 men and women participated, reveals that even in the area of recreational sport, traditional value orientations and sex-role stereotypes were evident (Bierstedt and Gras 1983). Women were disposed to be less motivated by performance-orientated kinds of sport than men, for whom the need to improve in their activity as well as the desire for comradeship and social gathering were in the foreground. Striving for a good figure was a considerably more frequently expressed motive for sports activity amongst women than men.

In spite of the different societal systems of respective specific sports structures and the different roles of the sexes, women demonstrated common interests in sport and their activities in the GDR and the then FRG. This common feature points to similar constructions of sex and sex order. The correlations between sport and sex are discussed in the next section of the chapter.

Women's sport today

Sporting activity among girls and women – attitudes and activities

Nowadays sport no longer seems to have any shortage of legitimation in Germany. There is a current trend towards a 'return' of the body, which is, however, accompanied by a simultaneous detachment from it. The liberation of the body had to be paid for with a simultaneous internalisation of pressures and with a growing need for disciplining the body. Fitness and health, slimming and 'sportiness' are the new fashion catchwords, the new ideals of the German middle classes. Today, sport, or rather here physical culture, which promises these ideals and also profits, among other things, from human striving after authentic experience and after excitement and diversion, plays a significant role in the somatic culture not only of boys and men, but also of girls and women.

In a number of surveys, the majority of the population of the Federal Republic of Germany (men and women) have been found to consider sport to be of great importance in society. This means that sporting activities are not only accepted but are also quite obviously viewed positively. 'Sportiveness', 'the hallmark of a whole life-style' (Kaschuba 1989: 163) is the present trend in everyday German culture. In addition there is, as a result of several empirical studies, a growing concern about the health, fitness and motor competencies of German children. The magic antidotal formula against obesity, posture faults, clumsiness and many other problems seems to be physical education and sport. A positive attitude to sport, however, does not necessarily go hand-in-hand with the active practice of a sport.

The 'leisure tastes' of the German population have changed significantly in the course of developments in society since World War II. There are crucial differences in the leisure profiles of the sexes: women favour communication- and relaxation-based leisure-time activities such as reading, calling friends and body care, whereas men are performance-active in their leisure-time, and are frequently manually active or they attend sports meetings. The most recent Shell Youth Study (2000) found that the everyday life of boys and girls differs. Technology, politics, computer games and the internet, sport and club life are male domains and social activities; looking after others, shopping, going for a walk and conservation are female domains.

In surveys, physical activities are not preferably rated in the list of leisure-time activities. Watching television, listening to music and reading the newspaper are the most frequently mentioned activities of both sexes. Doing sport ranks 28th for men and 30th for women. Only 12 per cent of women and 17 per cent of men interviewed by the BAT Leisure Research Institute indicated that they had participated in sport in the week before the interview. Among young people, the differences between the sexes was even greater: 38 per cent of 14–24 year old males, but only 21 per cent of females, listed sports activities among their leisure-time activities. In a representative poll carried out some years ago of the population (over fourteen years of age) in the Federal Republic of Germany, including West Berlin, Opaschowski (1987) identified only 45 per cent of those polled as being (at least minimally) active in sport (40 per cent of the women and 51 per cent of the men). In the interpretation of the data presented by Opaschowski, however, it is debatable whether those who 'occasionally practise a sport' (i.e. less than once a week on average) should be included among sports activists or sports abstainers. Whatever the case may be, the majority of women who are active in sport belong to this category. All in all, the survey brought to light quite patent dissimilarities between the sexes. Surveys carried out by the EMNID-Institute (1992) and by the Institut für Demoskopie, Allensbach (1991) showed the same trends. The research of the Allensbach-Institute included the five new federal *Länder* of the former GDR. The number of people engaged in sport was found to be lower than in western Germany. Women were even more under-represented than in the former West Germany. A representative survey in Berlin in 1994 showed again that 54 per cent of the male and 43 per cent of the female population was active in sport at least once a week (Senatsverwaltung 1995). In the BAT Leisure Research Institute survey carried out in 1994, many more women than men admitted to being 'sport killjoys': 46 per cent of female interviewees but only 22 per cent male interviewees indicated lack of interest as well as no participation in sport (Opaschowski 1995).

Apart from these surveys, membership lists of sports clubs also provide information on the participation of the population in organised sport, although both a high proportion of passive members and duplicated membership must be taken into account. Nevertheless, a distinct trend is observable. Since its foundation, the DSB has experienced a steady general increase as well as in the number of women members, which rose from 324,000 in 1950 to 7.5 million in 1989. The percentage of women DSB members rose from 10 per cent in 1950, to 28 per cent in 1970 and 37 per cent in 1989. According to DSB statistics, in 1990 roughly 19 per cent of the female population (over fifteen years of age) were members of sports clubs. After re-unification, the lower figures for the new federal *Länder* appeared: in 1990 the proportion of club members in the whole population dipped to 30 per cent; the proportion of women among club members and also among the sports-active in total was and is less in the new *Länder* than in the former FRG. In 2000, according to DSB statistics, more than 14 million boys and men and more than 9 million girls and women were members of the DSB, indicating that the proportion of female members was 39 per cent (DSB 2000).

The figures presented by Opaschowski and others clearly demonstrate that the majority of women active in sport, just like a great number of males active in sport, carry on their hobby outside the confines of a sports club. Whereas in most sports clubs they are still a minority, women make up the majority (in some cases up to 80 per cent) in sports courses offered by various other agencies, for example local authorities and institutes of further education. Women have also been discovered as consumers by commercial organisers as well as by the sport and leisure industries. Today, women are at home even in those strongholds of masculinity, the body-building institutes. Currently, the percentage of women members of such institutes lies between 50 and 60 per cent. A University of Hamburg empirical study showed that the fitness centres in this city had between 60.8 per cent and 39.2 per cent male users. The Veltins Sports Study (2000), which only registered physically active people between 16 and 39 years of age, indicated that about half of those interviewed played sport in a club and that 56 per cent of the club members were men. In contrast, 61 per cent of the clients of commercial leisure clubs were female. In the Bielefeld Youth Study (Kurz *et al.* 1996), a survey in North Rhine-Westphalia focused on club membership and physical activities outside of school and club. At interview, 51 per cent of the boys and 31 per cent of the girls (school years 3–13) were members of a club. A narrow definition of sport (according to the sample's interpretation) curtailed participation to 27 per cent boys and 17 per cent girls; a broad definition extended participation to 55 per cent boys and 47 per cent girls. It was concluded that there were significant differences between the sexes, especially in sports club settings, but also that the less 'sportive' sports are, the less sex-specific differences occur in sports engagement. Both the results of surveys as well as statistical data clearly show that even today fewer women than men are active in sport and that, therefore, there is a large group of girls and women that is still to be won over to sport.

Frequency and intensity of sporting activity

Membership of a sports club or the mere assertion that a person practises a sport is no indication of the frequency and intensity of sporting activity.

Among other things, one can infer from Opaschowski's (1987) survey that the percentage of women decreases with an increasing commitment to sport. The more hours per week that are invested in a sport, the smaller will be the number of women who take part. Significant differences between the sexes are also to be found in competitive sports: three times as many men take part in competitions as women (Opaschowski 1987; 1995). Differences between the sexes are also to be found in the frequency of visits to fitness studios: whilst 9 per cent of men and 18 per cent of women visit only once per week, and 58 per cent of men and 70 per cent of women visit 2–3 times per week, the group of so-called 'heavy users' (4–7 times per week) is clearly dominated by the men with 33 per cent, in comparison with women at 11 per cent (http://www.dssv.de/eckdaten. html).

Types of sport practised

From DSB statistics, it can be clearly seen which types of sport male and female members of sports clubs favour. The percentage of women in the different sports associations still varies considerably. While women are scarcely (or not at all) represented in certain types of combat sport, women's membership of the German Gymnastics Federation, which has nearly 3.5 million female and 1.5 million male members (DSB Bestandserhebung 2000), is nearly 70 per cent. Almost 40 per cent of all women members of the DSB belong to this federation. Women also make up the larger part of the horse riding, sport acrobatics, dancing and roller-skating associations. Thus it seems that women prefer an orientation towards 'sport for all', especially those activities which combine both aesthetic and recreational functions. Even today, the largest German sport federation, the German Football Federation, has less than 15 per cent female members, and many of its members do not play football but participate in 'sport for all' activities.

The above-mentioned University of Hamburg study also showed that male and female users of fitness studios prefer gendered physical activities: 12 per cent of the interviewed men and 29 per cent of the women participated in aerobics; 14 per cent of the men, but only 3 per cent of the women in combat sports; 22 per cent of the men and 42 per cent of the women in gymnastics; and 43 per cent of the men and 28 per cent of the women in fitness classes (http://www.dssv.de/eckdaten.html).

If all types of physical activities, including those practised privately and not as a member of a club, are taken into account, swimming and cycling are predominant among women (and to a little lesser extent among men). Whereas rhythmical gymnastics and aerobics are typical female activities, jogging and especially football still remain the domains of men (Opaschowski 1987; 1995; see also VeltinsGmbH/DSB 2000). It would be interesting to know whether 'swimming' is used synonymously for bathing, and to what extent cycling can be regarded as a sporting activity.

At present a much observed phenomenon in Germany is the growth (sometimes also decline) of so-called 'trendy' types of sport, though it should not be overlooked that these are the activities of a small minority of the population. Some of the new movement activities, like roller-skating, are attractive to both sexes and for many age groups; numerous other activities, from 'street ball' to skateboarding, are clearly located in a youth scene orientated to male values (Schwier 1998).

In summarising the development of women's sport in Germany, the following conclusions can be drawn. Recently, there has been a considerable change in women's engagement with sport. At the turn of the twenty-first century, women are participating in sports once thought to be exclusively male: marathon running, soccer and rugby, water polo, even boxing and weightlifting. However, it has to be borne in mind that it is a relatively small number of young women who are attracted by these 'unfeminine' types of sport. Whereas women are increasingly being integrated in the world of sport, which was formerly defined as a male domain, men, on the contrary, do not appear to be interested in 'female' physical activities.

When asked what types of sport they would wish to take up, women most frequently name tennis, horse-riding and sailing, whereas men choose tennis, sailing, surfing and football, and they also favour more adventurous types of sport such as sky-gliding, parachute-jumping and hang-gliding. According to Opaschowski (1987; 1995), the fitness and well-being movement is the female perspective; the trend towards thrill and adventure the male perspective in sport. Given that both these orientations involve specific ways of dealing with the body on the one hand and relating to the world, the self and to movement on the other, it is necessary to convince women (as well as men) of the advantages of extending both their sporting interests and their sporting activities.

The sport system is based not only on active participants, but also on the much larger group of sport consumers who watch sporting events in stadia or on television and who read sport reports in the print media. The gendered world of sport is mirrored in the sport coverage of the mass media, which for their part strengthen the gender differences and contribute to the construction of masculinity and femininity in sport. The majority of sport consumers are men, and the media orientate their reports to the values and tastes of men. Content analysis of mass media representations clearly indicates that the German media assign only a marginal role to women's sport, and that they present sex on the sporting stages. Thus the emphasis on appearance and the eroticism linked with female athletes is frequently the focal point of public interest (Pfister 2001c). Empirical research confirms our everyday knowledge: three times more men than women are among the crowds of sports spectators; and 56 per cent of women (33 per cent of men) asked in a representative survey said that they never visit sports events (Opaschowski 1995). In many sports, women cannot identify with the athletes, and there is not enough fun and entertainment in watching sports and games to attract women. Thus the lack of women as spectators and the emphasis on male sports combine to a produce a negative picture.

Problem groups

The extent to which a person is inclined to practise a sport is dependent on manifold, sometimes inter-related factors: age, education, social class, socio-ecological environment, ethnic origins, and so on. Women are influenced by these factors in a specific way, and combined with the factor of gender they form typical patterns. In German clubs, for instance, girls typically begin to withdraw from sports participation when they reach the age of fourteen, while boys continue to be quite active until they are at least eighteen (see DSB 2000). In particular, membership of the lower socio-economic groupings has a negative effect on sporting interests: older women from the lower social and income groups practise virtually no sport (Rittner and Breuer 2000). The dropout tendency from sports clubs among working-class girls begins during childhood, as Kleindienst-Cachay (1990) has demonstrated. Kleindienst-Cachay (1990) also found that working-class girls had little interest in school sport; they either played truant from physical education or found excuses (e.g. menstruation) not to take part in physical education lessons. While, after losing interest in sport as a result of adapting to a partner and the so-called 'family phase', middle-class women rediscover the enjoyment to be derived from participation in sporting activities, but women from the lower classes are lost to sport forever.

Religion and nationality also constitute decisive influences on girls' and women's chances of developing an interest in sport and putting this interest into practice. In Germany, Turkish girls and women in particular are subjected to social and cultural pressures which make sporting activity virtually impossible (Pfister 1999a). Only a very small percentage of members of German sports clubs are immigrants. In 1994 only 3 per cent of club members in Berlin were of Turkish nationality. Of these Turkish club members, more than 90 per cent were boys and men. Thus foreign girls and women take up sport in general, and especially physical activities in a sports club, to a far smaller degree than either Turkish males or German girls and women. Turkish females represented only 0.7 per cent of female members of sports clubs, even though they make up 4 per cent of the female population of Berlin. In some large cities, and especially in Berlin, immigrants have founded their own sports clubs. In Berlin there are around fifty sports clubs with a majority of non-German members; Turkish immigrants have founded sports clubs. In recent years the importance and attractiveness of 'ethnic' sports clubs has increased. In Berlin 50 per cent of Turkish men and boys who are members of a sports club belong to a Turkish club. These clubs offer sports (mainly soccer, but also the martial arts and sports of strength) almost exclusively for boys and men.

Suggestions on how to change the situation, however, are problematic: should, for example, integration and membership of German sport organisations, and hence the adoption of German norms and values, be recommended? This is a sure way of causing friction with girls' and women's social environments, especially with their families. Furthermore, the possibility of losing their cultural identity cannot be ruled out. If on the other hand, the case is made for the acceptance of other (in this case Turkish) values and ways of life, does this not mean depriving these girls and women of many of the physical and psychical possibilities of self-fulfilment? The only solution is to help Turkish and other foreign women to help themselves, with the implicit acknowledgement that they know best, and to take their needs and problems seriously.

Another problem group are handicapped women, who face much more discrimination than other women and handicapped men. Disabled persons are confronted with the ruling values and norms of society and measured according to the yardstick of normality. The few existing studies on the conditions of lives of handicapped women show that prevailing standards of beauty and femininity make it especially difficult for them to accept their handicap and to develop self-confidence and a positive identity. Disabled women have to struggle with many stereotypes and barriers when they claim a 'normal' life with sexual activity, family and children.

Because physical activity and sport are based on motor competency and bodily performance, and because sport needs and builds perfectly functioning bodies, disability and sport seem to be a contradiction. Despite this, disabled athletes have appropriated nearly all types of sport. But again, the barriers to women's participation are much higher than for men because, among other things, the stereotype of the 'weaker sex' seems to hold especially true for handicapped women. No wonder that women are a minority among athletes with disabilities. In the *Deutscher Behindertensportverband*, 40 per cent of members are female, but only a small minority of 2.5 per cent of all persons with disabilities are members of a sports club. However, there are numerous handicapped women who have made their way into sport at all levels, from grassroots to top-level sport. One of the most famous of all German female athletes (the able-bodied included) is Marianne Buggenhagen, a track-and-field athlete in a wheelchair, who won numerous medals in the Paralympics and who was elected several times as the athlete of the year.

Unfortunately there has been little research on special groups of women (for example, mothers with small children, older women or women in rural areas) and their engagement in sport. There is a clear need for more studies investigating the differences between women. Women are not one social group with the same needs, the same tastes and the same backgrounds.

Health and fun – motives for engagement in sport

For a number of reasons, investigations into the motives of those who practise a sport frequently provide only a very broad outline of trends. There is a tendency, particularly when it is a matter of socially accepted values such as sport, fitness and health, to give socially acceptable answers. Furthermore, the question of why a person practises a sport cannot be answered one-dimensionally except in the rarest of cases. The decision to practise sport or a certain type of sport tends not only to be based on rational considerations, but also on emotional and partly sub- or unconscious processes.

A further problem is that in many empirical studies the motives identified for practising sports are so stereotyped that their interpretation is extraordinarily difficult. In a survey undertaken by Opaschowski (1995), for example, 71 per cent of those interviewed named fun as a motive for their sporting activity, 60 per cent health, 48 per cent fitness and 37 per cent compensation for lack of movement. It is by no means clear what the interviewees understand by 'health' or 'fun'. These terms can be associated with entirely different, quite individual and also gender-related concepts. Rittner (1986) in particular made clear how widespread the stereotype of sport as a health factor is, and how little substance there is to the underlying notions. Since women express concern about their state of health more frequently than men, complain more often about psychosomatic ailments and are more inclined to be health conscious, the health aspect could play an important role in persuading women to take up a sport. Despite the problems mentioned above, the gendered sets of expectations and motivations, and the hopes connected with sports need to be addressed. A number of studies have revealed large differences between men and women with regard to keeping one's figure and being attractive as motives for taking up a sport. Four times as many women as men stated in Opaschowski's (1995) survey that 'they wanted to do something for their figure'. Men, on the other hand, wanted to become fitter more often than women. In a survey in Berlin (Senatsverwaltung 1995), 10 per cent more women than men named a 'good figure' as the reason for being active in sport, and more men (12 per cent) than women (5 per cent) reported that competition is one of the reasons to be active in sport.

Physical education

Interest in, and commitment to, sport are developed in school. In most German *Länder*, physical education is obligatory for girls and boys, but a 'hidden curriculum' contributes to the development of gender-specific competencies and interests in sport. For example, physical education for girls focuses very often on rhythmical exercises and gymnastics, whereas boys learn how to play soccer. In elementary school physical education lessons, co-educational classes are the norm. In many *Länder*, after grade 4, physical education is conducted normally with single-sex groups. The issue of co-education is contested territory in Germany. There is widespread debate on the advantages and disadvantages of co-educational gym lessons.

In mixed and in single-sex physical education classes, there are distinct signs that physical education in schools is not entirely free from blame in alienating many girls from physical activities. If too much emphasis is placed on performance and breaking records, it will deter those girls who are not able to reconcile this with their body ideals, their outlook and their identity. Girls who do not correspond to body ideals, or cannot perform the prescribed movements, or do not come up to the expected standards of performance, particularly often take an irreversible decision against sport, because they feel incompetent and uncomfortable or because they are afraid of making fools of themselves (Kugelmann *et al.* 1990).

Top-level sport

Discrimination also persists in elite sport, where women still play a secondary role. The financial support for women's sports, especially when there is sponsorship money, is still less than that offered to men. In Germany, with the exception of tennis and golf, opportunities for women to earn their living as openly professional athletes remains minimal. That 'proper' sport is men's sport, and that women's sport is only of marginal interest, is illustrated by the example of football, where male players are highly paid professionals and female players are amateurs who practise their hobby alongside their education or profession. A report about a workshop in which male and female mentors, as well as parents of competitive sportswomen, participated alongside the female athletes, provides a good overview of the framework of conditions of the sports performance careers of women (Anders and Braun-Laufer 1998). Despite the lower public significance of women's sport, female athletes who achieve valid performance norms are regarded in just the same way as men in the state promotion of sport. Moreover, with regard to the stress of training, no differences relating to sex can be discerned. German women are, therefore, also relatively successful in international top-class sport. In the Sydney 2000 Olympics, Germany's female athletes won twenty-one of their country's fifty-six medals. The higher percentage of medals won by

German males is explained by the higher number of medals in cycling, and by the fact that there are more events for men than for women.

Reasons for men's and women's different commitment to sport

Theoretical considerations

Reasons for men's and women's participation in different sports activities can be found by examining the historically developed conditions of life peculiar to each sex, which shape concrete, everyday behaviour patterns. It is the gender of individuals and the gender order of societies which also genders the world of sport. Gender is to be understood as 'a process of social construction, a system of social stratification, and an institution that structures every aspect of our lives because of its embeddedness in the family, the workplace, and the state as well as in sexuality, language and culture' (Lorber 1994: 5). The term 'gender' always has two perspectives: individual and institutional. People acquire 'female' and 'male' identities in life-long socialisation processes according to prevailing gender arrange-ments. Gender is one of the central ordinal principles of societies, principles which regulate the realisation and legitimisation of rights and duties, responsibilities and competencies in accordance with the centrally assigned criteria of sex, age, class and ethnic origin, whereby these assign-ments are realised and legitimised through norms and values, through institutions such as religion and science, law and administration, school and the media. Here the symbolically transmitted bi-sexuality is a funda-mental principle that corresponds with Western thinking in binary oppositions (Lehnert 1997).

Societal institutions and structures as well as gender relations are highly correlated with the organisation of work, which is characterised in indus-trial societies by the division of labour, principally through the separation of unpaid housework and paid employment. However, gender is not some-thing that we are or have, but rather what we produce, what we do: 'Gender is constantly created and re-created out of human interaction, out of social life, and it is the texture and order of that social life ... it depends on everybody constantly doing gender' (Lorber 1994: 13). Since sport is physical activity, and involves the presentation of the body and the demon-stration of the capacity to perform, it is always doing gender. The activity in sport is not only influenced by gender identity and the acting out of gender, but also by a deeply rooted gender order, since women and men develop preferences for certain sports and skills in certain disciplines in accordance with individual inclinations, motives, ideas and patterns of behaviour on the one hand, and social norms, values and expectations on the other. The experiences and emotions conveyed by sport are, in turn, filtered through gender identity and thus serve to reinforce this identity. In the course of their socialisation, boys and girls and men and women take over gender-related techniques and rules, patterns of interpretation, norms and values in an active exchange with their socio-ecological environment, and thus grow into conditions of life which are determined by the duality of gender.

There are many studies dealing with different aspects of socialisation into physical activity and sport; here the focus is on some other aspects, especially on the aspect of the body.

Body, body culture and femininity

The following considerations on the connections between physical activities and gender are applicable to the situation in Germany, but they perhaps also describe world-wide tendencies. If we transfer the above-mentioned constructionist view on the body, then it is clear that the body is not only the basis of our physical existence, but it is also a site of social control as well as an expression of the cultural superstructure. How we use our bodies, what we eat, how we sleep, the daily ritual of body care and how we do sports – our entire somatic culture is determined by the prevailing social structures and cultural patterns. This also means that men's and women's bodies are subjected to patterns of interpretation and social standardisation processes, in which the dichotomous and hierarchical relationships of the sexes are reflected. But what consequences does this have for the physical culture and exercise of girls and women?

1   Social control over the female body and women's adoption of their bodies as a social product result in women developing in many respects an ambivalent attitude to their bodies. Girls, for example, judge their athletic abilities less favourably than boys. Because of this they do not dare attempt many forms of movement and movement tasks, thus depriving themselves of many positive experiences. In surveys, moreover, adult women express dissatisfaction with their bodies and their health more frequently than men. Even today, orientation towards standards set from outside is of major significance for women. Representative surveys in Germany show that slimness and beauty is a major concern for most women (see among others Deuser *et al.* 1995). Whereas men judge their bodies more from a functional point of view, the female body is a medium of social and sexual attraction. The aesthetic styling of the body is, therefore, of the utmost importance for girls and women. Their models are the ideal bodies which are constantly reproduced and modified by the media, especially by advertising. The models presented in German newspapers, magazines or on television are young, slim and flawless. However, the

ideals presented by the media are in principle unattainable – not least because the criteria undergo constant change. On account of the discrepancy between ideals and reality, girls and women frequently sense a 'deficit' with regard to their own bodies, and develop a relationship to them which is full of conflict and requires constant activity and astute body management. The adornment and presentation of the body, from using make-up and dieting to body styling, is thus an important part of everyday life for women.

2   Attractiveness is not only a question of the shape of the body but also of the styling of its movements. Elegant, gracious, smooth and harmonious movements, along with the culture associated with these (e.g. dancing, ballet or gymnastics) are regarded as 'female'. The refusal to adapt to such demands and concepts can lead, as demonstrated by Palzkill (1990) in statements made by competitive sportswomen, to conflicts of identity. Here processes of interaction can be observed. Girls' and women's preference for gymnastics and aerobics labels these movement forms as 'feminine', and the marketing of 'female body culture' strengthens women's interest in the kinds of sport that signal and promise attractiveness. In contrast, the movement and behavioural codes in football, as evidenced in a survey of German female players, were stigmatised as 'unfeminine' and therefore less attractive (Pfister 1999b). Nevertheless, pictures from Sydney, which glorify muscular female athletes in sports involving strength, demonstrate that the standard view of body and movement can also change.

3   In discussions of the physical appearance of girls and women, the subject of violence cannot be ignored. Girls learn at an early age that their bodies are no protection against violence, but on the contrary are a stimulus for it. Boys, on the other hand, learn that one can accomplish things with the body and that one can assert oneself in the face of opposition. Aggression against women, even if only potential aggression, has many different effects: a lack of self-confidence with regard to their bodies, limits to the extent of their appropriation of the physical environment, and a lack of experience concerning their bodies and movement. Girls and women learn, and world-wide know, that many activities – from jogging in the park or visiting a fitness studio after dark to cycling in the countryside – can be dangerous.

4   As a result of the above, women develop a different and in some respects more antagonistic relationship to their bodies than do men. The results of this troubled relationship of girls to their bodies are often eating disorders (anorexia or bulimia) and abuse of medicines, especially psychoactive drugs. In Germany, 10–20 per cent of girls and women are supposed to have eating disorders and around 90 per cent of persons with eating disorders are female (Deuser et al. 1995). However, as far as their state of health is concerned, women are far from

being the 'weaker' sex. Men suffer more frequently from serious illness than women and have, partly on account of their greater preparedness to take risks, a shorter life expectancy, all of which, however, has done little to shatter the myth of female weakness, which is also acknowledged by women. Physical strength and the ability to withstand strain, it seems, are simply not the main ingredients of a woman's identity (see Pfister 1991). It is not only ideals of beauty, eating habits, rituals of body care and styles of dressing which are determined by people's body- and self-concepts; these concepts also determine the nature of their engagement in sport.

In summary, the gender order, gendered identities and the 'ecology of the female body' described above also finds its expression in the form of specific needs and activities with regard to sport. Girls and women are 'doing gender' on the sports grounds as well as in all other situations of everyday life. Therefore they favour types and forms of sport which are in keeping with their body techniques and body ethos, and which do not provoke any conflicts with the gender arrangements of their society. Like any social institution, sport provides gendered scripts, which are appropriated by individuals and which contribute to the gender order as a whole. Doing gender in sport is strengthened by manifold processes in the course of socialisation, especially in the family, the peer group and at school.

Possibilities and deficits

To a large extent, sporting activities are determined by the opportunities available. Since the types of sport provided are often oriented towards men's tastes, the sporting needs of girls and women are not uncommonly left unfulfilled. Girls seem to prefer to have more recreational sport provided, while clubs and coaches attach more importance to performance and competition, thus taking boys' interests into account instead of those of girls. Whereas large clubs (with over 1,000 members) in Germany offer a wide variety of sports for women, and for this reason have a large female membership amounting to nearly 50 per cent, the numerous small clubs outside the towns provide few types of sport which attract girls and women (Jütting 1996; Heinemann and Schubert 1999), with the result that in these clubs women account for only 25 per cent of the membership.

Because of the location and design of a great number of sports facilities, men predominantly frequent the large football stadiums. Women, especially women from the lower classes, older women and single mothers, need sports facilities which are near their homes because they lack both mobility and flexibility. Nevertheless, local authorities tend to close down small, unprofitable sports facilities like swimming baths, referring people to the large sports centres on the outskirts of town. Marie-Louise Klein

(1992) was able to demonstrate in the case of Bochum (a town in North Rhine-Westphalia) that this has led to a serious curtailment of sporting activity, and also social contact, among many, particularly older, women.

Finally, in the evaluation of opportunities provided for sport generally, it must be taken into account that the possibilities offered by parks, lakes and woods are taken advantage of much less frequently by women than men (Klein 1992), a fact which is most certainly largely attributable to the fear of sexual harassment. A systematic survey of playgrounds in Berlin revealed that 86 per cent of the users were boys. Girls had no chance to participate in games like football or to gain access to space for themselves. Other studies reveal the same findings (Pfister 1991).

A further concrete problem arising from the circumstances of women's lives is their lack of leisure time. The results of published studies clearly reveal (not only in respect of the Federal Republic of Germany) that subjectively and objectively women have less spare time at their disposal than men, regardless of demographic variables (Opaschowski 1989). The time available to them is limited above all because of their family commitments. The period between the children coming home from school and, for example, taking the daughter to a recorder lesson and the son to a sports club, can only be used for sports activities in a very restricted way. It is therefore not surprising that 31 per cent of the women interviewed gave 'too much housework' as a reason for their lack of sporting activity, whereas none of the men did (Klein 1987: 12). As a result of their limited spare time, as shown for example in a survey of men and women who attend fitness studios in Berlin, women value the possibility of flexible use of facilities much more highly than men do. However, although the numerous opportunities offered near the home by commercial organisations meet women's requirements insofar as they take account of their lack of mobility and flexibility, many women cannot take advantage of them for financial reasons. It must be pointed out that on average women earn much less than men, that fewer women own a car and that women, especially, are threatened by the so-called 'new poverty' (Klein 1992).

Besides the lack of sporting opportunities for women, there is also the problem of the one-sidedness of the sports offered. Gymnastics in particular, which caters for the majority of women active in sports, also has its negative effects. The hoped-for styling of the body is usually not achieved, or if at all, then only with the greatest of effort and never indefinitely. This can give rise to frustration, resignation and the abandonment of sport altogether, which is indicated by the high fluctuation of visitors to fitness studios. Moreover, so-called 'women's sports' convey one-sided experiences with regard to the body and movement: they establish a specific way of handling the body, one which is closely linked to the female role, i.e. with its restrictions and exclusions.

Abstinence from sport may, as already mentioned, have to do with social background, ethnic origins and/or with negative experiences in physical education. A further problem which may, either directly or indirectly, have a negative influence on the sporting activity of girls and women is the predominance of men in all the decision-making bodies of sport and among the coaches (Pfister 1998b): in the German Gymnastics Federation, 70 per cent of whose members are female, for example, only two of the seven members of the leading committee were women; only 24 per cent of positions on the decision-making committees of the Federation were held by women. Women are also under-represented in sport science. In Germany, sport science is integrated in the universities. There are around sixty institutes of sport science, and females account for 41 per cent of sports students and 28 per cent of the teachers of practical courses, but only 7 per cent of professorial staff are female (Pfister 1993). The DSB has developed a programme to increase the number of women in decision-making committees, and a certain percentage of positions (depending on the number of female members of a federation) is reserved for women. Whether this initiative has led to true equality remains to be seen.

The barriers described in this chapter that make girls' and women's access to sport more difficult are a concrete expression of the theoretical connections recounted above. Ideals and norms, organisations and institutions follow – in everyday behaviour as well as in the sporting activity of women and men – 'gendered scripts', which are drawn from the order of the sexes and which in turn strengthen them. In discussing the opportunities and problems for women in sport the question arises: Which findings and explanations are typical of Germany? Presumably, women in other countries encounter similar opportunities and problems in society and sport. In any case, the structural similarities and culturally conditioned differences in women's sport would have to be identified and interpreted. This is a topic for another text.

References

Anders, G. and Braun-Laufer, E. (eds) (1998) *Karrieren von Mädchen und Frauen im Leistungssport*, Cologne: Strauss.

Baur, J., Spitzer, G. and Telschow, S. (1997) 'Der DDR-Sport als gesellschaftliches Teilsystem', *Sportwissenschaft*, 27 (4) 369–90.

Bierstedt, H. (1981) 'Sportliche Betätigung in der Lebensweise der Jugend', *Theorie und Praxis der Körperkultur*, 30, 120–4.

Bierstedt, H. and Gras, F. (1983) 'Sportbezogene Wünsche, Bedürfnisse und Motive der Bürger der DDR', *Theorie und Praxis der Körperkultur*, 32, 263–71.

Deuser, K., Glässer, E. and Köppe, D. (1995) *90.60.90. Zwischen Schönheit und Wahn*, Berlin: Zyankrise.

Deutsche Shell (ed.) (2000) *Jugend 2000*, 2nd edn, Opladen: Leske & Budrich.

Diemer, S. (1994) *Patriarchalismus in der DDR*, Opladen: Leske & Budrich.

DSB (2000) *Bestandhebung*, Frankfurt am Main: DSB.

EMNID-Institut (1992) *Sportliche Betätigung und Interesse an Sportangeboten*, Bielefeld: EMNID.

Frevert, U. (1986) *Frauen-Geschichte. Zwischen bürgerlicher Verbesserung und Neuer Weiblichkeit*, Frankfurt am Main: Suhrkamp.

Heinemann, K. and Schubert, M. (1999) 'Sports clubs in Germany', in Heinemann, Klaus (ed.) *Sport Clubs in Various European Countries*, Schorndorf: Hofmann, 143–69.

http://www.dssv.de/eckdaten.html.

Institut für Demoskopie Allensbach (1991) 'Sportmuffel werden selten. Ein Allensbacher Langzeitvergleich zum Breitensport', *Allensbacher Berichte*, no. 3, February.

Jütting, D. (1996) 'Ansichten zu Sportvereinen in der Bundesrepublik', in Wopp, Christian (ed.) *Sport der Zukunft – Zukunft des Sports*, Aachen: Meyer & Meyer, 66–86.

Kaschuba, W. (1989) 'Sportivität: Die Karriere eines neuen Leitwertes', *Sportwissenschaft*, 19 (2) 154–71.

Klein, M. (1987) *Frauen im Sport – gleichberechtigt?*, Stuttgart: Kohlhammer.

Klein, M-L. (1992) 'Sozialräumliche Bedingungen des Frauensports – Das Beispiel Ruhrgebiet', in Kröner, Sabine and Pfister, Gertrud (eds) *Frauen – Räume, Körper und Identität im Sport*, Pfaffenweiler: Centaurus, 146–60.

Kleindienst-Cachay, C. (1990) 'Die vergessenen Frauen – Zum Sportengagement von Mädchen und Frauen aus sozialen Unterschichten', in Gabler, H. and Göhner, U. (eds) *Für einen besseren Sport*, Schorndorf: Hofmann, 192–212.

Kugelmann, C., Knetsch, H. and Pastuszyk, M. (1990) *Handreichungen für den Sportunterricht mit weiblichen Auszubildenden*, Munich: Hintermaier.

Kurz, D., Sack, H-G. and Brinkhoff, P. (1996) *Kindheit, Jugend und Sport in Nordrhein-Westfalen*, Düsseldorf: Sylvia Moll, 361–430.

Lehnert, G. (1997) *Wenn Frauen Männerkleidung tragen*, Munich: dtv.

Lorber, J. (1994) *Paradoxes of Gender*, New Haven/London: Yale University Press.

Opaschowski, H. W. (1987) *Sport in der Freizeit. Mehr Lust als Leistung. Auf dem Weg zu einem neuen Sportverständnis*, Hamburg: BAT.

——(1989) *Freizeitalltag von Frauen*, Hamburg: BAT.

——(1995) *Neue Trends im Freizeitsport*, Hamburg: BAT.

Palzkill, B. (1990) *Zwischen Turnschuh und Stöckelschuh. Die Entwicklung lesbischer Identität im Sport*, Bielefeld: AJZ Verlag.

Pfister, G. (1990) 'The medical discourse on female physical culture in Germany in the 19th and early 20th centuries', *Journal of Sport History*, 17, 183–99.

——(1991) 'Mädchenspiele – zum Zusammenhang von Raumaneignung, Körperlichkeit und Bewegungskultur', *Sportunterricht*, 40, 165–76.

——(1993) 'Vom Blaustrumpf zur Alibifrau? Zur Geschichte und Situation von Frauen an den Universitäten', *dvs-Informationen*, 4, 9–18.

——(1996) 'Physical activity in the name of the Fatherland: *Turnen* and the national movement (1810–20)', *Sporting Heritage*, 1, 14–36.

——(1998a) 'Keine förmliche Gymnastik für die Mädchen – Über die Bildung des weiblichen Geschlechts bei Gutsmuths', in Lämmer, Manfred and Geßmann, Rolf (eds) *Beiträge und Biographie zur GutsMuths-Forschung*, St Augustin: Academia, 55–81.

——(1998b) 'Mehrheit ohne Macht? Frauen in der Turn- und Sportbewegung', in Krüger, M. (ed.) *Innovation aus Tradition. Zukunftskongreß für Gymnastik, Turnen und Sport*, Schorndorf: Hofmann, 42–50.

——(1999a) 'Health, fitness, leisure and sport among girls of ethnic minorities', in Aland Islands Peace Institute (ed.) *Girl Power*, Mariehamn: Aland Islands Peace Institute, 35–65.

——(1999b) *Sport im Lebenszusammenhang von Frauen*, Schorndorf: Hofmann.

——(2001a) 'Umstrittene Geschichte', in Talbot, Margaret (ed.) *Gender, Culture and Power: a Celebration of 100 Years of Women in the Olympics*, Aachen: Meyer & Meyer (in press).

——(2001b) 'Geschlechterarrangements in der DDR – zur Rolle der Frauen in der Gesellschaft und im Spitzensport', in Kramer, H. and Naegele, R. (eds) *Geschlechterarrangements im Zeitalter der Globalisierung*, Berlin: Philoverlag.

——(2001c) 'Das Kournikova-Syndrom: Doing gender, Massenmedien und Sport', in Pfister, G. (ed.) *Frauen im Spitzensport*, Hamburg: Czwalina (in press).

Pfister, G. and Langenfeld, H. (1980) 'Die Leibesübungen für das weibliche Geschlecht – ein Mittel zur Emanzipation der Frau?', in Ueberhorst, H. (ed.) *Geschichte der Leibesübungen*, vol. 3/1, Berlin/Munich/Frankfurt: Bartels & Wernitz, 485–521.

Rittner, V. (1986) 'Veränderungen der Gesundheitsvorstellungen und des Sports im gesellschaftlichen Kontext', in Franke, Elk (ed.) *Sport und Gesundheit*, Reinbek: Roholt, 63–74.

Rittner, V. and Breuer, C. (2000) *Soziale Bedeutung und Gemeinwohlorientierung des Sports*, Cologne: Strauss.

Schwier, Jürgen (1998) *Spiele des Körpers*, Hamburg: Czwalina.

Senatsverwaltung für Schule, Berufsbildung und Sport (ed.) (1995) *Sportbericht Berlin 1991–1994. Leistungsbilanz und Perspektiven*, Berlin: Runze & Casper.

Spitzer, G. (1998) 'Doping in der DDR. Ein historischer Überblick zu einer konspirativen Praxis. Genese-Verantwortung-Gefahren', in *Wissenschaftliche Berichte und Materialien des Bundesinstituts für Sportwissenschaft*, vol. 3, Cologne: Strauß.

Teichler, H-J. (1997) 'Staatsplan ohne "Sportobjekte". Anmerkungen zur wirtschaftlichen Talfahrt', in Hartmann, G. (ed.), *Goldkinder – Die DDR im Spiegel ihres Spitzensports*, Leipzig: Forum Verlag, 243–8.

Wonneberger, I. (1983) 'Zur Ausprägung von sportlichen Bedürfnissen bei Frauen', *Theorie und Praxis der Körperkultur*, 32 (5) 276–8.

Veltins GmbH/DSB (eds) (2000) *Veltins-Sportstudie 2000*, Meschede: Veltins.

Chapter 11

Sport facilities

Frieder Roskam

Introduction

At the end of World War II, sports facilities in Germany were either seriously damaged or, for lack of care and maintenance in the pre-war and war years, in a pitiful state. Nevertheless, the facilities available prior to the war (in 1935, for instance, there were about 150,000 facilities for a population of 67 million) had formed an excellent basis for club and school sport at the time. This situation in the sports facility sector was achieved with carefully prepared orchestration and encouragement on the part of the sports organisations at the beginning of the twentieth century and immediately after World War I. As noted in earlier chapters, the state and status of sport itself was suffering in 1945: the Allies had dismantled the organisational structure of sport as it was in the Third Reich, and the intellectual leadership elite at that time had its reservations about sport. Not until the formation of new sports associations in 1949–50 did sport begin to get back on its feet. What has been achieved in sport and in the facilities sector since then has been remarkable.

The main reason for such positive post-World War II development lies in the harmonisation of the interests of the sports organisations united in the DSB with the promotion of school and club sport, and the will of the German Olympic Society (DOG) to provide the requisite sports facilities. The DOG above all called upon federal, *Land* and local governments to finance and build at least a so-called 'basic-level of sports facilities' (playgrounds, sports grounds, sports halls and swimming pools). For decades, the tasks involved were shared according to an unwritten agreement whereby government took responsibility for the construction and maintenance of facilities, and the sports organisations for their part injected life into the facilities. The mutual trust pervading this relationship for a period of about thirty years made success possible.

The procedure from the 1950s onwards, described here in simplified terms, was possible because the driving force behind sport in the 1920s and 1930s was still active after World War II. Carl Diem, the 'grand old man' of sport and promoter of sports facilities, founded the Cologne College of Physical Education in 1947. Through his efforts and those of the College, the body of knowledge (planning principles and ideas for facilities) amassed between the wars was now activated within the boundaries of the then Federal Republic (West Germany). The initial ideas for the systematic provision of play and sports opportunities for the population go back to the period preceding World War I. In 1911 at Diem's instigation, the German Imperial Committee for the Olympic Games (DRAfOS) debated an 'Imperial Playing Fields Act', which would obligate local government to build and maintain such facilities. In 1920, the German Imperial Committee for Physical Training then proposed a draft law to this effect to the Weimar Constitution. The draft law proposed a specified quantity (in total three square metres) of playing fields, gymnasia and swimming pools per head of population (a guide value for town planners). The draft was not enacted. However, during the years in which its content was debated, the goal of a nationwide provision of sports facilities for the population was taken up by town planners and put into practice, culminating, as mentioned above, in the number of facilities available to the population in 1935. For the planning of the facilities themselves, for project planning, suitable sports facility literature was available early on. After the establishment of the German College of Physical Education in Berlin in 1920 (again at Diem's instigation), a 'playing field advisory office' was set up and the subject of 'exercise facility construction' was included in the syllabus.

The immediate post-war period

Alongside parallel developments in public sports administration and non-governmental-organised sport, Diem was able to gather experts around him and take a number of landmark decisions, including, for example, the founding of the Working Party of German Sports Departments, publication of the 'Ten-year plan for facility construction' of the German local government associations, initiating the 'Recommendations for the promotion of physical education in schools' and initiating the 'Guidelines for the creation of recreational, games and sports facilities'. In 1954, Diem facilitated the foundation of the DSB Institute for Sports Facility Construction (after one preliminary year as an institution within the Cologne College of Physical Education). Three years later the Institute was elevated in status by the German local government associations to the Central Advisory Institute for Local Authority Sports Facility Construction.

In 1956, the DOG published the 'Guidelines for the provision of recreational, games and sports facilities' calculated on a per capita basis (see Table 11.1), which was a further development of the principles of the 1911 Imperial Playing Fields Act. As the associated working group succeeded in bringing together recognised town planners and notable representatives of the local authorities and sports associations, these guidelines met with widespread approval. The comparison of demand (calculated on the basis of the town planning guide values) with existing facilities (from surveys carried out by the Federal Statistical Office at the end of 1955) revealed a considerable shortfall in facilities. Specifically, shortfalls were identified in children's playgrounds (31,000), general and school sports grounds (14,700), sports halls and gymnasia (10,400), small gymnasia (5,500), learner swimming pools (2,625), outdoor pools (2,420) and indoor pools (435). The investment required to remedy this deficiency was estimated in 1959 to be DM6.315 billion (without land and ancillary building costs). The DOG, therefore, advocated the 'Golden plan for recreation, games and sport' at the end of 1959, which was given a period of fifteen years to overcome the shortage of facilities, with the financial support of national (20 per cent), *Land* (50 per cent) and local governments (30 per cent). The 'Golden plan' and the associated memorandum received cross-political party support as well as the approval of national, *Land* and local governments.

Table 11.1   Guidelines for the provision of recreational games and sports facilities (per capita basis)

Category		1956 (I), m²	1967 (II), m²	1976 (III), m²
II	Play/sports grounds for young children up to the age of 6	0.5ᵃ(0.25)ᵇ	0.5	0.5
II	Play/sports grounds for children aged 7–12	0.5	0.5	0.5
III	Play/sports grounds for adolescents aged 13–17	1.0	0.5	0.5
IV	General sports facilities (sports grounds)	3.0	3.5	4.0
V	Gymnasia, games and sports halls (sports halls)	0.1	0.1	0.2
VI	Indoor swimming pools			
	30,000–50,000 inhabitants	1 pool	0.025–0.0005ᶜ	0.025–0.01ᶜ
	Smaller local districts	At least 1 small pool		
	Schools covering at least 13 school years	1 instruction pool		
VII	Outdoor swimming pools	0.1	0.2–0.065ᶜ	0.15–0.05ᶜ

Notes:
ᵃ Closed design of settlement
ᵇ Open design of settlement
ᶜ Depending on the size and density of settlement
Unless otherwise marked, all areas refer to 'effective playing area' or 'effective water surface'.

The 'Golden plan' era (1960–75)

In 1960, each of the then 27,000 local authorities of the Federal Republic with its population of about 60 million, received a manual entitled the 'Golden plan in the communities' as a guide to the implementation of the plan at local government level. The manual, with the aid of numerous examples, explained the various steps that had to be taken, ranging from ascertaining local demand and designating suitable building land through to the setting of priorities, facility finance, and facility design and construction.

In the 1960s, many towns produced their own 'sports facility development plan', in which the *status quo* was set against the demand for basic-level facilities and for special facilities for individual sports. These special plans contributed to the general urban development plans, and particularly to the land use plans. During this period, work on the planning principles, guidelines and standards for project planning was intensified. Systematic research was conducted in the facility sector for the first time. Conferences were held to facilitate the exchange of experience and the dissemination of knowledge. The implementation of the 'Golden plan' was critically monitored. It soon became obvious that the forecast of demand on which the guidelines were based in 1956 was too conservative. A revised version was approved in 1967 (Guidelines II; see Table 11.1), which in some cases specified higher town planning guide values, and in other cases, taking developments in sport into account, recommended different design units (e.g. the standard size of sports halls was increased from 12×24m to 15×27m). The fast-expanding demand for sport reflected by the growth in sports clubs and club membership finally prompted a further revision. The third version of the guidelines was published in 1976 (see Table 11.1).

The review of the accounts in 1975, at the end of the 'Golden plan', which reveals investments of DM17.384 billion as against the originally forecast DM6.315 billion, underlines the broad acceptance of this plan at all levels. However, the rounded DM11 billion overshoot is only partly explained by the increase in the number of facilities. The main reasons for the far higher investment total were the greater size and multi-functionalism of the facilities, the superior safety and hygiene standards, and the use of higher-grade materials and equipment – combined not least with the increase in the index of building costs over the fifteen years.

This period also coincided with the phase of international contacts in the sports and leisure facility sector. Starting with informal European cooperation launched from Cologne in 1957, this loose association was put on a sounder footing in 1965 with the founding of the non-profit International Working Group for Sports Facilities (IAKS), the idea of which was spread to other continents. 'Leisure facilities' were included in the association's name in 1973. The present name of International

Association for Sports and Leisure Facilities was adopted in 1993. The location of the headquarters of the IAKS and the DSB Institute of Sports Facilities Construction respectively to the Department of Sports and Leisure Facilities of the Federal Institute for Sports Science in Cologne (and in the immediate vicinity of the German College for Physical Education) has encouraged successful cross-fertilisation.

Post-'Golden plan' to re-unification (1975–90)

With the 'Golden plan' coming to its natural end in 1975, sports facility construction, carried by its momentum dating back to 1960, was sustained with annual investments of about DM1.2 billion (see Table 11.2 for development of basic facilities, 1955–88). As before, the funding for basic-level sports facilities was mainly provided by local authorities and *Land* governments. Sports clubs, aided by grants from the *Land* governments, or by commercial operators, built the special facilities required for individual sports. The principles behind the assessment of demand for these types of facility, essentially based on a certain minimum number of active users to justify the construction of the facility in question, were not published until 1984. However, it was soon realised that the successful completion of the 'Golden plan' had left a vacuum. The DOG relinquished its involvement in the sports facility sector in about 1980, leaving the field to the DSB. Those groups in society interested in sports facilities in fact expected a continuation of this sports- and social policy orientated programme. These expectations were not fulfilled. This shortcoming gave rise to a serious problem, which still besets sports facility construction today: the lack of a general guide in times of low public spending has resulted in a considerable undervaluation of sport and sports facilities. Those with an active interest in sports facility construction are still confronted with this problem today.

A considerable growth in the number of sports clubs and members in organised sport, under the umbrella of the DSB, accompanied the enhanced quantity and quality of sports facilities from the end of World

Table 11.2   Development in basic-level sports facilities from 1955 to 1988

	1955	1965	1976	1983	1988
Sports grounds	15,143	28,335	33,206	39,900	52,000
Sports halls	6,143	14,315	21,775	24,800	28,500
Indoor pools	198	1,119	2,960	3,400	3,700
Outdoor pools	2,135	2,212	2,713	3,000	2,700
total	23,619	45,981	60,654	71,100	86,900

War II to re-unification. Even since 1988, the DSB has had an average increase in members of about half a million people per year. At that time, it was assumed that on average about 25 per cent of the population participated in organised club-based sport. The percentage of the population engaged in informal or casual sport outside clubs on a perhaps less regular basis was cautiously estimated to be 30 per cent.

The beginning of the 1980s marked the commencement of social and demographic changes. These changes were accompanied by a shift in demand, which had an effect on the facilities offered (project planning) and on the estimation of demand for facilities. The calculation of the facilities required with the aid of the town planning guide values was no longer considered appropriate. This led in 1985 to the formation of a Sports Facility Development Planning Working Group at the Federal Institute forSports Science, which, as in the immediate post-war years, brought together experts from sport, architecture, the social sciences, town planning and all three tiers of government. The purpose of the Working Group was to devise a new method, which would give more precise and flexible consideration to the huge spectrum of sports practised and the diverse interests of the population.

Re-unification in 1990

Having discovered that the sports facilities in the former GDR were in a catastrophic state, qualitatively and quantitatively, in 1992 the DSB published its 'Golden plan East' for the five new eastern German *Länder*. The aim was to bring the standard of sports facility provision in eastern Germany into line with that of the rest of the country. The plan was based on the successful principles of the 'Golden plan' of 1959. The new plan incorporated the experience and findings gathered during the implementation of the original plan and during the subsequent years. Since, at the time of the publication of the 'Golden plan East', the work on a new method of assessing demand for western Germany had not been completed (this took until the year 2000), the old 'guide value' method was retained (town planning guide values), although this was varied in accordance with the population of the particular planning district. The results of the survey of basic-level facilities show higher *per capita* values in smaller districts than in towns and cities.

The statistical surveys of the number and quality of facilities, the latter involving classification in four categories, by the responsible ministries of the eastern German *Länder* showed that only 11.3 per cent of the existing sports grounds were in a serviceable condition (category I). These were 10.6 per cent of the sports halls, 17.5 per cent of the indoor pools and 8.6 per cent of the outdoor pools. Table 11.3, in which the demand for sports facilities according to the guidelines for the creation of recreational, games and sports facilities for eastern Germany is compared with those available, reports on this and on the classification of the remaining facilities in category II (in need of renovation with major defects), category III (in need of renovation with serious defects) and category IV (beyond repair).

Table 11.3   Sports facility balance sheet: result of a comparison of supply and demand, 'Golden plan East', 1992

Comparison of supply and demand	Sports grounds Playing area (m²)	%	Sports halls Playing area (m²)	%	Indoor pools Water surface (m²)	%	Outdoor pools Water surface (m²)	%
I Demand in accordance with Part II (guidelines)	69,128,000	100	4,890,800	100	257,300	100	1,104,000	100
2 Supply (existing facilities)	53,241,800	77	2,061,600	42	79,300	31	1,519,600	138
their share of facilities in category I	5,987,400	9	218,500	4	13,900	5	131,400	12
Facilities in need of modernisation								
in category II	21,016,600		751,500		30,400		559,400	
in category III	20,502,700		779,100		20,000		606,600	
in category IV	5,735,000		312,500		14,900		222,200	
3 Modernisation requirements in	47,254,300	68	1,842,100	38	65,300	25	972,600	88
category II	21,016,600	30	751,500	15	30,400	12	391,900	35
category III	20,502,700	30	779,100	16	20,000	8	425,500	38
category IV	5,735,000	8	312,500	6	14,900	6	155,700	14
4 Shortage; new facilities required	15,886,200	23	2,829,200	58	178,000	69	0	0

Investment needs to the tune of DM24.772 billion were estimated in 1992, broken down into DM11.095 billion for renovation and DM13.677 for new facilities (see Table 11.4), and this just to bring eastern Germany up to the western German standard.

Like the 'Golden plan' of 1959, the 'Golden plan East' was expected to take fifteen years to remedy the deficiencies. As far as implementation and finance are concerned, the memorandum accompanying the plan states:

> The provision of funding of this magnitude and the distribution of the costs among several sources of public finance only makes sense if federal, *Land* and local government are asked to shoulder burdens according to their ability to do so. This joint project demands a federal contribution of 50 per cent and a joint contribution of a further 50 per cent from *Land* and local government. It therefore demands the consistent widening of all grant and investment programmes to encompass sports facilities as well.

The immense financial burdens imposed in Germany and on each individual citizen by re-unification, combined with the political constellations, have so far prevented the basic acceptance of this cost allocation principle. The grant and investment programmes of federal government are not tied in any way to sports facilities. These programmes can fund facilities of this kind, but there is no statutory obligation. The federal government for the first time introduced a funding item for sports facilities under the 'Golden plan East' in the year 1999! In view of the minimal allocation of funds associated with it, it must be regarded as more of a reminder than active assistance – a drop in the ocean, so to speak. Nevertheless, local and *Land* governments in eastern Germany have undertaken in the last ten years or so to overcome the problems inherited from the GDR by allocating land, rescuing buildings from decay, modernising existing facilities and building new ones.

Table 11.4   Cost of basic-level sports facilities (DM, million), 'Golden plan East', 1992

Facility type	Cost of modernisation	Cost of new facilities	Total
Sports grounds	3,277	1,825	5,101
Sports halls	3,823	6,665	10,488
Indoor pools	1,035	4,479	5,514
Outdoor pools	2,960	709	3,669
total	11,095	13,678	24,772

Consequences of the change in demand for sport in western Germany

In the immediate post-war years, clubs and schools were the only sources of demand for sports facilities. These two user groups, therefore, also determined the type and characteristics of the various kinds of facility. They established the requirement profiles for these facilities, guided either solely by competition rules or, in the case of facilities used jointly by schools and clubs, by the school curricula for physical education. Over the years, the traditional sports, with a greater or lesser bias in favour of competition, have been joined by an array of leisure- and health-orientated sports. This development has been accompanied by an increase in the number of athletes whose main interest has not been in competitive sport. The shift is well illustrated in the swimming pool sector. It is here that the change in user habits is particularly noticeable, with the first commercially operated fun pools, equipped with sauna landscapes, thermal pools, giant flumes, varied water attractions and food outlets, being established at the end of the 1970s and beginning of the 1980s. This new form of pool attracted a considerable proportion of users away from the competition-orientated swimming pools built in large numbers in earlier years.

Figures 11.1 and 11.2 illustrate the conceptional changes in sports ground provision between 1967 and 1990, from sports-orientated facilities for track and field and soccer to multi-facility complexes for a broad range of sport and leisure activities.

Figures 11.3 and 11.4 illustrate the development in indoor swimming pools provision between 1965 and 1994, from a rectangular training and competition pool to an attractive landscaped aquatic centre with pools for swimming (in the background) and for 'bathing' and enjoying water in the foreground.

The change in demand called into question the estimation of facility demand on the basis of the 'guide value' method (number of inhabitants in the planning district multiplied by a specific figure of square metres of effective sports space). A method had to be found which would reliably reflect the diversification in the sports catered for. In the mid-twentieth century, only thirty core sports had to be provided for; in today's climate of diversification and innovation, a hundred or so sports may easily be counted, the vast majority of which can only be practised in sports facilities. The 'guide value' method has now been superseded by the 'sport behaviour' method, following the publication of the Federal Institute for Sports Science's 'Guide to sports facility development planning' (see Figure 11.5).

With this method, a survey of sport currently practised and of the frequency and duration of practice per week, with details of possible seasonal variations, yields a certain quantity of sport demand. This survey distinguishes sex and sport-related age groups. The results yield a relatively

Figure 11.1 Athletics and soccer ground (1967)

Figure 11.2 Multi-facility complex (1990)

Figure 11.3 Indoor swimming pool (1965)

Figure 11.4 Landscaped aquatic centre (1994)

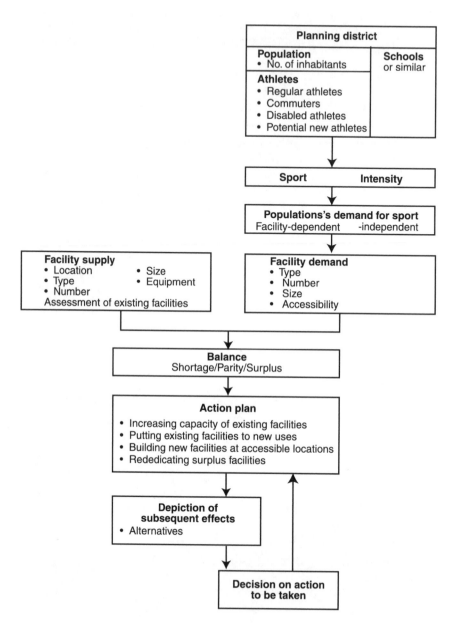

Figure 11.5 Sports facility development planning – planning steps

reliable forecast of future sport behaviour. In simple terms, this survey of the practised sport(s) yields for each individual sport a certain volume of demand, calculated from the number of available hours of use per week, the number of people practising the sport simultaneously and the size of the facility unit. The comparison may then show a shortage, a surplus or parity. The outcome thus defines the plan of action for sports facility development.

Sports facilities of the future

The earlier reference to the example of swimming pools only superficially highlighted the effects of changes in user behaviour on action to be taken by the planner. However, it is not only pools for swimming and bathing alone in which changes have taken place in what swimming pools have to offer. There are also extra demands relating to health and communication (e.g. fitness facilities with or without apparatus, more generously designed relaxation and rest areas, and cafeterias and restaurants). In addition there are changes affecting the ancillary areas and rooms on which the functioning of sports surfaces ultimately depends. The consequences of this are easier to formulate for conventional sports facilities, which have evolved over a longer period, than for facilities for entirely new activities. Decisions on facilities for 'trend' sports in particular, with the associated uncertainty of user interest and viability, are particularly difficult to take. This is where known territory is abandoned; cautious reaction to what are in many cases fleeting trends generated by industry is called for here.

If the sports facility of the future is to be characterised, it must stand apart from the mass of existing sports facilities in having an attractive agenda and appearance, and offering a varied range of uses for a broad spectrum of age groups, interest groups and abilities. It must be suitable and adaptable for new forms of exercise and games activities. It must contain leisure-orientated, social and cultural amenities and encourage communication in the widest sense. It must exhibit a strong health-promotion bias. Finally, it should be built and operated economically and with minimum impact on the environment. Such a facility, therefore, complies in the broadest sense with the goals of Agenda 21 of Rio 1992, which the International Olympic Committee in 1999 declared as 'the Olympic movement's Agenda 21' for sport and sports facilities. Agenda 21 – the original and the IOC version – appeals to all to heed the economic, ecological and social significance of decisions taken, and to be taken, for the sustained development of the Earth. Applied to sports facilities, this means present-day and future plans must ensure cost-effective construction (so that the facilities can be managed economically), little or no environmental pollution, and the care and conservation of non-renewable resources. With facilities like these, we can bequeath to future generations a social inheritance that will enhance both health and communication.

Further reading

2 History of sport and physical education in Germany, 1800–1945

Bois-Remond, du E. (1862) *Über das Barrenturnen und über die sogenannte rationelle Gymnastik*, Berlin: E. H. Schroeder.

Bukh, N. (1924) *Grundgymnastik*, Berlin: Teubner.

Digel, H. (ed.) (1988) *Sport im Verein und Verband: historische, politische und soziologische Aspekte*, Schorndorf: Hofmann.

Eichel, W. *et al.* (eds) (1965–9) *Geschichte der Körperkultur in Deutschland*, vols 1–3, Berlin: Sportverlag.

Euler, C. (1891) *Die Geschichte des Turnunterrichts*, 2nd edn, Gotha: Thienemann.

Gasch, R. (ed.) (1928) *Handbuch des gesamten Turnwesens*, Vienna/Leipzig: Pichler.

Kleindienst-Cachay, C. (1980) *Die Verschulung des Turnens*, Schorndorf: Hofmann.

Krüger, A. (1999) 'Breeding, bearing and preparing the Aryan body. Creating Super Man the Nazi way', in Mangan, J. A. (ed.) *Shaping the Superman. Fascist Body as Political Icon – Aryan Fascism*, London: Frank Cass, 42–68.

Krüger, M. (1996) *Körperkultur und Nationsbildung*, Schorndorf: Hofmann.

Kuhse, B. (1908) *Schülerrudern, Geschichte und Betrieb*, Berlin: Weidmannsche Buchhandlung.

Lion, J. C. (1873) *Statistik des Schulturnens in Deutschland*, Leipzig: Keil.

Naul, R. (1985) 'Sport in der Schule', in Twellmann, W. (ed.) *Handbuch Schule und Unterricht*, vol. 7, part 2, Düsseldorf: Schwann, 751–76.

——(1990) 'The Renaissance of the history of school sports: back to the future?', *Journal of Sport History*, 17, 199–213.

——(1994) 'Physical education teacher training – historical perspectives', in Mester, L. (ed.) *Sport Science in Europe 1993. Current and Future Perspectives*, Aachen: Meyer & Meyer, 588–610.

——(1994) 'Historical perspectives of sport pedagogy', *Sport Science Review*, 3 (1) 11–17.

Naul, R. and Lämmer, M. (eds) (1999) *Willibald Gebhardt – Pionier der Olympischen Bewegung*, Aachen: Meyer & Meyer.

Naul, R. (ed.) (1985) *Körperlichkeit und Schulturnen im Kaiserreich*, Wuppertal: Putty.

——(1997) *Contemporary Studies in the National Olympic Games Movement*, Frankfurt/Berlin/Bern/NewYork/Paris/Vienna: Lang.

Neuendorff, E. (1934) *Geschichte der neueren deutschen Leibesübungen von Beginn des 18. Jahrhunderts bis zur Gegenwart*, 4 vols, Dresden: Limpert.

Orlwasky, E. (1838) *Die Wiedereinführung der Leibesübungen in die Gymnasien*, Lissa/Leipzig: Guenther.

Rossow, C. (1908) *Zweite Statistik des Schulturnens*, Gotha: Thienemann.

Rothstein, H. (1862) *Die Barrenübungen, in zwei Abhandlungen besprochen*, Berlin: E. H. Schroeder.

Schodrok, K. H. (1989) *Militärische Jugend-Erziehung in Preussen 1806–1820*, Olsberg: Jofesheim Bigge.

Spiess, A. (1842) *Gedanken über die Einordnung des Turnwesens in das Ganze der Volkserziehung*, Basel: Richter.

——(1847) *Turnbuch für Schulen*, Basel: Schweighauser.

Ueberhorst, H. (1980; 1982) *Die Geschichte der Leibesübungen in Deutschland*, vols 3.1. and 3.2, Berlin: Bartels & Wernitz.

3 Sport and physical education in the two Germanies 1945–90

Bergner, K. and Gabler, H. (1976) 'Modelle und Maßnahmen zur Förderung des Schul- und Leistungssports', in Gabler, H. (ed.) *Schulsportmodelle in Theorie und Praxis*, Schorndorf: Hofmann, 25–62.

Bette, K. H. and Neidhardt, F. (1985) *Fördereinrichtungen im Hochleistungssport*, Schorndorf: Hofmann

Emrich, E. (1996) *Zur Soziologie der Olympiastützpunkte*, Niedernhausen/Ts.: Schors.

Gessmann, R. (1984) 'Sportunterricht heute: zwischen Sportartenlernen, Sozialerziehung, Bewegungsarrangement und Körpererfahrung', in Allmer, H. (ed.) *Sport und Schule*, Reinbek: Rowohlt, 10–34.

Martin, D. (1972) *Schulsport in Deutschland*, Schorndorf: Hofmann.

Naul, R. and Schulz, N. (1992) '20 Jahre Leistungsfach Sport – Versuch einer Bilanz', *Sportunterricht*, 41, 274–83.

Schulz, N. (1985) 'Schulsport – Die aktuelle Diskussion um Aufgaben, Ziele und Inhalte im Überblick', in Denk, H. and Hecker, G. (eds) *Texte zur Sportpädagogik*, Schorndorf: Hofmann, 190–213.

Wolf, N. (1984) 'Die strukturelle und inhaltliche Entwicklung des Schulsports von 1945 bis zur Gegenwart', in Carl, K., Kayser, D., Mechling, H. and Preising, W. (eds) *Handbuch Sport*, vol. 2, Düsseldorf: Schwann, 795–819.

Reichenbach, M. and Schwidtmann, H. (eds) (1976) *Sozialistische Erziehung und Schulsport*, Berlin: Volk und Wissen.

4 Sport and physical education in re-unified Germany (1990–2000)

Brettschneider, W. D. and Brandl-Bredenbeck, H. P. (1997) *Sportkultur und jugendliches Selbstkonzept: eine interkulturell vergleichende Studie über Deutschland und die USA*, Weinheim: Juventa.

Deutscher Sportbund (DSB)(1994) *Memorandum zur Förderung der Sportwissenschaft in der Bundesrepublik Deutschland*, Frankfurt am Main: DSB.

——(1995) 'Goldener Plan Ost', Frankfurt am Main: DSB.

EadS (ed.) (2001) *Physical Education: From Central Governmental Regulation to Local School Autonomy*, Velen: EAdS.

Einigungsvertrag (Unification Treaty) (1990) 'Vertrag zwischen der Bundesrepublik Deutschland und der DDR über die Herstellung der Einheit Deutschlands vom

31.8.1990', in Münch, I. (ed.) *Die Verträge zur Einheit Deutschlands*, 2nd edn, Munich: Beck, 43–67.

Hartmann-Tews, I. (1996) *Sport für alle!? Strukturwandel europäischer Sportsysteme im Vergleich: Bundesrepublik Deutschland, Frankreich, Grossbritannien*, Schorndorf: Hofmann.

Hummel, A. (2000) 'Schulsportkonzepte zwischen totaler Rationalisierung und postmoderner Beliebigkeit', *Sportunterricht*, 49, 9–13.

Kultusministerium Nordrhein-Westfalen (1995) (ed.) *Gesundheitserziehung in der Schule durch Sport. Bilanz und Perspektiven*, Frechen: Ritterbach.

Marburger Sportpädagogen (1998) "Grundthemen des Bewegens". Eine bewegungspädagogische Erweiterung der Sportlehrerausbildung', *Sportunterricht*, 47, 318–24.

Naul, R. (1997) 'Comparative physical education and sport studies in Germany in the 1990s', *International Journal of Physical Education*, 34, 80–102.

Naul, R., Telama, R. and Rychtecky, A. (1997) 'Physical fitness and active lifestyle of Czech, Finnish, and German youth', *AUC-Kinanthropologica*, 33 (2) 5–15.

NOK (2000) *Zehn Jahre Wiederbeginn der olympischen Einheit Deutschlands*, Frankfurt am Main: NOK.

Petry, C. (2000) *Mythos Chancengleichheit. Sportwissenschaftlerinnen in Deutschland und England*, Aachen: Meyer & Meyer.

Scherler, K. H. (ed.) (1990) *Normative Sportpädagogik*, Clausthal-Zellerfeld: Greinert.

Schwier, J. (ed.) (1998) *Jugend-Sport-Kultur: Zeichen und Codes jugendlicher Sportszenen*, Hamburg: Czwalina.

Tokarski, W. and Petry, C. (1993) *Das Europa des Sports. Sport und Sportpolitik ohne Grenzen*, Cologne: Strauss.

Tokarski, W. and Steinbach, D. (2001) 'Spuren', in *Sportpolitik und Sportstrukturen in der Europäischen Union*, Aachen: Meyer & Meyer.

5   Physical education in schools

Balz, E. (1999) 'Zur Bedeutung der sportdidaktischen Entwicklung für die Sekundarstufe I', in LSW (ed.) *Sport in der Sekundarstufe I. Dokumentation einer Fachtagung (Curriculumrevision im Schulsport*, book 6), Soest: LSW, 16–29.

Bannmüller, E. (1977) 'Schritte zu einem "offenen Bewegungskonzept" für die Grundschule', *Sportwissenschaft*, 7, 374–85.

Bannmüller, E. and Röthig, P. (1990) *Grundlagen und Perspektiven ästhetischer und rhythmischer Bewegungserziehung*, Stuttgart: Klett.

Baur, J. and Bräutigam, M. (1980) 'Zielperspektiven für den Sportunterricht in der Sekundarstufe I', *Sportunterricht*, 29, 206–14.

Baur, J., Bräutigam, M. and Brettschneider, W. D. (1984a) 'Sport in der Sekundarstufe I', *Sportwissenschaft*, 14, 229–51.

——(1984b) 'Sport in der Sekundarstufe I', in Carl, K., Kayser, D., Mechling, H. and Preising, W. (eds) *Handbuch Sport*, vol. 2, Düsseldorf: Schwann, 701–36.

Blankertz, H. (1977) 'Die Verbindung von Abitur und Berufsausbildung', *Zeitschrift für Pädagogik*, 23, 329–43.

Diem, L. (1977) 'Sport und Sportunterricht im Elementar- und Primarbereich. Didaktische Überlegungen', *Sportwissenschaft*, 7, 26–41.

DSB (ed.) (1978) *Sport für Jugendliche in berufsbildenden Schulen und Betrieben*, Frankfurt am Main: DSB.

Eulering, J. and Hiersemann, D. (1974) 'Vom "Schulversuch Sportgymnasium" zum Leistungsfach Sport in Nordrhein-Westfalen', *Sportunterricht*, 23, 333–7.

Falkenberg, G. (1988) *Kognitives Lernen im Sport. Struktur und Entwicklung kognitiver Kompetenzen im Sportunterricht der Sekundarstufe II*, Wuppertal: Putty.

Fischer, J. (1983) 'Rahmenlehrplan Sport (Hessen) – Konzeption und Aufgabe eines Curriculums für die Berufsschule', in Hartmann, H. (ed.) *Sport in der Berufsschule*, Bad Homburg: Limpert, 118–26.

Fischer, B. (1989) *Einstellungen zum Sport. Eine empirische Untersuchung über Einstellungen von Schülern zu Lernfeldern des Sportunterrichts in der Sekundarstufe II*, Münster/New York: Waxmann.

Fouqué, A. (2000) 'Health education as a part of the P.E. Curricula in Sweden and Germany (State of North Rhine Westphalia) within the last ten years', in Tolleneer, J. and Renson, R. (eds) *Old Borders, New Borders, no Borders. Sport and Physical Education in a Period of Change*, Aachen: Meyer & Meyer, 355–62.

Frankfurter Arbeitsgruppe (1982) *Offener Sportunterricht: Analysieren und Planen*, Reinbek: Rowohlt.

Gessmann, R. (1977) 'Die Konzeption der Grundkurse Sport der Oberstufe allgemeinbildenden Schulen', in Evangelische Akademie Hofgeismar (ed.) *Sport und Oberstufenreform Protokoll nr. 119*, Hofgeismar: Eigenverlag, 23–47.

Grotefent, R. (1968) 'Zweite Stellungnahme des Bundesverbandes Deutscher Leibeserzieher (e.V.) zur Frage einer stärkeren Förderung sportlich begabter Kinder und Jugendlicher', *Die Leibeserziehung*, 17, 121–5.

Groth, E. and Groth, K. (1980) 'Elf Bundesländer – elf Versuche zur Neugestaltung des Sportunterrichts in der Gymnasialen Oberstufe', *Sportunterricht*, 29, 88–98.

Grupe, O. (2000) *Vom Sinn des Sports*, Schorndorf: Hofmann.

Grupe, O., Bergner, K. and Kurz, D. (1974) 'Sport und Sportunterricht in der Sekundarstufe II', in Deutscher Bildungsrat (ed.) *Gutachten und Studien der Bildungskommission*, vol. 40, Stuttgart: Klett, 109–40.

Hartmann, H. (1978) 'Freizeitsport als Schulsport an Berufsschulen', *Sportunterricht*, 27, 171–8.

Hartmann, H. and Witzel, R. (eds) (1993) *Sport in der Berufsschule – Sport mit Zukunft?*, Wetzlar: DSLV.

Hildebrandt, R. (1993) 'Lebensweltbezug – Leitmotiv für eine Neuorientierung der Bewegungserziehung in der Grundschule', *Sportwissenschaft*, 23, 259–75.

——(1999) *Bewegte Schulkultur: Schulentwicklung in Bewegung*, Butzbach-Griedel: Afra.

Klupsch-Sahlmann, R. (1999) *Mehr Bewegung in der Grundschule: Grundlagen*, Berlin: Cornelsen.

KMK (1976) *Einheitliche Prüfungsanforderungen in der Abiturprüfung Sport vom 7.11.1975*, Neuwied: Luchterhand.

KM NRW (1974) *Curriculum – Berufliche Schulen-Sport*, book 22, Düsseldorf KM.

——(1980) *Lehrpläne und Richtlinien für den Schulsport in Nordrhein-Westfalen*, vol. I, Frechen: Ritterbach.

——(1981) *Lehrpläne und Richtlinien für den Schulsport in Nordrhein-Westfalen*, vol. V, Frechen: Ritterbach.

Kottmann, L., Schaller, H. J. and Stibbe, G. (eds) *Sportpädagogik zwischen Kontinuität und Innovation*, Schorndorf: Hofmann.

Kreidler, H. (1968) 'Zur pädagogischen Begründung des Sportgymnasiums', *Die Leibeserziehung*, 17 (4) 127–9.

Kreiter, C. (1983) 'Aspekte der historischen Entwicklung des Berufsschulsports', in Hartmann, H. (ed.) *Sport in der Berufsschule*, Bad Homburg: Limpert, 7–16.

Kröner, S. (1976) *Sport und Geschlecht*, Ahrensburg: Czwalina.

Kröner, S. and Pfister, G. (1985) *Nachdenken über Koedukation im Sport*, Ahrensburg: Czwalina.

Kugelmann, C. (1984) 'Sport in der Berufsschule', in Carl, K., Kayer, D., Mechling, H. and Preising, W. (eds) *Handbuch Sport*, vol. 2, Düsseldorf: Schwann, 737–56.

LSW (ed.) (1987) *Bildungsgangbeschreibung 'Freizeitsportleiter/Allgemeine Hochschulreife'*, Soest: Verlagskontor.

Lutter, H. (1978) 'Zum Curriculum Sport an berufsbildenden Schulen', in DSB (ed.) *Sport für Jugendliche in berufsbildenden Schulen und Betrieben*, Frankfurt am Main: DSB, 68–75.

Lutter, H., Liefländer, H. and Held, H. J. (1980) 'Sport an beruflichen Schulen: Curricularer Neuansatz unter Berücksichtigung der Realsituation', *Sportunterricht*, 29, 294–302.

MSWWF (2000) *Grundschule. Richtlinien und Lehrpläne Sport*, Frechen: Ritterbach.

Naul, R. (1977) 'Das Normenbuch Sport und seine Folgen für die Reform der Sekundarstufe II', *Sportunterricht*, 26, 184–9.

——(1978) *Das Sportprofil der Kollegstufe*, Münster: WBK.

(1990) 'Volleyball: Wissenschaftspropädeutisch lernen', *Sportpädagogik*, 14 (2) 76–80.

Naul, R., Fischer, B. and Falkenberg, G. (1992) 'Kognitives Lernen im Leistungsfach Sport der gymnasialen Oberstufe', *Sportunterricht*, 41, 101–14.

Pfister, G. (1983) *Geschlechtsspezifische Sozialisation und Koedukation im Sport*, Berlin: Bartels & Wernitz.

Pühse, U. (ed.) (1994) *Soziales Handeln im Sport und Sportunterricht*, Schorndorf: Hofmann.

Quanz, D. (1976) 'Oberstufensport im Umbruch', in Decker, W. and Lämmer, M. (eds) *Kölner Beiträge zur Sportwissenschaft*, St Augustin: Academia, 130–51.

Quanz, D. (1976) 'Zum Schulbuchproblem im Sportunterricht', in Hecker, G., Kirsch, A. and Menze, C. (eds) *Der Mensch im Sport*, Schorndorf: Hofmann, 135–46.

Recktenwald, H. D. (2000) 'Zur "Problematik" einer Prüfung im Sport als 4. Abiturfach', *Sportunterricht*, 49, 289–92.

Scherler, K. H. (1977) 'Die Regelung von Bewegungsspielen als Thema des Sportunterrichts', *Sportwissenschaft*, 7, 341–60.

Schmidt, B. (1967) 'Das "Sportgymnasium" im Spannungsfeld von Leistungssport und Leibeserziehung', *Die Leibeserziehung*, 16, 360–5.

Schmidt, W. (ed.) (1996) *Kindheit und Sport – gestern und heute*, Hamburg: Czwalina.

Schulz, N. (1985) 'Schulsport – Die aktuelle Diskussion über Aufgaben, Ziele und Inhalte im Überblick', in Denk, H. and Hecker, G. (eds) *Texte zur Sportpädagogik*, part II, Schorndorf: Hofmann, 190–213.

——(1997) 'Sport in der Grundschule für Kinder von heute – Überlegungen zum Kindgemässen', in Kottmann, L., Schaller, H. J. and Stibbe, G. (eds) *Sportpädagogik zwischen Kontinuität und Innovation*, Schorndorf: Hofmann, 77–91.

Schwidder, D. (1978) 'Zur Situation des Sportunterrichts in den berufsbildenden Schulen in der Bundesrepublik Deutschland', in DSB (ed.) *Sport für Jugendliche in berufsbildenden Schulen und Betrieben*, Frankfurt am Main: DSB, 21–56.

Stibbe, G. (ed.) (1998) *Bewegung, Spiel und Sport als Elemente des Schulprogramms. Grundlagen, Ansätze, Beispiele*, Baltmannsweiler: Schneider.

Thiele, J. (1999) 'Un-Bewegte Kindheit?' Anmerkungen zur Defizithypothese in aktuellen Körperdiskursen', *Sportunterricht*, 48, 141–9.

Uhler-Derings, H. G. and Haenisch, H. (1995) *Sport in der Berufschule und in den teilzeitschulischen Bildungsgängen der Kollegschule*, Soest: LSW.

Witzel, R. and Hartmann, H. (1983) 'Anforderungen an neue Lehrpläne für den Sportunterricht an beruflichen Schulen', in Hartmann, H. (ed.) *Sport in der Berufsschule, Didaktische Grundlagen*, Bad Homburg: Limpert, 107–17.

Zimmer, R. and Cicurs H. (eds) (1992) *Kinder brauchen Bewegung – Brauchen Kinder Sport?*, Aachen: Meyer & Meyer.

6 Physical education teacher training

Artus, H. G. (1980) 'Organisation Schulpraktischer Studien im Studiengang Sport an der Universität Bremen', in Manfred Wiegand (ed.) *Praxisbezug in der Sportlehrerausbildung*, Bad Homburg: Limpert, 78–85.

Becker, U. (1983) 'Schülerbücher für den Theorieunterricht im Leistungsfach Sport', *Sportunterricht*, 32, 133–41.

Brettschneider, W. D., Bräutigam, M. and Miethling, W. D. (1987) 'Sportlehrer und Schüler in neuer Perspektive. Die Hinwendung zum Subjektiven', in Peper, D. and Christmann, E. (eds) *Zur Standortbestimmung der Sportpädagogik*, Schorndorf: Hofmann, 109–30.

Dassel, H. (1980) 'Die Zielsetzung Schulpraktischer Studien in der 1. Phase der Sportlehrerausbildung aus der Perspektive des Seminarleiters (2. Phase)', in Wiegand, M. (ed.) *Praxisbezug in der Sportlehrerausbildung*, Bad Homburg: Limpert, 53–7.

DSB (ed.) (1979) *Training of Physical Education Teachers. Analysis and Reform*, Frankfurt am Main: Hassmüller.

Friedrich, G. (1999) 'Bewegungslernen im Sportunterricht – Konsequenzen für eine Neubestimmung der Aufgaben von Sportleherinnen und Sportlehrern', in Heinz, B. and Laging, R. (eds) *Bewegungslernen in Erziehung und Bildung*, Hamburg: Czwalina, 195–202.

——(2001) 'Increasing autonomy in schools: new qualifications for physical education teachers and new challenges for universities', in EAdS (ed.) *Physical Education: From Central Governmental Regulation to Local School Autonomy*, Velen: EAdS, 164–71.

Köppe, D. and Kottmann, L. (eds) (1989) *Integration von Theorie in die sportpraktische Ausbildung*, Clausthal-Zellerfeld: Greinert.

Köppe, D. and Kuhlmann, D. (eds) (1986) *Der Sportlehrer als Vorbild*, Clausthal-Zellerfeld: Greinert.

Kuhlmann, D. (1999) 'Ausbildung im Sport – Aufgaben für die dvs. Elemente eines Arbeitsprogramms für das nächste Jahrtausend', *dvs-Informationen*, 14 (1) 10–17.

Kultusministerium NW (1981) *Richtlinien und Lehrpläne für den Sport in den Schulen im Lande Nordrhein-Westfalen, vol.V: Gymnasiale Oberstufe*, Frechen: Ritterbach.

Miethling, W. D. (1986) *Belastungssituationen im Selbstverständnis junger Sportlehrer*, Schorndorf: Hofmann.

Naul, R. (1992) 'Teaching physical education teachers in the Federal Republic of Germany: a collaborative enterprise', in Graham, G. M. and Jones, M. A. (eds) *Collaboration between Researchers and Practioners in Physical Education: An International Dialogue*, Reston: AAHPERD, 127–31.

Naul, R. and Schulz, N. (1992) '20 Jahre Leistungsfach Sport – Versuch einer Bilanz', *Sportunterricht*, 41, 274–83.

Perle, H. J. (1980) 'Zur Struktur Schulpraktischer Studien am Erziehungswissenschaftlichen Fachbereich der Universität Göttingen', in Wiegand, M. (ed.) *Praxisbezug in der Sportlehrerausbildung*, Bad Homburg: Limpert, 65–77.

Pfister, G. (1992) 'Turnlehrerinnen auf dem Weg zur Professionalisierung (1880–1914)', in Lämmer, M. and Spitzer, G. (eds) *Sport als Beruf*, St Augustin: Academia, 83–108.

Rehbein, E. (1980) 'Zielsetzung der Studien zur Unterrichtspraxis im Rahmen der Sportlehrerausbildung', in Wiegand, M. (ed.) *Praxisbezug in der Sportlehrerbildung*, Bad Homburg: Limpert, 34–40.

Schröder, J. (1984) 'Studien zur Unterrichtspraxis als Prinzip didaktischer Veranstaltungen in der Sportlehrerausbildung', in Altenberger, H. and Köppe, G. (eds) *Schulpraktische Studien – Modelle und ihre Verwirklichung*, Bad Homburg: Limpert, 187–212.

Simons, H. (ed.) (1996) *Sportwissenschaft und Sportlehrerausbildung*, Freiburg: Selbstverlag.

Thierer, R. (1999) 'Studiengänge/Ausbildungsgänge im Berufsfeld Sport/Sportwissenschaft', *dvs-Informationen*, 14 (1) 18–21.

Voigt, H. F. and Jendrusch, G. (eds) (2000) *Sportlehrerausbildung wofür?*, Hamburg: Czwalina.

Wiehusen, D. (1980) 'Zur Struktur der Schulpraktischen Studien in der Sportlehrerausbildung aus der Perspektive des Seminarleiters für Referendarausbildung Sport', in Wiegand, M. (ed.) *Praxisbezug in der Sportlehrerausbildung*, Bad Homburg: Limpert, 86–9.

Zimmermann, H. (1997) 'Zweiphasige (Sport-)Lehrerausbildung: Ein Auslaufmodell? Ausbildungsdidaktische Überlegungen aus einem aktuellen Anlaß', in Kottmann, L., Schaller, H. J. and Stibbe, G. (eds) *Sportpädagogik zwischen Kontinuität und Innovation*, Schorndorf: Hofmann, 197–208.

7 Coach education and training

Bergmann Drewe, S. (2000) 'An examination of the relationship between coaching and teaching', *Quest*, 52 (1) 79–88.

Bernett, H. (1979) 'Wissenschaft und Weltanschauung. Sportlehrerausbildung im Dritten Reich', in Krüger, A. and Niedlich, D. (eds) *Ursachen der Schulsportmisere in Deutschland*, London: Arena Publications, 32–44.

Buss, W. and Becker, C. (eds) (2001) *Aktionsfelder des DDR-Sports: Die frühe Entwicklung*, Cologne: Strauss (in press).

Cachay, K., Thiel, A. and Meier, H. (1999) 'Berufsfeld Sport – Ergebnisse aus zwei Forschungsprojekten', *dvs-Informationen*, 14 (4) 20–9.

Claude, R. (1995) 'Berufsbild und Einsatz von hauptamtlichen Trainern in der Europäischen Union (EU)', in J. Kozel (ed.) *Trainerakademie Cologne e.V. 20 Jahre Trainerakademie. Internationales Trainersymposium*, Cologne: Strauss, 50–61.

Del Fabro, M. (1992) *Der Trainervertrag*, Bern: Haupt.

Derkatsch, A. A. and Issajew, A. A. (1986) *Der erfolgreiche Trainer. Das pädagogische Können des Trainers und Übungsleiters*, Berlin-East: Sportverlag.

Fischer, H. (1986) 'Sport und Geschäft', *Professionalisierung im Sport*, Berlin: Bartels & Wernitz.

Führungsakademie des Deutschen Sportbundes (ed.) (2000) *Arbeitsmarkt Sport. Dokumentation*, Berlin: Führungsakademie.

Gahai, E. and Holz, P. (1986) *Zur Rolle des Trainers im Leistungssport*, Cologne: Sport und Buch.

Grossböhmer, R. (1994) *Die Geschichte der preussischen Turnlehrer*, Aachen: Meyer & Meyer.

Hagedorn, G. (1987) 'Trainer – die soziale Rolle eines integrierten Aussenseiters. Versuch einer Provokation', *Leistungssport*, 17 (1) 5–8.

Heinemann, K. and Schubert, M. (1992) *Ehrenamtlichkeit und Hauptamtlichkeit in Sportvereinen*, Schorndorf: Hofmann.

Hoberman, J. (1992) *Mortal Engines. The Science of Performance and the Dehumanization of Sport*, New York: Free Press.

Hotz, A. (1990) 'Was zeichnet einen "guten" Trainer letztlich aus?', *Leistungssport*, 20 (5) 45–6.

Kreiss, F. (1995) 'Die Entwicklung der Trainerausbildung in Deutschland', in J. Kozel (ed.) *Trainerakademie Cologne e.V. 20 Jahre Trainerakademie. Internationales Trainersymposium*, Cologne: Strauss, 110–23.

Krüger, A. (1975a) *Sport und Politik. Vom Turnvater Jahn zum Staatsamateur*, Hanover: Fackelträger.

——(1975b) 'Die Trainerausbildung im Rahmen des Bildungssystems in der Bundesrepublik', *Leistungssport*, 5 (3) 214–17.

——(1986) 'Curriculum for the training of coaches and sports trainers in Europe – with special emphasis on Germany', in *Curriculum Improvement for the Training of Physical Education Teachers and Sport Instructors, vol. 1*, Yokohama: Nippon College, 71–106.

——(1989) 'Trainer brauchen Pädagogik!', *Leistungssport*, 19 (5) 31–3.

——(1991b) 'Hat sich die Sportpädagogik aus dem Leistungssport verabschiedet?', *Leistungssport*, 21 (6) 15–18.

——(1995) 'Die Rolle der Trainerschaft in der Gesellschaft. Die Verantwortung für die Sportkultur', in J. Kozel (ed.) *Trainerakademie Cologne e.V. 20 Jahre Trainerakademie. Internationales Trainersymposium*, Cologne: Sport und Buch, 80–91.

——(1998) 'Viele Wege führen nach Olympia. Die Veränderungen in den Trainingssystemen für Mittel- und Langstreckenläufer (1850 – 1997)', in Gissel, N. (ed.) *Sportliche Leistung im Wandel*, Hamburg: Czwalina, 41–56.

——(1999) 'Breeding, rearing and preparing the Aryan body: creating the complete Superman the Nazi way', *International Journal of the History of Sport*, 16 (2) 42–68.

Krüger, A. and Casselman, J. (1982) 'A comparative analysis of top level track and field coaches in the USA and West Germany', *Comparative Physical Education and Sport* 4 (3) 20– 9.

Lamnek, S. (1999) Ansätze zu einer Soziologie der Professionalisierung', in Hartmann-Tews, I. (ed.) *Professionalisierung und Sport*, Hamburg: Czwalina, 13–29.

Mrazek, J. and Rittner, V. (1991) *Übungsleiter und Trainer im Sportverein*, Schorndorf: Hofmann.

Patsantaras, N. (1994) *Der Trainer als Sportberuf*, Schorndorf: Hofmann.

Sarfatti-Larson, M. (1977) *The Rise of Professionalism*, Berkeley: University of California Press.

Volkamer, M. (1989) 'Zum Problem der Laienkompetenz', *Sportunterricht*, 38 (1) 6–32.

von Krockow, C. (1990) 'Der Wetteifer in der industriellen Gesellschaft und im Sport', in ADL (ed.) *Spiel und Wetteifer*, Schorndorf: Hofmann, 212–26.

Weber, W., Schnieder, C. Kortlüke, N. and Horak, B. (1995) *Die wirtschaftliche Bedeutung des Sports*, Schorndorf: Hofmann.

10 Sport for women

Baur, J. (1989) *Körper- und Bewegungskarrieren*, Schorndorf: Hofmann.

Becker-Schmidt, R. (1994) 'Geschlechterverhältnis, Technologieentwicklung und androzentrische Ideologieproduktion', in Beckenbach, Nils and Treeck, Werner van (eds) *Umbrüche gesellschaftlicher Arbeit*, Göttingen: Schwartz, 527–38.

Bernett, H. (1960) *Die pädagogische Neugestaltung der bürgerlichen Leibesübungen durch die Philanthropen*, Schorndorf: Hofmann.

Bierstedt, H. (1981) 'Die Einbeziehung der sportlichen Betätigung in die Lebensweise der Familien', *Theorie und Praxis der Körperkultur*, 30, 32–4.

Boutilier, M. A. and San Giovanni, L. F. (1991) 'Ideology, Public Policy and Female Olympic Achievement: a Cross-National Analysis of the Seoul Olympic Games', in Landry, F., Landry, M. and Yerlès, M. (eds) *Sport...the Third Millennium*, Sainte-Foy: Les Presses de l'Université Laval, 397–409.

Brinker-Gabler, G. (ed.) (1979) *Frauenarbeit und Beruf*, Frankfurt: Fischer.

Brinkhoff, K-P. (1998) *Sport und Sozialisation im Jugendalter*, Weinheim/Munich: Juventa.

Czech, M. (1994) *Frauen und Sport im Nationalsozialistischen Deutschland*, Berlin: Tischler.

Dordel, S. (1992) 'Kindheit heute', *Sportunterricht*, 49, 341–8.

Esch, H. (1990) *80 Jahre Sport in Spornitz. Eine Chronik 1909–1989*, Spornitz: Eigenverlag.

Fechtig, B. (1995) *Frauen und Fußball*, Dortmund: eFeF.

Freckmann, B. (1982) 'Wesen und Formen der Gymnastik', in Ueberhorst, Horst (ed.) *Geschichte der Leibesübungen*, vol. 3/2, Berlin: Bartels & Wernitz, 1008–26.

Freizeit–Monitor 2000 (2000) *Daten zur Freizeitforschung*, Hamburg: BAT.

Gottschall, K. (1995) 'Geschlechterverhältnisse und Arbeitsmarktsegregation', in Becker-Schmidt, R. and Knapp, G.-A. (eds) *Das Geschlechterverhältnis als Gegenstand der Sozialwissenschaften*, Frankfurt: Campus, 125–63.

Hagemann-White, C. (1984) *Sozialisation: Weiblich – Männlich?*, Opladen: Leske & Budrich.

——(1993) 'Die Konstrukteure des Geschlechts auf frischer Tat ertappen? Methodische Konsequenzen einer theoretischen Einsicht', *Feministische Studien*, 11 (2) 68–78.

Hartmann-Tews, I. (1990) 'Weibliche Körper-Verhältnisse – Wandel und Kontinuitäten', *Brennpunkte der Sportwissenschaft*, 4 (2) 146–62.

Helwig, G. and Nickel, H. M. (eds) (1993) *Frauen in Deutschland 1945–1992*, Bonn: Bundeszentrale für politische Bildung.

Hirschauer, S. (1996) 'Wie sind Frauen, wie sind Männer. Zweigeschlechtlichkeit als Wissenssytem', in Eifert, C., Epple, A., Kessel, M., Michaelis, M., Nowak, C., Schicke, K. and Weltecke, D. (eds) *Was sind Frauen? Was sind Männer? Geschlechterkonstruktionen im historischen Wandel*, Frankfurt: Suhrkamp, 240–57.

Klein, G. (1997) 'Theoretische Prämissen einer Geschlechterforschung in der Sportwissenschaft', in Henkel, U. and Kröner, S. (eds) *Und sie bewegt sich doch*, Pfaffenweiler: Centaurus, 103–25.

Klein, M-L. (1986) *Frauensport in der Tagespresse*, Bochum: Brockmeyer.

Knapp, G-A. (1995) 'Unterschiede machen: Zur Sozialpsychologie der Hierarchisierung um Geschlechterverhältnis', in Becker-Schmidt, R. and Knapp, G.-A. (eds) *Das Geschlechterverhältnis als Gegenstand der Sozialwissenschaften*, Frankfurt: Campus, 163–95.

Kurz, D. and Tietjens, M. (2000) 'Das Sport-und Vereinsengagement der Jugendlichen', *Sportwissenschaft*, 30 (4) 384–408.

Nurbe, U. (ed.) (1995) *Spieglein, Spieglein an der Wand. Der Schönheitskult und die Frauen*, Munich: Heyne, 11–22.

Petry, K. (1990) 'Zur Situation der Frauen in den Führungsgremien des organisierten Sports – eine Bestandsaufnahme', *Brennpunkte der Sportwissenschaft*, 4 (2) 233–43.

Pfister, G. (1987) 'Macht Euch frei – Frauen in der Arbeiter- Turn- und Sportbewegung', in Teichler, J. and Hauk, G. (eds) *Illustrierte Geschichte des Arbeitersports*, Berlin/Bonn: Dietz, 48–56.

——(1989) *Fliegen – ihr Leben. Die ersten Pilotinnen*, Berlin: Orlanda.

——(1992) 'Biologie als Schicksal. Zur Frauen-, Körper- und Sportpolitik im Nationalsozialismus', in Kröner, S. and Pfister, G. (eds) *Frauen – Räume, Körper und Identität im Sport*, Pfaffenweiler: Centaurus, 41–61.

——(1997) 'Body culture, myths of femininity and the discourse of gender in Germany (1919–1933)', in Krüger, A. and Teja, A. (eds) *La Commune Eredità dello Sport in Europa*, Rome: CONI, 199–211.

——(2000) 'Doing gender – die Inszenierung des Geschlechts im Eiskunstlauf und im Kunstturnen', in Norberg, Johan R. (ed.) *Studier Idrott, historia och samhälle. Tillägnade professor Jan Lindroth pa has 60-arsdag*, Stockholm: HLS Förlag, 170–201.

Pfister, G. and Langenfeld, H. (1982) 'Vom Frauenturnen zum modernen Sport – Die Entwicklung der Leibesübungen der Frauen und Mädchen seit dem Ersten Weltkrieg', in Ueberhorst, H. (ed.) *Geschichte der Leibesübungen, vol. 3/2*, Berlin/Munich/Frankfurt: Bartels & Wernitz, 977–1008.

Pfister, G. and Reese, D. (1995) 'Gender, body culture, and body politics in National Socialism', in Pfister, G. (ed.) 'Sport history', *Sport Science Review*, 4 (1) 91–122.

Rittner, V. (1985) 'Sport und Gesundheit. Zur Ausdifferenzierung des Gesundheitsmotivs im Sport', *Sportwissenschaft*, 15, 136–54.

Schlagenhauf, K. (1977) *Sportvereine in der Bundesrepublik Deutschland*, Schorndorf: Hofmann.

Schlüter, A. (1986) 'Diskriminierungen von Frauen in der Wissenschaft', in Schlüter, A. and Kuhn, A. (eds) *Lila Schwarzbuch. Zur Diskriminierung von Frauen und der Wissenschaft*, Düsseldorf: Schwann, 10–34.

Teichler, J. and Reinartz, K. (1999) *Das Leistungssportsystem der DDR in den 80er Jahren und im Prozeß der Wende*, Schorndorf: Hofmann.

Index